Shakespeare's Others in 21st-century European Performance

GLOBAL SHAKESPEARE INVERTED

Global Shakespeare Inverted challenges any tendency to view Global Shakespeare from the perspective of 'centre' versus 'periphery'. Although the series may locate its critical starting point geographically, it calls into question the geographical bias that lurks within the very notion of the 'global'. It provides a timely, constructive criticism of the present state of the field and establishes new and alternative methodologies that invert the relation of Shakespeare to the supposed 'other'.

SERIES EDITORS

David Schalkwyk, Queen Mary, University of London, UK
Silvia Bigliazzi, University of Verona, Italy
Bi-qi Beatrice Lei, National Taiwan University, Taiwan

ADVISORY BOARD

Douglas Lanier, University of New Hampshire, USA
Sonia Massai, King's College London, UK
Supriya Chaudhury, Jadavpur University, India
Ian Smith, Lafayette College, USA

Eating Shakespeare: Cultural Anthropophagy as Global Methodology
Edited by Anne Sophie Refskou, Marcel Alvaro de Amorim and Vinicius Mariano de Carvalho

Shakespeare in the Global South: Stories of Oceans Crossed in Contemporary Adaptation
Sandra Young

Migrating Shakespeare: First European Encounters, Routes and Networks
Edited by Janet Clare and Dominique Goy-Blanquet

FORTHCOMING TITLES

Disseminating Shakespeare in the Nordic Countries: Shifting Centres and Peripheries in the Nineteenth Century
Edited by Nely Keinänen and Per Sivefors

Shakespeare's Others in 21st-century European Performance

The Merchant of Venice and *Othello*

Edited by
Boika Sokolova
and Janice Valls-Russell

THE ARDEN SHAKESPEARE
LONDON • NEW YORK • OXFORD • NEW DELHI • SYDNEY

THE ARDEN SHAKESPEARE
Bloomsbury Publishing Plc
50 Bedford Square, London, WC1B 3DP, UK
1385 Broadway, New York, NY 10018, USA
29 Earlsfort Terrace, Dublin 2, Ireland

BLOOMSBURY, THE ARDEN SHAKESPEARE and the Arden Shakespeare logo are trademarks of Bloomsbury Publishing Plc

First published in Great Britain 2022
This paperback edition published in 2023

Copyright © Boika Sokolova, Janice Valls-Russell and contributors, 2022

Boika Sokolova, Janice Valls-Russell and contributors have asserted their right under the Copyright, Designs and Patents Act, 1988, to be identified as the authors of this work.

For legal purposes the Acknowledgements on pp. xii–xiii constitute an extension of this copyright page.

Cover image: Hold On , Ella Baron (2017) (© www.ellabaron .com)

All rights reserved. No part of this publication may be reproduced or transmitted in any form or by any means, electronic or mechanical, including photocopying, recording, or any information storage or retrieval system, without prior permission in writing from the publishers.

Bloomsbury Publishing Plc does not have any control over, or responsibility for, any third-party websites referred to or in this book. All internet addresses given in this book were correct at the time of going to press. The author and publisher regret any inconvenience caused if addresses have changed or sites have ceased to exist, but can accept no responsibility for any such changes.

Library of Congress Cataloging-in-Publication Data

Names: Sokolova, Boika, editor. | Valls-Russell, Janice, editor.
Title: Shakespeare's others in 21st-century European performance: The merchant of Venice and Othello / edited by Boika Sokolova and Janice Valls-Russell.
Description: London; New York, NY: The Arden Shakespeare, 2021. |
Series: Global Shakespeare inverted | Includes bibliographical references and index.
Identifiers: LCCN 2021020334 (print) | LCCN 2021020335 (ebook) |
ISBN 9781350125957 (hardback) | ISBN 9781350260795 (paperback) |
ISBN 9781350125971 (ebook) | ISBN 9781350125964 (epub)
Subjects: LCSH: Shakespeare, William, 1564-1616–Stage history–Europe. |
Shakespeare, William, 1564-1616. Othello–Adaptations–History and criticism. |
Shakespeare, William, 1564-1616. Merchant of Venice–Adaptations–History and criticism. |
Other (Philosophy) in literature. | Strangers in literature. | Ethnicity in literature.
Classification: LCC PR3109.E2 S535 2021 (print) | LCC PR3109.E2 (ebook) |
DDC 792.9/50905–dc23
LC record available at https://lccn.loc.gov/2021020334
LC ebook record available at https://lccn.loc.gov/2021020335

ISBN: HB: 978-1-3501-2595-7
PB: 978-1-3502-6079-5
ePDF: 978-1-3501-2597-1
eBook: 978-1-3501-2596-4

Series: Global Shakespeare Inverted

Typeset by Deanta Global Publishing Services, Chennai, India

To find out more about our authors and books visit www .bloomsbury.com and sign up for our newsletters

CONTENTS

Notes on contributors viii
Acknowledgements xii

Introduction Boika Sokolova and Janice Valls-Russell 1

PART ONE Relocating otherness: The Other-within 23

Induction 1 *Lawrence Guntner* 24

1 'Venice' is elsewhere: The Stranger's locality, or Italian 'blackness' in twenty-first-century stagings of *Othello* Anna Maria Cimitile 29

2 Refracting the racial Other into the Other-within in two Bulgarian adaptations of *Othello* Boika Sokolova and Kirilka Stavreva 49

3 Estranged strangers: Krzysztof Warlikowski's Shylock and Othello in *African Tales after Shakespeare* (2011) Aleksandra Sakowska 69

4 Drags, dyes and death in Venice: *The Merchant of Venice* (2004) and *Othello* (2012) in Belgrade, Serbia Zorica Bečanović Nikolić 89

5 *The Merchant of Venice* in France (2001 and 2017): Deconstructing a *malaise* Janice Valls-Russell 108

PART TWO New nationalisms, migrants: Imperfect resolutions 127

Induction 2 *Lawrence Guntner* 128

6 'Barbarous temper', 'hideous violence' and 'mountainish inhumanity': Stage encounters with *The Merchant of Venice* in Romania *Nicoleta Cinpoeş* 131

7 Staging *The Merchant of Venice* in Hungary: Politics, prejudice and languages of hatred *Natália Pikli* 152

8 Dutch negotiations with otherness in times of crisis: *Othello* (2006) and *The Arab of Amsterdam* (2008) *Coen Heijes* 171

9 'Were I the Moor, I would not be Iago': Radical empathy in two Portuguese performances of *Othello* *Francesca Rayner* 190

10 A tragedy? *Othello* and *The Merchant of Venice* in Germany during the 2015–16 refugee crisis *Bettina Boecker* 209

PART THREE Performative propositions 229

Induction 3 *Lawrence Guntner* 230

11 *The Merchant in Venice* in the Venetian Ghetto (2016): Director Karin Coonrod in conversation with Boika Sokolova and Kirilka Stavreva 233

12 Inverting *Othello* in France (2019): Director Arnaud Churin in conversation with Janice Valls-Russell 245

13 Migrant *Othello* (2020) in Bulgaria: Director Plamen Markov in conversation with Boika Sokolova and Kirilka Stavreva 258

Coda: Staging Shakespeare's Others and their biblical archetype *Péter Dávidházi* 269

Index 281

CONTRIBUTORS

Zorica Bečanović Nikolić is Associate Professor at the Department of Comparative Literature and Literary Theory, Faculty of Philology, University of Belgrade. She is the author of three monographs in Serbian: *Hermeneutika i poetika* (1998), *Šekspir iza ogledala* (2007) and *U traganju za Šekspirom* (2013). Her work is focused on Shakespeare and contemporary literary and philosophical theory. She has also published academic articles in Serbian, French and Spanish on Shakespeare in relation to Erasmus, Machiavelli and Montaigne, as well as on Serbian culture in the European context.

Bettina Boecker is Senior Lecturer at the University of Munich, as well as Executive Officer and Research Librarian at the Munich Shakespeare Library. She has published on a variety of early modern topics, but is particularly interested in the popular culture of the period and Shakespeare's afterlives. Other interests include children and children's literature in the early modern period, Cold War Shakespeare and Shakespeare in performance.

Anna Maria Cimitile is Associate Professor of English Literature at the University of Naples 'L'Orientale'. Her interests range from Shakespeare's playtexts and their stagings, especially with respect to tragedy and the tragic, to present rewritings and cinematic adaptations of Shakespeare, to postcolonial theory, literature and arts. She is Regional Editor for Global Shakespeares (globalshakespeares.mit.edu). Among her publications are *Shakespearean Orders* (2000), *Emergenze. Il fantasma della schiavitù da Coleridge a D'Aguiar* (2005) and a series of articles and essays on the topics of her interest.

Nicoleta Cinpoeș is Professor of Shakespeare Studies at the University of Worcester, UK. Author of *Shakespeare's Hamlet in Romania 1778–2008* (2010), and contributor to *Doing Kyd* (2016), *Europe's Shakespeare(s)* (2018), and *Viewing & Reviewing* (2019), she regularly contributes articles to specialist journals and collections, and peer-reviews. For the new Shakespeare's *Complete Works* in Romanian, she wrote introductions to *Hamlet* (2010) and *Titus Andronicus* (2019). Her current project is on Shakespeare Festivals as Shakespeare tourism.

Péter Dávidházi, Member of the Hungarian Academy of Sciences (MHAS), is Research Professor Emeritus at the Institute for Literary Studies and Professor Emeritus of English Literature at Eötvös Loránd University, Budapest. He is the author of *The Romantic Cult of Shakespeare: Literary Reception in Anthropological Perspective* (1998), has published monographs on Hungarian literature and edited *New Publication Cultures in the Humanities: Exploring the Paradigm Shift* (2014). His recent work focuses on biblical allusions in Shakespeare and the appropriation of biblical patterns in Hungarian poetry.

Lawrence Guntner taught Literature, Cultural Studies and Film Studies at the Technical University of Braunschweig (Germany). His publications on Shakespeare include *Re-Defining Shakespeare: Literary Criticism and Theater Practice in the German Democratic Republic* and a chapter in *The Cambridge Companion to Shakespeare on Film*. Most recently, he has published interviews with George Tabori and Heiner Müller in *Shakespeare Jahrbuch*.

Coen Heijes teaches Shakespeare, Presentism and Performance at the University of Groningen, the Netherlands. He combines Shakespeare and ethnic and racial studies in his research and has written/edited/participated (in) books on the abolishment of slavery, Dutch multicultural society, cross-cultural communication, and performing early modern drama today. His latest book is *Shakespeare, Blackface and Race* (2020). He is a member of the editorial board of *Multicultural Shakespeare* and of the board of directors of the British Shakespeare Association.

Natália Pikli is an Associate Professor of English Literature at Eötvös Loránd University, Budapest. Her research concerns cultural memory, both in Shakespeare's time and now, with special focus on Shakespeare in contemporary theatre and the traffic of popular discourses in Shakespeare, early modern theatre and print. She has published her findings in *Shakespeare Survey* 70, *Journal of Early Modern Studies* 2, and *European Journal of English Studies* 14:3. Her forthcoming book is *Shakespeare's Hobby-horse and Early Modern Popular Culture* (2021).

Francesca Rayner is Assistant Professor at the Universidade do Minho, Portugal, where she teaches undergraduate and graduate courses in Theatre and Performance. Her research centres on the cultural politics of performance, with a particular interest in the performance of Shakespeare in Portugal and questions of gender and sexuality. She is a member of the research project *The Presence of Shakespeare in Spain and the Mark of his European Reception* (University of Murcia, Spain).

Aleksandra Sakowska is a Research Associate at the Shakespeare Institute. She is the author of chapters in *Local and Global Myths in Shakespearean Performance* (2018), *Hamlet Translations: Prisms of Cultural Encounters across the Globe* (2021) and *The History of Polish Theatre* (2021). A frequent collaborator of *Cahiers Élisabéthains*, she co-edited a special issue of the journal, *Shakespeare and European Theatrical Cultures: Circulations, Hybridisations, and Negotiations* (2019).

Boika Sokolova teaches at the University of Notre Dame (USA) in England. She has published extensively on Shakespeare and performance and is co-editor of *Shakespeare in the New Europe* (1994), co-author of *Painting Shakespeare Red* (2001) and author of an ebook on *The Merchant of Venice* (2008). Her latest publications include '*The Merchant of Venice* East of Berlin', *Shakespeare Survey* 71 (2018) and a cluster of articles on post-communist Shakespeare appropriations in Bulgaria (2017), co-authored with Kirilka Stavreva. Her publications have appeared in a number of journals and collections.

Kirilka Stavreva is Professor of English at Cornell College, USA, author of *Words Like Daggers: Violent Female Speech in Early Modern England* (2015) and contributing editor of two ebook series on British literature for the Gale Researcher platform (2017). Her work on European Shakespeare and performance has appeared in numerous journals and edited collections. With Boika Sokolova, she is completing a book on key performances of *The Merchant of Venice*.

Janice Valls-Russell is a Principal Research Associate of France's National Centre for Scientific Research (CNRS), at the Institute for Research on the Renaissance, the Neo-Classical Age and the Enlightenment (IRCL), University Paul-Valéry, Montpellier. Her main areas of interest are the early modern reception of classical mythology and present-day engagements with Shakespeare in performance and education. She has co-edited *Interweaving Myths in Shakespeare and his Contemporaries* (2017), *Thomas Heywood and the Classical Tradition* (2021) and collections of essays on performance.

ACKNOWLEDGEMENTS

The idea for this collection of essays first took shape in the creative atmosphere of the 2017 Conference of the European Shakespeare Research Association, in Gdańsk. Internationally, this was a moment of post-Brexit and post-annexation of Crimea tensions, of the rise of populist nationalisms across Europe, mass migration from Africa and the Middle East. The 'form and pressure' of this time inevitably inform the current volume. The final stages of its preparation took place under national lockdowns across the continent, due to Covid-19, the stress of an abrupt shift to online teaching, and much personal anguish. Thus, our first words of appreciation and gratitude are to our authors and interviewees. Your courage, dear colleagues, your commitment, sense of duty and academic and professional dedication are what has made this volume possible. Your papers and comments were sent from hospital beds, in the aftermath of family loss, despite all manner of difficulties, to prove, yet once again, that an academic and artistic community is a power to reckon with. Thank you all!

As usual, the sources of expertise working behind the scenes of a multicultural undertaking like this are much wider. We owe thanks to Ángel Luis Pujante, Victor Huertas, Juan F. Cerdá, Susan L. Fischer, Jaceck Fabiszak, and to Michael Hattaway and Peter Holland.

In preparing this publication, we have used funding generously offered by the University of Notre Dame (USA) in England and by the Institute for Research on the Renaissance, the Neo-Classical Age and the Enlightenment (IRCL), a joint research unit of the French National Centre for Scientific Research (CNRS) and Université Paul-Valéry, Montpellier. Special thanks are due to Professor JoAnn DellaNeva and the extraordinary Alice Tyrell of Notre Dame; to Nathalie Vienne-

Guerrin and Florence March for their steadfast support; and Brigitte Belin and Vanessa Kuhner-Blaha for their valuable help with funding and logistics.

In Lara Bateman and Mark Dudgeon we had helpful and understanding house editors.

We are indebted to Ella Baron, for allowing us to use one of her marvellous drawings for the cover of this volume. Ella's artwork for the *Times Literary Supplement*, the *Guardian*, numerous NGOs and other venues offers sensitive artistic responses to major contemporary issues. Her drawing of a woman clasping a bundle of cut-outs seemed to us to engage visually with the multiple Others that crowd the performances discussed in this volume, and occupy European societies more widely.

We owe thanks and gratitude to our families for giving us mental space and comfort across this tense period. As ever, Elliot Leader and Yves Peyré offered calm water in the midst of storm. Joaquim and Sofia, too, were a source of relief, fun and inspiration. This book is for and because of them, too.

Introduction

Boika Sokolova and Janice Valls-Russell

In April 2018, the programme of the Craiova International Shakespeare Festival included a production of *Othello*. The director was Armenian; the company and the language of performance were Romanian; the play text was a translation of Boris Pasternak's Russian rendering of Shakespeare's play. Here is how it was received by an international team of reviewers:

> This production's agenda deliberately looked beyond a racialised identity . . . the actor [playing Othello] was not black, and no visual markers, whether in makeup, costume or props, pointed to an ethnic otherness. . . . The mutually damaging othering was created instead by the emphasis on the age difference [between Othello and Desdemona]. (Carson et al. 2019: 85)

Such emphasis is far removed from the dominant interpretations on stages where performances are shaped by race relations, as in the United States, Britain and other European countries with imperial histories, in other words, by the grim legacy of colonialism and slavery. Opting not to employ the race gauge to 'the Moor of Venice' comes to remind us of the complex relationship between a production, its context and the spectating eye. Instead of a black/white, racialized dichotomy, this *Othello* activated another web of interpretive possibilities. It invited audiences to think of the Other not in racial, but in ethnic terms, and to focus on the gender disparities in the play. It also allowed for an unexpected moment of empathy with Iago. If this individual example is something to go by, it points to the variety of perspectives on the Stranger to be encountered in this volume, and to examples of unsettling empathetic identifications in the process of performance. The essays presented here look at twenty-first-century European productions of *The Merchant of Venice* and *Othello*, two plays inflected by the history of European anti-Semitism and racism, in an unstable world shaped by residues of post-totalitarianism, post-communism, deepening regional tensions, rising nationalisms and massive internal as well as external migration.

Fears of the Other, which lurk behind the figure of the Stranger in the two plays, are themselves examples of the 'migrating' images of danger through the course of history. In her study of *Othello*, Sandra Young points to early modern fears of Ottoman aggression and the perilousness of the Mediterranean world, which impacted on the then emerging national (English) identity (2011: 22). Such tensions are apparent in the modern day as well, though the Stranger is different. Recent Spanish productions of the play, as Keith Gregor suggests, are embroiled in the identity debates triggered by the influx of immigrants from northern Africa, 'especially galling in a country, and indeed a region (Andalusia), which owes much of its present identity to the presence of Moors' (2010: 150). Taking a long view of the critical afterlife of *Othello*, Stephen Cohen describes another form of 'migration', a shift in twentieth-century critical interpretations of the play – as a tragedy of jealousy, of race, or of racism, with the processes of othering oscillating between exclusion and assimilation (Cohen 2011: 165–75). He makes a case for understanding the play as 'a tragedy of recognition and identification', enabling intercultural rather than assimilative identification 'with a Moor whom we recognize – and in whom we recognize ourselves – not despite, but because of, his otherness' (2011: 172–3, 179). In tracing the stage history of the play, Ayanna Thompson concludes that in a global context, *Othello* is characterized by malleability which 'invite[s] . . . revisions, retellings, appropriations and adaptations' (Shakespeare 2016: 114), that is, it engages with various alterities and histories. 'Migratory' shifts in the provenance of the dangerous Other and in the ways audiences identify with him mark the history of *The Merchant of Venice* as well. As Emma Smith points out, in Shakespeare's time, a variety of Others lurked behind the figure of the Jew – Catholics and Jesuits, Huguenot and Dutch Protestant immigrants, the stresses of 'multicultural city living' (2013: 219). During the twentieth century, the play's critical and performance focus has shifted away from Portia – the centre of earlier interpretations – to absorb the tragedy that befell the Jewish population of Europe in the 1930s and profoundly affect identification with Shylock as a victim. A push against this tradition has more recently allowed unpleasantly aggressive Shylocks (mirror images to unpleasantly aggressive Christians) to walk the boards, thus directing attention to Venetian society itself. By making Shylock an autonomous agent, and not a victim, productions, such as Peter Zadek's at Vienna's Burgtheater in 1988, have 'activated the play's potential of looking awry at the processes of representation, figuration, and identification', and turned the tables on the Christians, by showing them as Other to him (Ackermann and Schülting 2019: 170). The long shadow of anti-Semitism still dominates *The Merchant of Venice*, as racism does *Othello*, but the changing world in which performances exist continues to reformulate the tensions, dynamics and identification points with characters and their environments.

Just as in the sixteenth century, so in the globalized postcolonial and post-totalitarian twenty-first century, the plays articulate histories arising from the circumstances of their production (Smith 2013: 219). The Strangers in Venice now serve as a test for understanding how modern societies function and for exploring the invisible line between civilized and uncivilized behaviour. They enable productions to reflect on the difficulty of recognizing the otherness of the Other and of living as an Other in an outwardly civilized polity. The faces, races, ethnicities of the Venetian Others have multiplied; indeed, Shylock may or not be Jewish, but a Muslim, or a minority-culture rapper (Ackermann and Schülting 2019: 197–200), while Othello may, or may not, be black, but of another ethnic, social, or age group.

The theatrical engagements with the Stranger represented in this collection have appeared in circumstances of rising European nationalisms, violent reactions to multiculturalism and an influx of refugees from Muslim and African countries. Particularly since 2015, Europe has been awash with humans seeking refuge, as it has been many times before. Western countries have also seen a movement of workforce from the new European Union (EU) member states of Central Eastern Europe, which has further complicated relationships with the Stranger. The eternal bogeyman of history – the Other – is again out there to get us. A prime example of the perceived dangers of these developments was Britain's 2016 vote to leave the EU, driven by fear and suspicion, perhaps unsurprising for the downsized former colonial power. The contagion of extreme nationalism, however, is widespread and rife across the continent. Populist politicians from the smaller nations use it as a power tool in establishing their 'patriotic' credentials through opposition to the 'big' countries, and for attacking EU principles while accepting financial support.

The essays in this collection remind us of the resurgence of old malaises, like anti-Semitism, racism, xenophobia and patriarchal attitudes to gender in the twenty-first century. Some analyse stagings in parts of the continent which self-identify as Others. Not least, all discuss theatrical engagements in languages different from Shakespeare's, which makes them sites of further 'migrations', displacements and inversions. In this sense, as Dirk Delabastita has argued, they are also 'alternative Shakespeares' (2003: 113). Though aesthetically varied, all productions are presentist, seeking to involve the audience through linguistic contemporaneity, modern images, settings and technologies.

The narrowed temporal span allows for a close study of the way the two plays work in performance in the new century. The collection also seeks to address a long-standing need in Shakespeare performance studies to work towards a more transnational view of European histories of *The Merchant of Venice* and *Othello*. Both plays travelled early across the continent, gaining particular popularity during the nationalist revivals of the nineteenth century, becoming quintessentially European Shakespeare texts about the Other. Yet, in spite of their rich stage life, numerous translations and critical and theoretical interpretations, there are few comprehensive national, let alone transnational, studies of the kind of work they have been rallied to do across time – with Germany and Italy as conspicuous exceptions. Smaller studies have made headway, like Boika Sokolova's work on *The Merchant of Venice* in Eastern Europe (2018a). However, without larger national histories, such undertakings can only be partial.[1]

Recently, national histories of the plays have begun to appear, and a clearer picture is starting to emerge. Though in concise formats, such are Anna Cetera's Introduction, in the latest translation of *The Merchant of Venice* in Poland (2015: 211–49), Krystina Kujawińska Courtney's discussion of *Othello*'s Polish lives (2020: 243–53) and Zuzana Koblišková's overview of *Othello* on the contemporary Slovak stage (2018). Chantal Meyer-Plantureux (2005) has studied the stage Jew in France; Andrew Bonell, German Shylocks down to the Nazi period (2008); and Susan L. Fischer, the short but intense late twentieth- and twenty-first-century history of *Merchant* in Spain (2009: 267–303; 2017). The landmark national study is Zeno Ackermann and Sabine Schülting's history of *The Merchant of Venice* on the German stages, which extends to the early twenty-first century (2019).[2] For a long time Anna Busi's work on *Othello* in Italy was a rare example (1973).[3] Shaul Bassi's work on both Venetian plays is notable in its scope and sophistication. In exploring the metamorphoses of *Othello* in the Italian imagination (Bassi 2000), and in his work on race, he has introduced ideas applicable to a variety of regional

European contexts. Particularly productive is his choice to 'supplement' the notion of 'race' with the 'underutilized notion of *ethnicity*', which complicates 'the traditional dialectics of whiteness and blackness' (Bassi 2016: 13, 13–14). Bassi has also drawn attention to 'the different trajectories' Shylock and Othello follow in critical discourse, and to the need to 'attempt to think together [their] destinies' (Bassi 2011: 232–3).

Many of the essays in this volume foreground ethnicity as an issue of debate, while the structure of the book connects the current stage histories of the two plays by placing them together to enable comparisons.

Multi-layered European identities

In an important essay addressing the field of European Shakespeare, Sabine Schülting warns against a 'facile notion of a Europe that is made up of the (allegedly) more or less homogeneous cultures of the member states of the European Union' (2018: 162). Europe has a West, comprising of countries which in the past four centuries have colonized huge swathes of the globe and imagined themselves as the standard of civilized behaviour whereby otherness is defined. For all their differences, Britain, Portugal, Spain, Holland and France shed some of their colonial territories only late in the twentieth century. Europe also has a Centre East, large parts of which had been colonized by the Ottomans, and then damaged by communism; additionally, it has a number of historically formed regions. Apart from these fracture lines, there is also a North-South divide. Vast populations carry painful historical memories, whether as underdogs of the classical empires of yesteryear, of totalitarian regimes of different political stripes, or of life as minorities inside nation states whose borders have shifted more than once over the last century. This Europe's Other is most often the next-door neighbour, or a minority group. Writing about European identities, philosopher Tzvetan Todorov stresses how much they depend on difference. In his view, 'what is individual to the cultures of different countries and regions that make up Europe is of more significance to them than what they have in common' (2010: 171). Within the shifting and porous boundaries of Europe's national formations, past and recent, lies a dynamic diversity of cultures, languages, traditions, collective memories and experiences, a plurality which results in a multi-layeredness of self-identification (Todorov 2010: 171–2, 198), with the concomitant dangers of multi-lateral fractures. The sources of this fraught relationship with the Other, within and without, philosopher Giorgio Agamben traces back to the collapse of the multi-ethnic in-land European empires at the end of the nineteenth century and after the First World War, which resulted in the emergence of new nation states. This was the moment of birth of modern nationalism and the tyranny of streamlined national identity. The territorial consolidation of the new polities resulted in wars and the drastic suppression of the inevitable minority groups remaining inside newly drawn national boundaries (Agamben 2008 [1993]: 91). This caused major demographic distortions through the forced uprooting of whole populations. By the millions, people were pressed to 'return' to their now ethnically designated countries, a process recurring after the Second World War as borders shifted again. Brute pressure on those perceived as Others-within resulted in marginalization, if people refused to deny their religion, ethnicity or language. In the course of these massive shifts, certain sub-groups of Jews and Roma became what Agamben defines as *homo sacer*, 'forms of bare life', excluded from the normal limits of the state, left beyond the interest and protection of the law (Agamben 1998: 8, 71), a situation in which some of the people currently fleeing across the Mediterranean find themselves. Such forms of institutional non-recognition are deaf to Emmanuel Levinas's and Todorov's insistence on the imperative need to acknowledge the Other's humanity, vulnerability, or destitution (Levinas 1991; Todorov 2010).

The totalitarian regimes which emerged before and after the Second World War in the form of military dictatorships in the south and west, or communist states in the east, controlled much of the continent from the Iberian Peninsula to Central Eastern Europe, adding extreme ideologies to the mix. The long list of Others-within came to include the political non-conformist. At the same time, the states of Central Eastern Europe felt betrayed by the West, which consigned them to the Soviet sphere of influence on a piece of scrap paper, in 1944, creating a political othering on a transnational scale (Resis 1978).

After 1989, the post-communist situation created new fractures: new nation states appeared, whether peacefully (Czechoslovakia), or in the throes of war (Yugoslavia). The period produced drastically distorted economic circumstances, gangster elites, the unravelling of social networks, unstable democratic institutions, precipitous social change. This increased the 'migrant encounters' of the west with those driven out of their homes by the economic fallout of capitalist democratization. Europeans, whether from the new member states or not, migrated to the richer Western countries in search of work and triggered new racialized and ethnic divisions (Zorko 2019: 151–67). In 2008, the economic crash hit all populations across the continent. In these circumstances, the influx of refugees between 2015 and 2019 stoked the flames of ethno-nationalisms, with their familiar forms of virulent racism, xenophobia and gender-role normativity, disguised as a return to traditional 'patriotic' and family (i.e. patriarchal) values (Sokolova and Stavreva 2017; Kušić, Lottholz and Manolova 2019). Throughout Europe, immigration from Africa and the Middle East provoked nationalist rallies and outrages led by ideologies of exclusion, under the nostalgic banners of a resurgent extreme political right.

In these circumstances, Hannah Arendt's visionary essay 'We Refugees', written in 1943, at the height of the extermination of European Jews during the Second World War, has become again eminently prescient. Apart from creating a document of a human disaster, Arendt probes the fundamental sources of the tragedy, which she attributes to three basic factors. First, to the refusal of European nation states to allow the otherness of the Jews to exist without being pressurized; to allow their unproblematic identification, as Jews, with the political entities they lived in. Second, to the pressure to assimilate and suppress difference, something ultimately ineffective in saving the lives of those who yielded to it. Thirdly, Arendt points to the abandonment of the non-violent, civilized relationship with the otherness of the Other. At the root of this evil, lay the destruction of 'the comity of European peoples . . . [which] allowed its weakest member to be excluded and persecuted' (Arendt 2007: 274).

It is precisely the principles of diversity, plurality, non-violence, of comity, structured around common interests, embraced by the EU, that open a horizon for a collective European identity, in spite of the different historical experiences and memories of its population (Todorov 2010: 174–95). The current reaction against these principles has made the purportedly multicultural Europe look isolationist; unease hovers around discourses of solidarity; ultra-nationalist sentiment gains ground. Germany, whose official policy of welcoming refugees (*Willkommenskultur*, culture of welcome) had a wide social support during the refugee crisis, has seen a nationalistic backlash, while reactions, especially in post-communist countries, have been drastic. Throughout much of Europe, the 'fear of barbarians' has raised its head again: hate speech, proliferation of offensive images, marginalization, scapegoating and debasing, along with reductive debates on multiculturalism, have chipped away at the collective element in European identities. In this context, as Lieke Stelling suggests, *The Merchant of Venice* and *Othello* have acquired the edge of 'conversion plays', breathing with the apprehension of the Other and anxieties over stable collective identities (Stelling 2019: 2, 3).

Raising walls around 'fortress Europe' obliterates the memory of its own history of migration and internal strife which has taught us that being 'barbarian' is to forget that the Other is a being like ourselves and that we are 'obligated' to 'the stranger, the widow, and the orphan' (Levinas 1991: 215). Resonances of Arendt can be found in the work of a number of thinkers, referred to in this volume, like Levinas who locates his ethics in the face of the Other (1991: 197–201) and Todorov who defines civilized behaviour as 'the ability to *see* others as others and yet to accept . . . that they [are] as human as ourselves' (Todorov 2010: 195, our emphasis).

Time and again, European theatre has turned to the cultural capital of Shakespeare as a template for conceptualizing historical crises (Sheen and Karremann 2016; Bigliazzi 2020; NEW FACES 2016–19). Coming face to face with the Stranger, as Marta Gibińska notes, is 'the crisis we most often face in life' (Gibińska 2019: 2) and the essays in this volume relate recent performances of *The Merchant of Venice* and *Othello* to societal change.

What *Shakespeare's Others* offers, therefore, is a Shakespeare 'repositioned' (Cartelli 1999: 1), transposed into different languages, appropriated and adapted by cultures that are all European, but need to speak, sometimes even shout, in order to be heard.

Imperfect resolutions

The present volume features ten essays, each discussing two individual productions, and three interviews with directors. All consider the aspects of performances pertaining to the role of the Stranger within their specific political, geographic, cultural or linguistic contexts. Three contributions look at *Othello*: in Italy (Anna Maria Cimitile, Chapter 1), Bulgaria (Boika Sokolova and Kirilka Stavreva, Chapter 2) and Portugal (Francesca Rayner, Chapter 9). Three other essays consider *The Merchant of Venice*: in France (Janice Valls-Russell, Chapter 5), Romania (Nicoleta Cinpoeș, Chapter 6) and Hungary (Natália Pikli, Chapter 7). Four look at both plays jointly: in Poland (Aleksandra Sakowska, Chapter 3), Serbia (Zorica Bečanović Nikolić, Chapter 4), the Netherlands (Coen Heijes, Chapter 8), and Germany (Bettina Boecker, Chapter 10). The directors interviewed in the final section discuss their productions of *The Merchant of Venice*

(Karin Coonrod in the Ghetto Nuovo in Venice) and *Othello* (Arnaud Churin in France and Plamen Markov in Bulgaria). Additionally, Lawrence Guntner's brief inductions to each of the three parts of the book tease out connections across the essays. Péter Dávidházi's coda binds the collection together by reaching back to archetypal biblical negotiations between 'crisis' and 'the Stranger'; to the manipulative use of the Other for gain and as a scapegoat. He reminds us of 'Shibboleth', the language barrier used to disenfranchise the Other, and of the eternal conflict over land ownership. Dávidházi recalls the Geneva Bible, the version well-known to Shakespeare, where the Lord explains why land cannot be sold forever: because 'the land is mine, and ye be but strangers and sojourners with me' (Lev. 25.23), thus masterfully connecting the mythopoetic biblical archetypes with the questions at the heart of this volume.

The essays collected here reveal European societies struggling with their own self-image of being civilized and theatrical endeavours consciously, critically, or evasively, grappling with the challenges of living with Strangers. These find expression in the aesthetics of representation and the appropriative strategies that push against the Shakespearean text. Some productions use re-written play versions (Chapters 1, 3, 7), others challenge openly the original and its limitations (Chapters 8, 10). Sometimes, the Stranger is from an ethnic minority within a nation state (Chapter 6), or an immigrant (Chapter 10), an old man (Chapter 3), a woman (Chapters 2, 3, 9) or a gay person (Chapters 3, 4, 7).

Directors consciously complicate audience identification: Andrei Șerban (Chapter 5) and Horațiu Mălăele (Chapter 6) implicate the audience in the rejection of Shylock and in the need for him to plead for respect and dignity. During the filming of scenes from *Othello*, the inmates of a Bulgarian prison share their life stories, which reveal deep-rooted social injustice (Chapter 2).

To confront what theatrical tradition has led audiences to expect, several of the productions flaunted stereotypes by engaging with representational staples, like the prosthetic nose, disseminated by the way of the Western theatrical tradition (Meyer-Plantureux 2005; Sokolova 2018b: 41, 44). The Mohácsi brothers' Hungarian adaptation abounded in references to 'the Jewish nose' and the corrosive normalizing of stereotypes (Chapter 7). In Romania (Chapter 6), Shylock appeared in a pointed yellow hat and spoke with a heavy accent. In France, directors have used the black hat, side-locks, beard and gabardine, which French audiences associate to this day with Gérard Oury's film, *Les Aventures de Rabbi Jacob* (Chapter 5).[4] In *The Arab of Amsterdam*, director Aram Adriaanse exploded stereotypes by interpolating anti-Semitic content from Rainer Werner Fassbinder's controversial *Der Müll, die Stadt und der Tod* [*Garbage, the City and Death*] (Chapter 8).

Where directorial choices on the European continent move farthest away from mainstream Anglo-American representations and expectations is perhaps in the staging of *Othello*, whose production numbers are on the rise. Pragmatically, in European countries without colonial histories, the acting profession is still white; there are few, if any, black actors in places like Poland, Bulgaria or Serbia, which inevitably has an impact on approaches to the play. Racial dichotomies are substituted by ethnic differences, or by aesthetic choices which challenge the tradition of blackface. In countries where black actors are part of the profession, authors discuss and critique the choices made. The performance of race, as these essays suggest, continuously raises questions of representation and casting.

Arguably, a director like Krzysztof Warlikowski, whose *African Tales after Shakespeare* benefitted from international funding, could have cast a black actor for the section that draws on *Othello*. However, his concept used the figures of Lear, Shylock and Othello, all performed in sequence by one of his regular white actors, allowing him to shed light on patriarchy, age, anti-Semitism, race and gender – all questions relevant to Poland and beyond (Chapter 3). In Johan Doesburg's Dutch production (Chapter 8), Othello was also performed by a white actor, whose sole mark of difference was a residual circle of black make-up around his eyes, left there after he had removed his blackface. In the fallout of high-profile murders by members of an immigrant community in the Netherlands, this production addressed the vulnerability of the hybrid identity of the Stranger, even when he does his best to fit in. In a different aesthetic key, colour/ing was used in Miloš Lolić's Serbian production (Chapter 4), where Othello started life made up in black, a colour superseded by green and blue, to reflect his changing states of mind; as a result, at the end, a mingled gamut of hues covered both him and Desdemona. This production examined hybridity and the susceptibility of otherness to deconstruction, an exploration particularly relevant in a country where Iagos have dangerously flattened complexity through nationalistic agendas. In a different political context, the Bulgarian director Lyuben Grois had used a black mark on Othello's forehead to encourage spectators to examine their own – then communist – world where, 'with the stroke of a pen, a "black mark" could turn anyone into a [political] Other' (Chapter 2).

Erasure, or stylization of physical, racial or cultural signifiers, often invites explorations of social alienation. 'Difference', often, has less to do with skin colour (Chapters 1 and 12) than with displacement. In *Arab of Amsterdam* (Chapter 8), Shylock/Rafi introduces himself as a 'Jewish Arab, an Arab Jew', who has migrated to the Netherlands from Iraq: a Jew in an Arab country, he has become an Arab in the Netherlands, invariably marked out as an – or, indeed, *the* – outsider. The Bulgarian director Plamen Markov (Chapter 13) imagined Othello as a white-skinned Moor, originating from a West-African multiracial and multi-tribal empire, living in Venice within a Moorish community including Iago and the Clown, to explore the tensions inside a migrant group. Race and even ethnicity were laid aside, to look instead at the psychology of migration which has become a mass experience for Bulgarians during the post-communist period.

Language plays an important part in broadening the focus of performative appropriation. In Markov's *Othello*, it allowed Iago to manipulate the Clown for his ends, by conversing with him in their native Nigerian Ibo. As the director notes, 'Language is the country that immigrants inhabit. It is what turns them into a tribe' (Chapter 13). The same is true of the host culture and is also revealed as a source of manipulation. In Șerban's Paris production (Chapter 5), Shylock, who thinks that he has integrated to the extent of becoming invisible, has to give up this illusion, just like the character in Péter Valló's Hungarian *Merchant* (Chapter 7).

Language is also intimately connected with regionalism. Within European countries where regions retain a distinct sense of identity, tensions between the national and local are played out through its forms. The Italian productions discussed here (Chapter 1) reverse assumptions and politicize latent prejudices about 'provincial' dialects, accents or body language, to challenge dominant cultural codes. Such strategies have been used to construct a sense of a local 'blackness-within' and re-conceptualize alterity: in Luigi Lo Cascio's Sicilian production, Desdemona was the Stranger to Othello's 'regionally black' community. Code reversals can be used to other political effects, too. In Christian Weise's Berlin *Othello*, Roderigo's Saxon dialect allusively connected him to Germany's right-wing movement Pegida which started in Saxony. In Karin Coonrod's production at the Ghetto Nuovo, abuse in multiple languages suggested the far-reaching extent of anti-Semitism (Chapter 11). Polyglossia has also been employed to move the play beyond anti-Semitism as in Nicolas Stemann's *Merchant* (Munich) which used Shylock's speech about the humanity of the Jew to open space for the disenfranchised voices of Muslims, Roma and women (Chapter 10).

Excess, inversion and remapping expose the 'imaginary ethnicity' (Bassi 2000) of both Othello and Shylock. By placing a white Othello in a black community, Arnaud Churin de-naturalized the dominant status of whiteness, by performing it as otherness (Chapter 12). Such choices de-centre notions about 'those others who are different' and manipulate identification, but their effect is strongly dependent on the contexts of production and reception.

Of the countries presented in this collection, Germany (Chapter 10) and the Netherlands (Chapter 8; Heijes 2020) are perhaps the only ones where the performance of race has been the subject of serious debate within the theatre circles. In Weise's *Othello* (Chapter 10), all Venetians were heavily made up in white, in *commedia dell'arte* style – which contrasted with the minimal make-up on Othello's darker face, making it the only one not resembling a mask.

Gender inequality, or the position of women as Others-within, is explored in many of the productions presented here. In Liliya Abadjieva's *Othello*, which problematized multiple genres (Chapter 2), the women's plight emerged as the true subject of tragedy and became a vehicle for deconstructing a violent, militaristic, male culture. In many productions, tribal masculinity, with its ingrained intolerance and rivalries, holds up a mirror to a misogyny and homophobia still rampant in European post-totalitarian societies (Muharska 2019). Thus, the violence directed at Desdemona in Nuno Carinhas's Portuguese production made the performing actress herself psychologically uncomfortable, and she raised the question of enacting domestic violence with the company (Chapter 9), as did one of the actors in Churin's French production. Warlikowski's *African Tales* gave women space to speak of their traumas and alienation through soliloquies, while the production played with a mixture of patriarchal biases. The durability of the patriarchal model was evident in Markov's adaptation as well (Chapter 13). Productions also turn their eye to the way tribalism pounces on its own, as in the Mohácsis' *Merchant* (Chapter 7), with Antonio realizing that his homosexuality would always make him the odd man out in the Venetian/Hungarian tribe of anti-Semites.

In most of the productions of *Merchant of Venice* discussed here, Arragon, and especially Morocco, take on a significance they typically lack in many Anglo-American stagings. Put simply, they stop being a comic outlet for the darker energies of the play. The Mohácsis (Chapter 7) drove home the message about a deeply ingrained racism that cuts in more directions than one, by making the much-abused Shylock join the Venetians in their disgust at the African's supposed smell. In Laszlo Bocsárdi's Romanian production (Chapter 6), where the two characters were conflated, their strangeness and stereotyping were conveyed through a costume uncannily suggesting a suicide bomber. At the end of Şerban's production, Morocco and Arragon fleetingly reappeared, stripped of their stereotypical garments and make-up: these ghostly strangers embodied something of the ethical inviolability of Levinas's Other, whose gaze and destitution neither the golden world of success, nor the audience, could avoid. A dark-skinned servant's silent empathy with the two suitors produced a powerful juxtaposition to Portia's contemptuousness. The ethics of aesthetic choices invited the audience to look at the play from the margins, through the eyes of characters who frequently receive no greater consideration from them than they do from the other characters on stage.

As already mentioned, many of the productions are based on textual adaptation, but even where the language is substantially preserved, directors intervene in the structures of tragedy and comedy in decisively post-modern ways. The terror and pity associated with the central subject of tragedy and the delicate balances of comedy are displaced and reshuffled. New characters voice their versions of events, claim space for their grievances, aporia reigns over resolution. In Abadjieva's *Othello*, a character popped up to summarize events in a low stylistic key, giving the story the salaciousness of a gossip column (Chapter 2). In Jacques Vincey's *Merchant of Venice*, the actor playing Lancelet (and doubling as Salarino and the Duke) was given a prologue and asides which punctured the dramatic illusion (Chapter 5).[5] In Lo Cascio's version of *Othello*, a soldier figure acted as the Chorus of Greek tragedy, drawing on the deep cultural roots of Sicily (Chapter 1). In Weise's production (Chapter 10), a chorus of Cypriots added a political thrust by repeatedly venting their frustration with the succession of colonizers claiming their island. Sometimes, Shakespeare's text is openly challenged. At the end of Şerban's production of *Merchant* (Chapter 5), Antonio suggested that theirs could not be an adequate ending, if they followed

Shakespeare: 'We are not completely satisfied; ask us questions [and] we shall answer them all'. Similarly, in Weise's *Othello* (Chapter 10), the actors turned to the spectators to request an alternative playtext. In Adriaanse's *Arab of Amsterdam* (Chapter 8), the actors broke the fourth wall by launching a devastating attack on Shakespeare for creating a Jew who was such an easy vehicle for anti-Semitic propaganda.

As this volume suggests, however transformed, Shakespeare's plays remain a shared currency, enabling reflections on the state of Europe, its constituent cultures and their multiple Others. And when theatre-making is not enough, as it was not during the migrant crisis of 2015–19, theatre stepped out of its home and engaged in activism, as it did in Germany (Chapter 10). The productions presented here coalesce around global processes of Shakespearean appropriation (see Desmet, Iyengar and Jacobson 2020). They speak in local voices to audiences living and watching in post-colonial/post-totalitarian situations. Their Europe is an array of traumatized places and Shakespeare, a 'creative resource' (Schalkwyk 2019: xxiii) from a dynamic cultural legacy. Multiplicity is where the trajectories of *The Merchant of Venice* and *Othello* currently converge. While the former has long been the testing ground for reflecting on the Stranger, *Othello* is now coming into prominence to speak for the silenced and obscured Others-within.

On and off European stages, the character of the Other looms large. Holding the mirror up to our own natures and cultures, it challenges us all, as audiences and citizens, through its ever-morphing personations.

Notes

1 *Othello in European Culture* (2021), from John Benjamins (https://benjamins.com/catalog/sec), and a special issue of *Shakespeare* dedicated to *The Merchant of Venice* (18 (2), 2022) should provide further transnational perspectives.

2 The transmutations of both plays within the context of their overall German stage history are discussed in *Shakespeare on the German Stages* (Williams 1990; Hortmann 1998).

3 See also Sergievsky (2014).

4 Almost fifty years after it first came out, *Rabbi Jacob* remains enduringly popular with French audiences, thanks largely to its leading actor, Louis de Funès. During the Covid-19-related lockdown in the spring of 2020, this comedic film drew an audience of over four million when screened on French television (Franceinfo 2020), and a video was posted online to teach viewers the steps of the Hasidic dance that is one of the film's highlights.

5 The spelling of the name used here follows Drakakis's edition (Shakespeare [2010] 2014).

References

Ackermann, Z. and S. Schülting (2019), *Precarious Figurations: Shylock on the German Stage 1920–2010*, Berlin: De Gruyter.

Agamben, G. (1998), *Homo Sacer: Sovereign Power and Bare Life*, trans. D. Heller-Roazen, Redwood City: Stanford University Press.

Agamben, G. ([1993] 2008), 'Beyond Human Rights', *Social Engineering* 15: 90–5.

Arendt, H. ([1943] 2007), 'We Refugees', in J. Cohn and R. H. Feldman (eds), *The Jewish Writings*, 264–74, New York: Schocken Books.

Bassi, S. (2000), *Le metamorfosi di Otello, Storia di un'etnicità immaginaria*, Bari: Graphis.

Bassi, S. (2011), 'Barefoot to Palestine: The Failed Meetings of Shylock and Othello', in L. Tosi and S. Bassi (eds), *Visions of Venice in Shakespeare*, 231–41, London: Routledge.

Bassi, S. (2016), *Shakespeare's Italy and Italy's Shakespeare: Place, 'Race', Politics*, London: Palgrave Macmillan.

Bigliazzi, S. (2020), *Shakespeare in Crisis: One Hundred Years of Italian Narratives*, Amsterdam: John Benjamins.

Bonnell, A. G. (2008), *Shylock in Germany: Antisemitism and the German Theatre from The Enlightenment to the Nazis*, London: Tauris.

Busi, A. (1973), *Otello in Italia, 1772–1972*, Bari: Adriatica.

Carson, C., N. Galland, D. Monah, J. Seymour and J. Valls-Russell (2019), '*Othello*, directed by Suren Shahverdyan for Teatrul Tony Bulandra, Târgovişte, Romania; Teatrul Colibri, Craiova, 25 April 2018' (review), *Cahiers Élisabéthains*, 100 (1): 84–6.

Cartelli, T. (1999), *Repositioning Shakespeare: National Formations, Postcolonial Appropriations*, London: Routledge.

Cetera, A. (ed.), (2015), William Shakespeare. *Kupiec wenecki*, trans. P. Kamiński, Warszawa: Wydawnictwo WAB.

Cohen, S. (2011), 'I am What I am Not: Identifying with the Other in *Othello*', *Shakespeare Survey*, 64: 163–79.

Delabastita, D. (2003), 'More Alternative Shakespeares', in A.-L. Pujante and T. Hoenselaars (eds), *Four Hundred Years of Shakespeare in Europe*, 113–33, Newark: University of Delaware Press.

Desmet, C., S. Iyengar and M. Jacobson (eds) (2020), *The Routledge Handbook of Shakespeare and Global Appropriation*, London: Routledge.

Fischer, S. L. (2009), *Reading Performance: Spanish Golden Age Theatre and Shakespeare on the Modern Stage*, Woodbridge: Tamesis.

Fischer, S. L. (2017), 'Staging *The Merchant of Venice* in Spain (2015): Felicitous "Romancing" with Money and Willful Ambiguity?', *Shakespeare Bulletin*, 35 (2): 317–34.

Franceinfo (2020), 'Pourquoi Louis de Funès est un antidépresseur majeur en temps de confinement', 6 April, https://www.francetv info.fr/culture/patrimoine/pourquoi-l-acteur-louis-de-funes-reste-un-antidepresseur-majeur-en-temps-de-confinement_3902423.html (accessed 2 April 2021).

Gibińska, M. (2019), 'Crisis: Meeting the Other and the Philosophy of Dialogue', preprint, halshs-02145012 (accessed 2 April 2021).

Gregor, K. (2010), *Shakespeare in the Spanish Theatre: 1772 to the Present*, London: Bloomsbury.

Heijes, C. (2020), *Shakespeare, Blackface and Race: Different Perspectives*, Elements in Shakespeare Performance, Cambridge: Cambridge University Press.

Hortmann, W. (1998), *Shakespeare on the German Stage, vol. 2, The Twentieth Century*, Cambridge: Cambridge University Press.

Koblišková, Z. (2018), 'Othello and the Perception of Race Within the Cultural Context of Czech and Slovak Theatre', *Theatralia*, 21 (2): 127–40.

Kujawińska Courtney, K. (2020), '*Othello* in Poland, a Prevailingly Homogeneous Ethnic Country', in C. Desmet, S. Iyengar and M. Jacobson (eds), *The Routledge Handbook of Shakespeare and Global Appropriation*, 243–53, London: Routledge.

Kušić, K., P. Lottholz and P. Manolova (2019), 'From Dialogue to Practice: Pathways towards Decoloniality in Southeast Europe', in P. Manolova, K. Kušić and P. Lottholz (eds), *Decolonial Theory and Practice in Southeast Europe*, Special Issue, *dVERSIA*, 03/19: 7–30. Available online: https://issuu.com/dversiamagazine/docs/dversia-special-issie-decolonial-th (accessed 2 April 2021).

Levinas, E. ([1969] 1991), *Totality and Infinity: An Essay on Exteriority*, trans. A. Lingis, Pittsburgh: Duquesne University Press.

Meyer-Plantureux, C. (2005), *Les Enfants de Shylock, ou l'antisémitisme sur scène: images du Juif de 1880 à nos jours*, Paris: Éditions Complexe.

Muharska, R. (2019), 'Chalga Culture Meets the Istanbul Convention: A Grotesque Spectacle of Masculinity', in E. Slavova, A. Bagasheva and K. Slavova et al. (eds), *Traditions and Transitions*, vol. 1, 206–22, Sofia: Sofia University Press.

NEW FACES (2016–19), *Facing Europe in Crisis: Shakespeare's World and Present Challenges*, http://www.new-faces-erasmusplus.fr/ (accessed 2 April 2021).

Resis, A. (April 1978). 'The Churchill-Stalin Secret "Percentages" Agreement on the Balkans, Moscow, October 1944', *American Historical Review*, 83 (2): 368–87.

Schalkwyk, D. (2019), 'Foreword', in A. S. Refskou, M. Alvaro de Amorim and V. M. de Carvalho (eds), *Eating Shakespeare: Cultural Anthropophagy as Global Methodology*, xvii–xxiii, London: Bloomsbury.

Schülting, S. (2018), 'Imagined Communities: Reconsidering European Shakespeares', *Cahiers Élisabéthains*, 96 (1): 160–71.

Sergievsky, A. (2014), 'Othello in Italy', published online: https://www.academia.edu/12461671/ (accessed 2 April 2021).

Shakespeare, W. ([2010] 2014), *The Merchant of Venice*, ed. J. Drakakis, The Arden Shakespeare, third series, London: Bloomsbury.

Shakespeare, W. ([1997] 2016), *Othello*, ed. E. A. J. Honigmann, rev. ed., intr. A. Thompson, The Arden Shakespeare, third series, London: Bloomsbury.

Sheen, E. and I. Karremann (eds) (2016), *Shakespeare in Cold War Europe: Conflict, Commemoration, Celebration*, Basingstoke: Palgrave Macmillan.

Smith, E. (2013), 'Was Shylock Jewish?', *Shakespeare Quarterly*, 64 (2): 188–219.

Sokolova, B. (2018a), '"Mingled Yarn": *The Merchant of Venice* East of Berlin and the Legacy of "Eastern Europe"', *Shakespeare Survey*, 71: 88–102.

Sokolova, B. (2018b), 'The Bulgarian Fortunes of *The Merchant of Venice*', in J. B. Wild (ed.), *Shakespeare in Between*, 38–59, Bratislava: Vysoka skola muzickych umeni v Bratislave, Divatelna fakulta.

Sokolova, B. and K. Stavreva (2017), '"The Readiness is All", Or the Politics of Art in Post-Communist Bulgaria', *Bulgarian Shakespeares, Toronto Slavic Quarterly*, 60: 1–17. Available online: http://sites.utoronto.ca/tsq/60/SokolovaStavreva1_60.pdf (accessed 2 April 2021).

Stelling, L. (2019), 'Wheeling Strangers of Here and Everywhere: Present Issues of Integration and the Early Modern Crisis of Conversion', preprint, halshs-02268979 (accessed 2 April 2021).

Todorov, Tz. ([2008] 2010), *The Fear of Barbarians: Beyond the Clash of Civilizations*, Chicago: University of Chicago Press.

Williams, S. (1990), *Shakespeare on the German Stage*, vol. 1, *1586–1914*, Cambridge: Cambridge University Press.

Young, S. (2011), 'Imagining Alterity and Belonging on the English Stage in an Age of Expansion: A Reading of *Othello*', *Shakespeare in Southern Africa*, 23: 21–9.

Zorko, Š. D. (2019), 'Migrant Encounters Between Postsocialism and Postcolonialism', in P. Manolova, K. Kušić and P. Lottholz (eds), *Decolonial Theory and Practice in Southeast Europe*, Special Issue, *dVERSIA*, 03/19: 151–67. Available online: https://issuu.com/dversiamagazine/docs/dversia-special-issie-decolonial-th (accessed 2 April 2021).

PART ONE

Relocating otherness

The Other-within

Induction 1

Lawrence Guntner

The stagings of Shakespeare's Venetian plays discussed in Part One (Relocating otherness: The Other-within) probe the question of otherness within national European contexts: Italy, Bulgaria, Poland, Serbia and France. The theatre practitioners presented here liberate and redefine these received narratives to examine and challenge hegemonies, whether linguistic, religious, ethnic or ideological, which serve to silence singularities, assimilate them or relegate them to the margins in a variety of ways. Their strategies involve commissioning new translations and radical adaptations which contest official vernaculars with regional languages, relocating the action to contemporary settings, restructuring the dramaturgy of the plays through the replacement of dialogue with narrators and commentators, foregrounding minor characters and sometimes directly challenging Shakespeare's text for deficiencies, or intervening in its integrity and coherence – all techniques associated with post-dramatic theatre. Though not all of them can be brought under this heading, re-envisioning otherness in Shakespeare performance has meant politicizing Shakespeare. And while race, as skin pigmentation, has become the volatile marker for the Other throughout Europe, Othello's skin colour as a cultural marker has been diffused through the dissolution of black/white dichotomies, the foregrounding of gender and other forms of othering.

Recent Italian adaptations of *Othello* have chosen to concentrate on language and geography. This, Anna Maria

Cimitile argues, was an overt act of 'resistance to linguistic and cultural homogenization'. In her study, she follows Antonio Gramsci's discussion of the 'Southern Question', regarding the use of regional dialects to resist fascist ideas of marginalizing the local through the hegemony of a single national vernacular, a process where the translation of Shakespeare was used as a tool. Othello's 'blackness' was neither mentioned, nor suggested via make-up, but signified by regional verbal and body language, an act which redefined alterity as well as critiqued it as an act of regional othering with profound political implications. The rebalancing of the play thus underscored Desdemona's otherness, both in terms of gender and culture.

Boika Sokolova and Kirilka Stavreva also explore how recent Bulgarian productions have re-located *Othello*, protagonist and play, in twenty-first-century post-communist Bulgaria in order to probe otherness within. In the theatre, burlesque, slapstick, music and dance, and spatial upstaging of Othello's tragedy, foregrounded the brutalization of women. On film, *Othello* became 'a tragedy of exclusion', where the setting of a real prison, combined with the histories of the inmates, created a metaphor for post-communist Bulgarian society, its deprivations and arbitrary class justice. The authors use Tzvetan Todorov's ethical philosophy to suggest how the film peels away the otherness of the prisoners, while the production estranges the women through cross-gender casting to make these Others stand before the viewer in all their vulnerability as human beings.

Just as with the Italian and Bulgarian productions, Aleksandra Sakowska views Krzysztof Warlikowski's *African Tales after Shakespeare* in the context of the sensibilities, stereotypes and prejudices in twenty-first-century Poland. Through a theoretical approach deriving from Zygmunt Bauman, the essay discusses the radically reduced mélange of *The Merchant of Venice*, *Othello* and *King Lear*, supplemented with other modern texts and stark, shocking visual effects, which result in a 'multi-focal exploration of identity'. Warlikowski deconstructs stereotypes of ethnicity, race, gender, sexuality, age and disability to confront Polish and international audiences with universal examples of marginalization. By conjoining three iconic outcasts – Shylock (the Jew), Othello (the black man), Lear (the debilitated old man) – the production simultaneously de-historicized the characters and challenged the audience's perceptions of the 'normal' strange.

For Zorica Bečanović Nicolić, *The Merchant of Venice* and *Othello* are structured around 'intricate webs of interpretation', or rather, 'mis-interpretation', a hermeneutic approach, based on Hans-Georg Gadamer, which she applies in the discussion of their stagings in Belgrade. In Shylock's Venice, moved to the late 1920s, with Italian fascism on the rise, the Strangers – homosexuals, Jews and other foreigners – were to be ghettoized as a danger to the social order. A stylistically radical production of *Othello* used a mixture of colours to mark symbolically otherness, locations and states of mind, while characters remained on stage throughout the action, reminiscent of both television reality shows and pervasive surveillance. In both productions, events in Shakespeare's plays were projected onto the local context, where 'every representative of any ex-Yugoslav nation in any of the ex-Yugoslav republics and now separate states, is the Other'.

Janice Valls-Russell draws attention both to the reluctance of French theatre to stage *The Merchant of Venice* and the evasiveness of interpretation. The two productions which are the subject of her essay break with this tradition by placing the action in the world of high banking and a small supermarket respectively, referencing recent anti-Semitic attacks in France. Drawing on Jean-Paul Sartre's anatomization of the anti-Semite and Michel Maffesoli's theorization of urban neo-tribalism, Valls-Russell suggests that these two productions projected a similar message: the Stranger no longer seems equal in terms of the ideals of the French Republic, which have come under increasing pressure in the new millennium.

The close analysis of the strategies of representation, interpretation and re-imagining of local European alterities highlights a heightened sense of social inequality and gender difference. Directors simultaneously engage with national assumptions regarding a collective identity and invite their audiences to look beyond the limitations of national representations. This is an invitation to reconnect through presentist re-envisionings of Shakespeare's plays in a variety of European contexts, and the complexities, vulnerabilities and potentialities of living with the Other, both within and without.

1

'Venice' is elsewhere

The Stranger's locality, or Italian 'blackness' in twenty-first-century stagings of *Othello*

Anna Maria Cimitile

Locality and the literary global

In *Winter Sleep* (2014), directed by the Turkish director Nuri Bilge Ceylan, the protagonist is the owner of the Othello Hotel, in Cappadocia.[1] As it turns out, he is a former actor, writing a book on the history of Turkish theatre. In a stunning snowy landscape and picturesque village, in a country suspended between (and bridging) Europe and Asia, the name of the hotel, located in one of Cappadocia's troglodyte dwellings, expresses the protagonist's life-long love of drama and stands for theatre itself. In that exotic landscape the name, albeit unexpected, comes across as a scrap of the Western world that has reached a region otherwise remote from all that *Othello* would stand for: Western art, English literature, Shakespeare. To the viewer, the play has a double status: as a universal icon of theatre and as a specifically British canonical text.[2] Othello the character, on the other hand, is the Stranger in Venice and a Stranger in Turkey; not as 'an extravagant and wheeling stranger, / Of here and everywhere' (*Oth* 1.1.134–5), but because in the Anatolian space he is more evidently his 'real' self: an English, Anglophone 'Venetian' Moor.[3]

The sublime, desolate landscape of Cappadocia in Ceylan's film is a unique locality that helps foreground the Europeanness-as-foreignness of *Othello*, not least because it stands in stark contrast to the play's famous setting, Venice;[4] in this respect, one could even say that the allusion to *Othello* in *Winter Sleep* enhances the *locality* (Venice) of an otherwise *universal* play. Although not an adaptation, the film reveals the relevance of space and place in the tragedy. It poses a question about what happens when stagings of *Othello* translocate the original setting; to answer which, one should first consider what 'locality' means when referring to Shakespearean plays. 'Locality' can denote multiple sites: besides the setting (Venice in *Othello*), it can point to the actual location of site-specific performances (e.g. the Venetian Ghetto in the 2016 production of *The Merchant in Venice*),[5] or, following a trend in performance and reception studies, it can even refer to a wider space (nation, region, city) where the performance takes place.

For Alexa Huang, representing Shakespeare also means to represent the dynamics between different localities: Shakespeare's and the actors' (2007: 190). In the two Italian stagings I discuss here, those different levels of Shakespearean 'locality' are engaged by the directorial choices. To parallel the displacement of 'Venice' to another Italian region or city, the text is translated into a regional Italian dialect. As a result, the two versions invite a reflection on several related aspects:

on translocating Shakespeare, and on the specific, emerging theoretical positionalities that arise when the location is the Italian South; on how those positionalities contribute both to a re-envisioning of Italian regional culture and to globally significant readings of *Othello*.

In recent years, critics have variously acknowledged that a relationship is always in place between global and local Shakespeare. For Huang, '"global Shakespeares" seems to be able to answer competing demands that artists and scholars become more transnational in outlook while simultaneously sustaining traditional canons' (2013: 273). Sandra Young proposes to think of the two not as oppositional, but rather 'as the constitutive elements of an appropriative "global"' (2019: 15). Against the backdrop of, and in dialogue with, ongoing Shakespeare Studies developed in this vein, this chapter focuses on versions of *Othello* which move the setting from Northern to Southern Italy and from Shakespearean English to Italian dialects. What kind of theoretical impact on notions of global and local Shakespeare is potentially present in the specific literary interventions? How is the multi-layered otherness of Othello reconceptualized by a Neapolitan or Sicilian Otello? Can the discussion of two *Othellos* from the Italian South be related to, and actualize, Antonio Gramsci's discussion of a 'Southern Question'? I discuss Luigi Lo Cascio's *Otello* (2015), translated into, or rather rewritten in, the Sicilian dialect by Lo Cascio himself, and Giuseppe Miale di Mauro's *Otello* (2017), rendered into the Neapolitan dialect by Gianni Spezzano.[6] Both directors chose Southern Italian regional cultures to stage the tensions around identity and difference in Shakespeare's play, staging thereby the pressures over identity and difference experienced by those cultures.

Luigi Lo Cascio's Sicilian *Otello* (2015)

The Sicilian *Otello* only retains the three main characters: Iago, Otello and Desdemona (Lodovico appears once, briefly), but adds a Soldier who acts as the Chorus of ancient Greek tragedy.[7] He is a witness to the tragic events, which have already unfolded, and comes in mainly to address the audience and retell the story of the general and his wife. The past is made present, and the Soldier's retelling frequently refers to the characters on stage and to the moment they are 'living' there and then. He sometimes interacts with the others, but most of what we see or hear, even the most famous scenes from the play, is presented as a recounting of past events, whether by the Soldier or one of the other characters. The play is *a staging of the tale* of Otello and his wife, and to this end different textualities are employed: for example, the Soldier's central, oral narration, and the invention of letters Otello and Desdemona exchanged before marriage, which produce more stories of their respective past and present. Sometimes latching onto a single word of Shakespeare's text, the letters reveal new tragic 'secrets' or background stories, like that of Otello's brother's death on the battlefield, a long and detailed account originating in Iago's brief reference (*Oth* 3.4.135–8).[8] The characters each speak and enact their own letters, transforming the written word into a live 'exchange': in one of them, Otello mentions two accompanying gifts, a handkerchief and . . . a dagger, giving them to Desdemona before exiting, leaving 'our great captain's captain' (*Oth* 2.1.74) to slash at the air with her new weapon.

Lo Cascio's playtext is a literary work in its own right. Pirandellian stage directions describe the action about to take place and comment on it in a suggestive figurative language, as if to allow readers to identify with the atmosphere and sensations that audiences might experience. These stage directions are an intrinsic part of the text. Consider the opening of the first one:

Darkness in the house. The underground sound of a musical note has been delving into the ears of spectators [ha cominciato a scavare nel'ascolto degli spettatori] *for a few minutes; its volume, increasing in slow crescendo, seems to demand that the curtain should now finally open.* (Lo Cascio 2015: 13)[9]

Similarly, the second stage direction describes the characters on stage as being '*still as bas-reliefs carved in the stone of an ancient temple . . . [beings] of implacable rigidity, as if subject to a spell that blocked time and made movement impossible*' (16).

The action starts in medias res; in the darkness, a video, projected onto a huge white sheet which closes off the stage area, shows an animated drawing tracing the story of the handkerchief from the 'hallowed' worms that 'did breed the silk' (*Oth* 3.4.75) to the present moment. Otello's voice is heard, questioning Desdemona, we guess, about the handkerchief (*Oth* 3.4.51–99). Otello refuses the handkerchief Desdemona must have offered him, protesting that he does not want 'a handkerchief without a history' (14). He then tells her the story of the precious gift, following Shakespeare. The sheet comes down to reveal four figures, '*still as bas-reliefs*': Otello is sitting on a chair, almost in the proscenium, with his back to the audience – he will stay like that during most of the scene; next to him is Iago; upstage, right and left, are Lodovico and Desdemona. This is the moment when Otello slaps Desdemona in public, shortly before killing her. Iago, too, reveals his most characteristic features from the outset; as Lodovico comes forward ('*Enter LODOVICO . . .*', *Oth* 4.1.212sd) and asks how Cassio fares, Iago replies: 'Right now? He lives, still' (17). Iago's obscurely truthful answer is fully meaningful to those who know his plot – and his rhetorical abilities – from the original play.

The scenes follow fluidly, shrinking time and merging moments that are apart in Shakespeare's play. We move from the opening scene, when Otello strikes Desdemona, to the scene after her death, when Iago enters from the back of the auditorium, already a prisoner, with a rope around his neck, to deliver a metatheatrical monologue: 'What are you staring at? / This spectacle [of his own death] is not for you. It is not for your entertainment. / I'll get to the scaffold and to my torture for myself only' (21). Nothing will change after him, because audience and characters share the same destiny; the 'cancer' of jealousy (both Iago's envy and Otello's jealousy) will not go away: 'Man is cancer, / Cancer and mud. / Cancer without laws' (22). In a language that is even more violent than Shakespeare's, Iago describes the physical tortures he is about to suffer, and seems to rejoice in them. Through physical pain the body triumphs over the 'useless thoughts of the mind': 'Torture, [is] hygiene of the mind' (24).

The Soldier/Chorus, who holds the other end of Iago's rope, enters after Iago's monologue to report on Otello's speech – 'Soft you, a word or two before you go' (*Oth* 5.2.336–54) – and tell the whole story of Otello and Desdemona. As he says 'Let us begin', the scene returns to the moment when, in Lo Cascio's variation on the handkerchief motif, Desdemona and Otello secretly exchange love letters written on napkins in order to hide their love from her father.

Blackness is a problematic issue. The Sicilian Otello, like the actor (Vincenzo Pirrotta), is white. Mentions of his black skin seem to refer not to ethnicity, but rather to the darker hue sometimes associated with Southern Italians. At the beginning of his tale, the Soldier recalls how the first thing people noticed or remembered about Otello was his 'black skin' ('a peddi nivura' [30]). However, because he thinks it is not true that this was the cause of Otello's tragedy, the Soldier says that, in his account, he will not mention it – and indeed, he does not. For the Soldier, Otello's is the story of a tragic love, in which skin colour plays no part: 'In my memory and in my tale Otello has a new skin, bright and white like a full moon' ('Ntù me' ricordu e ntù me' cuntu Otello / ci havi na peddi nova, / lucenti e janca comu luna china' [32]).

Intertextuality characterizes the speeches of the two most metatheatrical figures, Iago and the Soldier. Iago quotes from other Shakespearean plays, like *Hamlet*'s 'The rest is silence' ('chiddu c'arresta è silenziu' [25], which he later poetically elaborates [96–7]), whereas the Soldier points to the textual dimension of all characters when, comparing Otello to other famous figures, he refers to Brutus, Cassius, Coriolanus, the 'Prince of Denmark' and Lear (30) – all in Shakespeare's plays. The play closes with the Soldier about to take Otello to the moon (an homage to Ariosto's *Orlando Furioso*); in the usual overlapping between staged past events (in this case, a past dream of the Soldier's) and their present recounting, he tells the story of the journey and converses with Otello while on the moon. He ends the play by pronouncing Iago's last sentence from Pier Paolo Pasolini's *Che cosa sono le nuvole?* reformulated in Sicilian, while taking Otello back to the Earth (Lo Cascio 2015: 109).

Sicily as a new location is only linguistically present. All the characters – except Desdemona, who speaks in Italian – speak Sicilian. As for references to the Sicilian setting, there are only two. In his 'Farewell the tranquil mind' speech (*Oth* 3.3.350-60), Otello mentions 'the mountain where Jove is' ('u munti unni sta Giovi' [70]), a possible allusion to Monte di Giove or Mongiove, a mountain in Sicily in the Messina province.[10] The other reference, also by Otello, is to 'Muncibeddu' (84), a variant spelling of Mungibeddu, a popular appellative for *the* mountain in Sicily, Mount Etna.

Giuseppe Miale di Mauro's Neapolitan *Otello* (2017)

Miale di Mauro's *Otello* is set in an underground world of illegality: Otello is a young Neapolitan crime boss, Iago a heavy cannabis user, Roderigo being his dealer. Iago's comedic features make him really likeable. There are only six characters, listed in a brief introductory note written by the director, where each figure is identified by its distinctive role or feature: Otello is the culprit, Iago the misogynist, Cassio the critical conscience, Desdemona the victim; Emilia is an unjust justice; Roderigo is the puppeteer. There are also wedding guests, unmentioned in the introductory note, who remain on stage throughout, as silent witnesses to the tragedy. In the note, the director explains that the production aims at denouncing femicide as a global scourge.

The play opens with Otello and Desdemona's wedding ceremony, which takes place when Brabantio is already dead. In an acceleration of the time line, their banquet lasts for the duration of the play, the action being concentrated to a single day. A red handkerchief is wrapped round the wedding rings Emilia hands Desdemona, a gift and pledge of love from Otello to his wife-to-be in accordance with family tradition. Here, too, the story is essentially that of a man and a woman, polarizing the wedding guests into groups: the men siding with Otello and the women with Desdemona.

Miale di Mauro's *Otello* was part of *Glob(e)al Shakespeare*, a cycle of six Shakespearean plays produced by Naples's Teatro Bellini in 2017, to celebrate the 400th anniversary of the playwright's death. Metatheatricality characterized all six productions, somewhat playfully in *Otello*: 'William the poet' ('Guglielmo 'o poeta') entered his own play to the music of a 'jealousy rap'. The newly wedded couple and their guests had come in from the far end of the auditorium, walking to the stage between the wooden benches which had replaced the velvet armchairs, while spectators threw rose petals.[11] Intermediality was also used: Otello's fantasy of Desdemona's unfaithfulness was a video, hardcore style, of her and Cassio.

The characters occasionally spoke Neapolitan, but mostly Italian with Neapolitan inflection, except for Desdemona and Cassio, the two Strangers in this production, who only spoke in Italian. The Neapolitan setting was recognizable from typically Neapolitan hand gestures or attitudes, as well as the dialect, with Iago the most colourful Neapolitan.

Both Lo Cascio's and Miale di Mauro's Otellos were white-skinned 'locals', rooted in their respective cultures. The Strangers were the two Desdemonas, victims of male jealousy, linguistically and culturally Other to surrounding communities used to witnessing and stereotypically adumbrating femicide. The way the local cultures were represented made 'recognition' of what the two productions were obviously condemning the pre-eminent experience of audiences. In Miale di Mauro's *Otello* the topical context was recognizable in the day-long wedding ceremony; in Lo Cascio's, there were almost no material references to the Sicilian setting: jealousy was at once a marker of locality and the key to an intimate and universal tale of unwise love. In their Southern Italian localities both productions recast *Othello* as a story that is both contemporary and timeless. By using the stereotype of the Southern Italian jealous man (especially the Sicilian *Otello*), they made Shakespeare *current*.[12] As Neapolitan and Sicilian share a certain 'refusal to assimilate into canonical forms',[13] the cultural translation from Venice to Southern Italy gave a renewed sense to this *currency*, with imports for *Othello*'s representation of 'blackness' and difference.

Venice, Naples, Sicily: The literary and political status of dialects

In 1611 Thomas Coryat's *Crudities* defined Venice as 'the most glorious, peerelesse, and mayden Citie of Venice . . . mayden, because it was never conquered' (Coryat 1905: 301). The city held a fascination for its visitors in Shakespeare's time. As the setting for *Othello* it would evoke for London audiences a place of thriving commerce and wealth that was also a melting pot of races, religions and cultures, a place at once beautiful, exotic and possibly dangerous.

Naples seems to have invited the same kind of reaction from travellers: Goethe quoted the famous proverb 'Vede Napoli e poi muori!' ('See Naples and die!') (1885: 179). Yet, the city was also ungovernable, at once scandalous and seductive according to Fernand Braudel (quoted in Maresca 2012: 319–23). Naples was the universal city for Curzio Malaparte:

> When Naples was one of the most illustrious capitals in Europe, one of the greatest cities in the world, it contained

a bit of everything. It contained a bit of London, a bit of Paris, a bit of Madrid, a bit of Vienna – it was a microcosm of Europe. Now that it is in its decline nothing is left in it but Naples. What do you expect to find in London, Paris, Vienna? You will find Naples. It is the fate of Europe to become Naples. If you stay in Europe for a bit you will become Neapolitan yourselves. (Malaparte 1952: 130)

As for Sicily, Goethe wrote: 'Italy without Sicily leaves no image on the soul; here is the key to all' (1885: 240). In the eyes of foreign travellers, the fascination of these two new settings parallels that of Venice.

In the Neapolitan *Otello* the displacement to Naples was achieved by replacing the eighteen references to Venice by generic references to 'this city'; the Sicilian *Otello* left out all cues that mention the city. The dis/relocation of Venice was effected by the aural impact of dialects, the characteristic hand gestures and ways of speaking. As the divide between the North and South of Italy remains a highly politicized question, translating Shakespeare into Southern dialects is evidently a political as well as a literary act.

'One does not inhabit a country; one inhabits a language', writes E. M. Cioran (2012: 12), while Jacques Derrida declares: 'I only have one language; it is not mine' (1998: 1). Taking our cue from these two statements on (un)belonging, intended in the Heideggerian terms of being-in-a-language, what can we say about the progress of the Moor in the Shakespearean tragedy, when we find him inhabiting another language – not the imagined Italian and real English of the play, but a Southern variation of Italian? Or literary variations of the Neapolitan or Sicilian dialects? How would these refashion the tragic character, alter our perception of his otherness? Also, what would the use of regional dialects bring to: (1) the staging of Shakespeare; (2) the perception of those dialects and the regional cultures associated with them; and (3), more specifically, the historically residual vision of subaltern Southern Italy?

In literature as in cinema, the presence of characters talking in dialect adds to the realism of the story. This is as true of Shakespeare as it is of Victorian novels or Ken Loach's films. Criticism has always been alert to the ideological bias in the use of dialects in literary texts, especially in the erroneous conflation of geographical belonging and cultural status, already present in George Puttenham's *Arte of English Poesie* (1589) (Puttenham 1811: 120). Writing about Shakespeare and his contemporaries, Brian Gibbons considers how accents and dialects in early modern texts are often 'borders marking historical and cultural as well as merely geographical difference', alongside 'class differences' (2011: 76). He recalls the ambivalent responses to dialects: while a shared accent or dialect may contribute to solidarity and bonding, hearing a different accent may either give pleasure, or produce a feeling of hostility. At the turn of the seventeenth century some dialects were 'stage-conventionalized': they were employed as 'signals' and 'socio-cultural indicators', which audiences would have been able to recognize (Gibbons 2011: 88). English would have been enhanced by the contrast with what the dialects represented on stage. The two Southern *Otellos* inverted this convention. Italian was relegated to a minority status, a sign for foreignness – doubly displaced, as it signalled not the Moor's, but Desdemona's, foreignness.

Over the years, Italy has seen few translations of Shakespeare into dialects. Eduardo De Filippo translated *The Tempest* into seventeenth-century Neapolitan language in 1984. Pasolini had previously adapted *Othello*, evoking the Sicilian Teatro dei Pupi in *Che cosa sono le nuvole?* (1968), in which actors spoke in different accents: Sicilian, Roman, Neapolitan. More recently, Roberta Torre moved *Romeo and Juliet* to Palermo in *Sud Side Stori* (2000), and Andrea Camilleri translated *Much Ado about Nothing* into Sicilian in *Troppu trafficu ppi nenti* (2009). Such dialectal translations of Shakespeare aim to consolidate a sense of belonging to regional communities, raising questions of cultural authority that concern both Shakespeare and the regional dialect and culture appropriating it.

These Shakespeare translations belong to the wider practice of translating the classics, Dante's *Comedy* above all, as a mode of survival and literary self-affirmation. Translations into Neapolitan range from Vergil's *Bucolics* (1835) to Carlo Collodi's *Pinocchio*, translated by Antonio Del Deo in 1978 – and into Sicilian *sestine* by Giuseppe Ganci Battaglia in 1927. The practice is comparable with other world dialects or minority literatures – such as Catalan, to take another European example – as a proactive instrument of identitarian politics and survival.[14] The two *Otellos*, however, do more than seek recognition for their respective dialects and cultures; hereon, I focus on what they do to re-appraise Othello's 'blackness' by using as critical lenses the Gramscian vision of the 'Southern Question' and Pasolini's view of regional cultures and dialects.

Dialects in early modern Italian literature were already associated with class and cultural difference, and used to fashion and assert local identity. The sixteenth-century Paduan playwright Ruzante used the *pavan* (the Paduan variety of Venetian) or a mixture of dialects, in his most popular comedies, to represent the everyday life of lower classes, peasants and others. In the twentieth century attention to the use of dialects, especially in the theatre, was still high: Nobel Prize Laureate Dario Fo noted its subversive character and acknowledged his own debt as a dramatist to Ruzante, in particular for *Mistero buffo* (1969), in which he adopted a combination of Italian, dialectal forms and the invented 'grammelot'. Even Italo Calvino, who was unenthusiastic about dialects, conceded that literary Italian should look to the vernaculars to renew itself, provided it did not annihilate itself in the process (Calvino 1980: 3–18). For Luigi Meneghello, the use of dialect in literary texts was about truth and truthfulness, as opposed to falsehood or fakeness (Meneghello 1986). Carlo Emilio Gadda, Eugenio Montale and Pasolini also wrote in defence of dialects.

In the first part of the twentieth century, with fascism looming large, anti-fascist intellectuals, like Gramsci, Piero Gobetti and Meneghello, saw Italian dialects as a bridge between the sterile Italian taught at universities – which, they contended, was unable to express the real life of the people or indeed relate to them – and the people themselves. Meneghello stressed the huge gap 'between the humanistic Italian he was taught in his formative years and the world of things'; in his view, as summed up by David Ward, 'to make up for the shortcomings of *lingua*, dialect and low register Italian take on a vital, almost cleansing role' (Ward 2010: 164). The project was overtly political because fascism sought to strengthen national identity by campaigning against dialects, which were deemed dangerous since they encouraged particularism. For Gramsci, the linguistic question was connected with cultural and political issues and related to hegemony (Gramsci 1977: Prison Notebook 29 §3). In a brief overview of the history of Italian written in prison (Prison Notebook 3 §76), Gramsci viewed the preservation of dialects in periods of language homogenization as a sign of popular resistance against linguistic hegemony.[15] He pointed to the political significance of the '[v]ernaculars [as opposed to Latin] [which] are written when the people regain importance' (Gramsci 1996: 73). Gramsci famously opposed a perception of the South as 'the ball and chain which prevents the social development of Italy', of 'the Southerners [as] biologically inferior beings, semi-barbarians or total barbarians, by natural destiny', of 'Nature' having made them 'lazy, incapable, criminal and barbaric' (Gramsci 2000: 173). Taken together, Gramsci's call to stand against a disparaging stereotype of the South, alongside his and other anti-fascist views on language, provide an analytical framework for exploring the use of Southern dialects in the *Otellos* under discussion.

For Lo Cascio, the use of Sicilian was a 'necessity'. Being an ancient dialectal language, Sicilian retains an aulic and poetic richness of tonalities; as a popular form, it is also very 'concrete', 'adhering-to-reality' and direct (Lo Cascio in Sciancalepore 2015). On stage and page, it comes across as a powerful medium for the tragedy, almost as if it were the only suitable alternative to Shakespeare's English. As Lo Cascio states in his introductory note to the published text, in its written form, his dialect is unconventional, it does not always follow the rules of transcription. In order to preserve its 'authenticity' and potency, he employs a mixture of invented and accepted spellings for a single word. The sound of the dialect takes priority over the philological accuracy of its transcription, to the effect that the text becomes an aural text, whose potency is further enhanced by the verse forms, hendecasyllables and heptameters. Those who understand the dialect experience an interesting form of identification with Otello, which is not part of the experience in the original play. For those who do not read or speak Sicilian, one might venture a parallel between Lo Cascio's dialect and James Joyce's language in *Finnegans Wake*: words as sounds, their meaning *intuited* rather than fully grasped, a new creation by every reader/listener as well as the author. The 'intuited' text resists the unintelligibility often associated with dialects, and allows for an identification with Otello – 'identification' being one process through which his alterity is reworked in both productions.

Bearing in mind the Gramscian take on dialects and the Southern question, I further discuss the dialectal *Otellos* in relation to their appropriation of the Shakespearean tragedy of the Moor of Venice to stage a difference 'within'. The Moor's blackness, turned into Southern Italian difference, works as a critical tool for reconsidering the idea of foreignness in the original play.

Othello's Italian blackness

A Sicilian or Neapolitan Othello is still a Stranger, a foreigner in Italy because a foreigner to the Italian language. Of the Neapolitan Otello, Iago disparagingly says that he cannot put two words of Italian together (Miale di Mauro and Spezzano 2017: 10), although he often speaks in standard Italian. As the South has been traditionally (although not exclusively) depicted as Italy's vilified Other, productions of *Othello* turning the Moor into an Italian Southerner are of interest. The cultural translations, however, do more than reflect or adapt, at a national or local level, the alterity of Shakespeare's character. The use of dialects adds new perspectives which work against the erroneous association of dialect with low cultural and social status, by rejecting the idea that vernaculars are non-literary. Pasolini wrote of the local cultures of the South (in cities like Rome, Naples, Palermo) as 'surviving culture[s]' (1972: 60). He noted that 'Naples is still the last plebeian metropolis, the last great village with cultural traditions . . . that are not strictly Italian; this general and historical fact levels the social classes physically and intellectually' (Pasolini 1987: 18). Today, the system of social classes he refers to is altered, replaced by new groups or corporations, but the statement is still valid. Naples was especially dear to Pasolini, who viewed it as the last outpost of resistance to cultural homologization and the Neapolitans as Italy's 'last tribe', unaltered by technology and progress:

> This tribe has decided . . . to become extinct, rejecting the new power, that is, what we call history, or otherwise modernity. . . . This refusal, this subtraction from history, is right and sacrosanct. . . . The Neapolitans have decided to become extinct, remaining Neapolitans to the last – that is, unrepeatable, irreducible and incorruptible. (Pasolini 1976: 15–16; my translation)

It is precisely this *irreducible otherness*, coming from the past and resisting modernity, that the two Southern *Otellos* offer. Their tie with the past (which in the Sicilian *Otello* is also evident in references to ancient Greece) does not mean stasis, but resistance to linguistic and cultural homogenization. Since 2013, Italy has been celebrating dialects on a National Day, 17 January, with a wide range of local events. The two *Otellos* promote the actuality of the dialects and cultures of two worldwide if stereotypically renowned regions. They assert a 'blackness-within' that radically reworks Shakespearean alterity, by making Othello a citizen in his own community and Desdemona a stranger to it. While this choice is also a strategy to condemn jealousy, it carries other implications too. First, dialects offer a new insight into the world-famous story by enhancing it through their specificity, since dialects 'are not vibrations of the air characterizing the word, but different vibrations of the mind' (Meneghello 1986: 28). Second, because the dialects redouble the sense of belonging for readers and spectators who share the same culture, the two Otellos' local 'blackness' questions the invention of the ethnic difference of the original Moor, exposing his 'imaginary ethnicity', to borrow a phrase from Shaul Bassi (2000). Third, locality becomes a critical 'agent' of displacement: not only of cultural difference (from 'Venice' to Southern Italy), but also on the level of interpretation. Displacement to regional dialectal cultures effects a vision of local otherness as agent of resistance. In the tradition of Italian intellectuals, from Gramsci to Pasolini, this radically capsizes the view of Othello based solely on the plot. While Otello is condemnable at the level of the plot, dialects make him a tool of resistance for identitarian affirmation at a theoretical level.

The two *Otellos* open up to and resonate with what Young writes about the Global South Shakespeare:

> [O]penness to nontraditional Shakespeares has the potential to unsettle normative cultural practices and, in a truly 'ex-centric' fashion, bring into view the racisms that have structured global relations since early modernity. (2019: 13)

At a national level, this is, I think, an achievement of the two productions. Italy still reflects the space-bound distinction, made by the Western Enlightenment, between a knowledge-driven North, and a Global South, envisioned 'primarily as a place of parochial wisdom, of antiquarian traditions, of exotic ways and means', a '[reservoir] of raw facts: the minutiae from which Euromodernity might fashion its testable theories and transcendent truths' (Comaroff and Comaroff 2012: 114).[16] The two productions may be read as rejecting any such view of the Italian South; by inverting the hierarchical terms, they contribute, in my view, to the current re-envisioning of the Global South. Might it be that 'the so-called "Global South" . . . affords privileged insight into the workings of the world at large?' (Comaroff and Comaroff 2012: 114).

The move to include 'other' Shakespeares in Global Shakespeare Studies, 'not just in terms of case studies . . . but in terms of thought and theoretical models' (Refskou, de Amorim and de Carvalho 2019: 15) and 'recast the global South as a source of innovative critical theory in its own right' (Young 2019: 3) derives from an invigorated study of the Global South. The Italian 'Southern Question', in Gramsci's analysis, established a fruitful paradigm for analysing other contexts, as testified by the Subaltern Studies in India in the 1980s. The two *Otellos* prove that Southern Italy is as relevant as ever, that literary engagements with Shakespeare in dialect are acts of resistance against cultural colonization or acculturation, offering a critical tool for analysis *from* the South.

Notes

1 A thematic link between the Palme d'Or film and Shakespeare's play lies in the relationship between the protagonist and his young wife.

2 For a critical reclaiming of the notion of Shakespeare's universality see Ryan (2015) and, for a problematization, Thurman (2014).

3 All Shakespeare quotations are from the Arden Third Series.

4 Although only Act 1 is set in Venice, *Othello* is iconically associated with the lagoon city. Cyprus remains somehow 'Venetian' in our imaginary. For analyses of the Shakespearean Venice see Tosi and Bassi (2011: more especially 1–18).

5 See the interview in this volume with Karin Coonrod, who directed *The Merchant in Venice*.

6 Lo Cascio's *Otello* was co-produced by Teatro Stabile of Catania, Emilia Romagna Teatro (ERT) Fondazione; Lo Cascio played Iago. Miale di Mauro's *Otello* was staged by the Compagnia NEST and co-produced by Fondazione Teatro di Napoli – Teatro Bellini, Fondazione Campania dei Festival and Napoli Teatro Festival. When referring to these productions and their protagonists, I retain the Italian spelling, Otello.

7 The same actor plays the Soldier and Lodovico.

8 References to *Othello* are to Shakespeare, not to the Italian productions.

9 All subsequent quotations from *Otello* are in the text, page numbers in parentheses. All translations are mine.

10 This could also be a reference to Mount Olympus in Greece.

11 This was the case in the performance of 7 October 2017.

12 In this they share a common ground with indigenous Shakespeare, which, understood in Young's acceptation, 'can also render Shakespeare *current*, within the complex contemporaneity of the globalized twenty-first century' (2019: 49–50).

13 Young (2019: 57) is writing of the resistance to canonical forms produced by indigeneity in India.

14 As Helena Buffery notes of Catalan, 'a minority Shakespeare [was] employed to achieve cultural majority' (2007: 1). Neapolitan and Sicilian are listed in the UNESCO *Atlas of the World's Languages in Danger* (2010).

15 Gramsci referred to the time when, in the Renaissance, Venice and the Venetian dialect represented a local resistance, of historical import, to the spread of the Florentine dialect as a sort of national language (Gramsci 1996: 74). In *Othello*, Cassio is an obscurely 'counter-caster' Florentine for Venetian Iago (1.1.30).

16 Young sees 'southerliness' as a concept already present in early modernity, when geographers referred to 'southern climes' or 'southern nations' or the 'south', thus formulating 'subtle forms of racializations' that legitimized 'colonial exploitation' (2019: 4).

References

Bassi, S. (2000), *Le metamorfosi di Otello: Storia di una etnicità immaginaria*, Bari: B. A. Graphis.

Buffery, H. (2007), *Shakespeare in Catalan: Translating Imperialism*, Cardiff: University of Wales Press.

Calvino, I. (1980), 'Il midollo del leone' (1955), in G. Einaudi (ed.), *Una pietra sopra. Discorsi di letteratura e società*, 3–18, Torino: Einaudi.

Cioran, E. M. (2012), *Anathemas and Admirations*, trans. R. Howard, New York: Arcade Publishing.

Comaroff, J. and J. L. Comaroff (2012), 'Theory from the South: Or, How Euro-America is Evolving Toward Africa', *Anthropological Forum*, 22 (2): 113–31.

Coryat, T. (1905), *Coryat's Crudities*, London: Macmillan and Co.

Derrida, J. (1998), *Monolingualism of the Other; or, The Prosthesis of Origin* (1996), trans. P. Mensah, Stanford: Stanford University Press.

Gibbons, B. (2011), '"He shifteth his speech": Accents and Dialects in Plays by Shakespeare and His Contemporaries', in C. Jansohn, L. C. Orlin and S. Wells (eds), *Shakespeare Without Boundaries: Essays in Honour of Dieter Mehl*, 76–91, Newark: University of Delaware Press.

Goethe, J. W. (1885), *Goethe's Travels in Italy*, London: George Bell and Sons.

Gramsci, A. (1977), *Letteratura e vita nazionale*, Roma: Editori Riuniti.

Gramsci, A. (1996), 'The Question of the Language and the Italian Intellectual Classes', in J. A. Buttigieg (ed. and trans.), *Prison Notebooks*, vol. 2, 72–6, New York: Columbia University Press.

Gramsci, A. (2000), 'Some Aspects of the Southern Question' (1926), in D. Forgacs (ed.), *The Gramsci Reader: Selected Writings 1916–1935*, 171–85, New York: New York University Press.

Huang, A. (2007), 'Shakespearean Localities and the Localities of Shakespeare Studies', *Shakespeare Studies*, 35: 186–204.

Huang, A. (2013), 'Global Shakespeares as Methodology', *Shakespeare*, 9 (3): 273–90.

Lo Cascio, L. (2015), *Otello*, Messina: Mesogea.

Malaparte, C. (1952), *The Skin*, trans. D. Moore, London: Alvin Redman.

Maresca, G. (2012), *Era di maggio. La storia stracciata*, Cologno Monzese: Lampi di stampa.

Meneghello, L. (1986), '"Vorrei far splendere quella sgrammaticata grammatica"', in *Il tremaio. Note sull'interazione tra lingua e dialetto nelle scritture letterarie*, with C. Segre, E. Pellegrini and G. Lepschy, 11–42, Bergamo: Pierluigi Lubrina Editore.

Miale di Mauro, G. and G. Spezzano (2017), *Otello*, Firenze: Nardini Editore.

Moseley, C. (ed.) (2010), *Atlas of the World's Languages in Danger*, 3rd edn, Paris: UNESCO Publishing.

Pasolini, P. P. (1972), 'Diario linguistico' (1965), in G. Einaudi (ed.), *Lingua*, 45–63, Torino: Einaudi.

Pasolini, P. P. (1976), '[La napoletanità]' (1971), in A. Ghirelli, *La Napoletanità*, 15–16, Napoli: no publisher.

Pasolini, P. P. (1987), *Lutheran Letters* (1976), trans. Stuart Hood, New York: Carcanet.

Puttenham, G. (1811), *The Arte of English Poesie* (1589), ed. J. Haslewood, London: Robert Triphook.

Refskou, A. S., M. A. de Amorim and V. M. de Carvalho (eds) (2019), *Eating Shakespeare: Cultural Anthropophagy as Global Methodology*, London: Bloomsbury.

Ryan, K. (2015), *Shakespeare's Universality*, London: Bloomsbury.

Sciancalepore, M. (2015), *Retroscena – I segreti del teatro*, Interview with Luigi Lo Cascio and Vincenzo Pirrotta, *TV2000*, TV programme, broadcast 24 February.

Shakespeare, W. (2016), *Othello*, ed. E. A. J. Honigmann, rev. edn, intr. A. Thompson, The Arden Shakespeare, third series, London: Bloomsbury.

Thurman, C. (ed.) (2014), *South African Essays on 'Universal' Shakespeare*, Farnham: Ashgate.

Tosi, L. and S. Bassi (eds) (2011), *Visions of Venice in Shakespeare*, Farnham: Ashgate.

Ward, D. (2010), *Piero Gobetti's New World: Antifascism, Liberalism, Writing*, Toronto: University of Toronto Press.

Young, S. (2019), *Shakespeare in the Global South: Stories of Oceans Crossed in Contemporary Adaptation*, London: Bloomsbury.

2

Refracting the racial Other into the Other-within in two Bulgarian adaptations of *Othello*

Boika Sokolova and Kirilka Stavreva

The Tragedy of Othello was among the most popular Shakespeare plays on the amateur and professional stages in the nineteenth century, when Bulgarian theatre was taking its first steps by appropriating repertoires and emulating European performance styles. Arguably, the family plot appealed to the sensibilities of a patriarchal culture, but as importantly, the status of Othello as a Stranger in the white Venetian world found an emotional resonance with an audience whose cultural identification with the Other had been cemented during the long colonization of the country by the Ottoman Empire (Shurbanov and Sokolova 2001: 47). In the post-Second World War communist era, however, *Othello* was rarely staged; when it was, the mark of otherness was blackface, as was the established theatre practice in Europe. Two mutually reinforcing interpretative frameworks specified what *Othello* was 'about' and 'what Shakespeare meant' by the character of the Moor of Venice. On the one hand, the play was a visionary analysis of tensions characteristic of Shakespeare's own historical moment, defined as the birth of capitalism, characterized by self-interest and double standards. Thus, Venice was construed as a marketplace where talent could be bought for the need of state preservation, while it only grudgingly accepted otherness. Parallel to this interpretive approach, within the Cold War context, the play was supposed to deliver a critique of racial disenfranchisement and discrimination by the ideological imperialist enemy who used the labour of black people without accepting their humanity. In both frameworks, Othello's character was posited as a torchbearer for progressive, humanist ideals – a character that wrests victory out of defeat and points the way to a brighter historical future (Shurbanov and Sokolova 2001: 239; Tenev 1968). Presumably living in that better world, contemporary audiences could appreciate both the heroics of the play and the achievements of their own time. Relatively small attention was paid to Desdemona, to the familial and the personal.

This interpretative tradition was challenged in 1975, when visionary director Lyuben Grois chose not to mark Othello as racially different and assigned to him a new kind of otherness – an otherness-within. He thus refracted the play's racial problem to shine a light on a distinctive aspect of the communist system itself: the pressure to conform and the suppression of individuality. The productions analysed in this chapter – Liliya Abadjieva's 2005 experimental theatre appropriation and Ivan Mladenov's 2008 prison documentary incorporating Shakespeare's play – follow a similar path to that first charted by Grois in identifying the Other of their specific here-and-now and localizing the play politically without paying lip service to dominant ideologies. Their Others are not 'extravagant and wheeling stranger[s] / Of here and everywhere' (*Oth* 1.1.134–

5), but victimized women, members of violent militaristic neo-tribes and little people serving long sentences for crimes that pale in comparison to those of the political elite of the Bulgarian post-communist transition.

When Grois first introduced a racially unmarked Othello, he was himself already marked as politically suspect and consigned to work outside the capital. Thus, the first Bulgarian Othello without blackface or mask walked the boards of a regional theatre, in Blagoevgrad.[1] The production proved groundbreaking in several respects. Apart from erasing Othello's race and relocating his otherness within a local context of cultural traumas inflicted by communist society, Grois placed the audience in the uncomfortable position of silent witnesses to a dialogue about the all-too-familiar methods of Othering. Furthermore, he visually redefined the space of the tragedy, translating the contraction of time in Shakespeare's play into an oppressive scenic enclosure.

In Grois's *Othello*, the protagonist was a white man with a large black mark on his forehead, smudged there at the beginning of the performance. In his notebook, the director explains that his concept was that of 'a man branded . . . discriminated against, kept on the fringes, a man without rights' (Grois 1986: 99). Fellow theatre director Nikola Petkov recognized in the protagonist Grois's own social status as an artist of unconventional talent, deemed ideologically suspect (Dimova 2018). This emotionally charged reading of Othello as the Other-within was reinforced by an aphoristic refrain recurring throughout the play:

> It is hard to live in the world here and now
> If you bear a black mark on your brow. (Shurbanov and
>   Sokolova 2001: 245)

The verse prompted spectators to examine their own world where, with a stroke of a pen, a 'black mark' could turn anyone into an Other, right 'here and now'. Venice and Cyprus were also reconceptualized as locally recognizable, albeit in accordance with Grois's associative theatrical style. The set was a curved white-tiled space evoking 'a bath house, an arena where wild animals kill each other, or a laboratory'. A metal grille rose above the tiles, sections of it sliding down to close off tiny doorways. Crowned with a menacing array of small sheet-iron flags (Grois 1986: 99), this slaughterhouse/social-experimentation site was clean, efficient and merciless.

Grois's de-raced interpretation of the play was acutely sensitive to issues of institutionalized discrimination against the Other-within. Addressing the racially homogeneous Bulgarian public, he turned the edge of the tragedy on his communist home society, a society demanding uniformity, branding and ostracizing talent, insidiously invading the most intimate corners of human relationships. Over thirty years later, during the trying era of the post-communist transition, Abadjieva and Mladenov developed similarly de-raced and socially engaged approaches to *The Tragedy of Othello, the Moor of Venice*. They also refracted racially marked otherness to bring forth culturally invisible traumas of marginalized groups, as well as the normalization of the deceit and violence of entitled men. They, too, caged their characters within claustrophobic spaces, and held the audience captive. Both generated overt dialogues between Shakespeare's tragedy and contemporary discourses – discourses high and low, poignant and burlesque. Calling attention to their explorations of the Others-within, both Abadjieva and Mladenov used only male actors, which resulted in an estrangement of the female characters and foregrounded the processes of their Othering. At the same time, Mladenov's work in particular shines a light on social injustice that stunts and warps masculinity.

These twenty-first-century appropriations of *Othello* came out of the social and cultural crises of the Bulgarian post-communist transition.[2] In the first decade of the new century, the social elation about the democratic changes following the fall of the Berlin Wall had given way to profound disillusionment. The ideals of freedom, justice and economic prosperity were hijacked by mushrooming oligarchic groups of the apparatchiks of the Communist Party (now rebranded as Socialist), their families and cronies. One self-serving government followed another, their election promises belied by the reality of economic distortion, pervasive corruption, severely compromised social cohesion, mass emigration, civic apathy and desperation. By 2011, over 49 per cent of Bulgarians risked poverty or social exclusion; 43.6 per cent lived in dire poverty that cut across ethnic divides (Directorate General 2013: 5). As the social fabric unravelled, basic civility yielded to the adoration of the tough man, 'the embodiment of the archaic *kratos*, the brutal pre-political natural force' (Manchev 2004–6). It was not long before flaunted masculinity and militant nationalism became assets in electoral politics, fusing mafioso 'power groups' with the political elite. Among those othered by the processes were women and the large swathes of economically disadvantaged men who, ironically, often buy into the ideology of militant neo-tribalism. In 2005, the year of Abadjieva's *Othello*, domestic violence became a criminal offence for the first time in Bulgarian history. Since then, crime statistics have measured a steady increase in the number of its victims. By 2019, every third victim of premeditated murder was a woman killed by a domestic partner (Nikolov 2019). Abadjieva's experimental theatre project focuses on the othering of these victims of toxic masculinity, while Mladenov's prison documentary initiates a provocative dialogue about thwarted masculinity.

Liliya Abadjieva's *Othello* (2005): A tragedy of gender[3]

Aggressive masculinity was highly visible in Abadjieva's *Othello*, performed on a tiny studio stage in the National Theatre 'Ivan Vazov' in Sofia.[4] Vassil Abadjiev's scenography created a stark, claustrophobic world. A scaffolding spanned the width of the stage, its four openings vaguely evocative of a cartoon strip. Beyond it was the most private space where powerful passions unfolded with the characters' backs literally against the stage wall. In such bare quarters, harshness of sound, violence and profane humour grated on the senses, while ephemeral beauty and trusting vulnerability grabbed audience members by the throat.

As part of a long-term aesthetic programme, Abadjieva uses all-male casts, extracting from her actors performances of explosively dynamic and refined physicality. In *Othello*, she also deployed post-modernist episodic structure, alternating the poetry of Shakespeare's playtext with burlesques, improvisations and metatheatrical gags; the effect was a parodic visualization of the rituals of masculine tribalism. At the same time, the production layered visual and musical structures, binding audience and performers through their intensity as it exposed women's cultural estrangement and mourned their ritualistic destruction. Though Abadjieva refuses to call herself a feminist, her choices resolutely put gender forth as the subject of tragedy.

This approach resonates with Michel Maffesoli's ideas about the post-modern paradigm shift of tragedy from 'ego-centred' to 'place-centred'. For him, social space, which used to be defined by the 'primacy [of] the rational individual living in a contractual [relationship with] society' has changed under the cyclical pressures of besieging neo-tribes, while the individual self has been lost in the primacy of the tribe (Maffesoli 2004: 134). Along similar lines, Abadjieva's *Othello* is set in spaces where private and classical tragic discourses are interrupted, again and again, by burlesque neo-tribal entertainment, to be ultimately destroyed by relentless male wrestling for control over physical and psychological space. Among the recurrent and unresolved conflicts driving the production are the overpowering of ennobling passion by puny ambitions, the displacement of the momentum of history by the interruption of the event, the erasure of the promise of renewal offered by the end of classical tragedy.

The play opened with a meticulously choreographed mechanical number of Othello (Deyan Donkov) and Desdemona (Vladimir Karamazov) in the upstage area. Immersed in golden light against the blackness surrounding them, the two take turns setting in motion a swing on which they are precariously perched; they bring it to a halt, pausing to consider, to take courage, then purposefully yield to the next pendular motion. This wordless scene evokes the image of a giant upside-down metronome, its slow swaying underscored by a hypnotic musical motif. It conveys something of the inexorability of fate. The lovers' passionate commitment, body and soul, is marked when Desdemona pulls out a lemon and feeds it to Othello; he reciprocates with a fruit of his own. For all the provocativeness of dripping juice and hungry reaching of mouths for the fruit, the rhythm of the movement is never broken, and the tableau-like presentation retains the quality of a ritual created for the ages. Before long, however, we witness the vulnerability of the lovers in this idealized tableau, the unobstructed incursion of maliciousness into the space of love.

The principal upholder of this masculine maliciousness is Iago (Dimitar Rachkov) who moves deftly across all performance spaces. Visually, he comes across as the embodiment of self-serving machismo: short and stocky, he hogs space with his knees wide apart, ruthlessly domineering the frail, bespectacled, jumpy Roderigo (Vladislav Violinov). Iago's militancy is marked by the green and red flag he clutches, a prop which conveniently flaunts his 'Venetian' patriotism. Here, the translated text resonates with concepts key to social displays of aggressive masculinity: connections to men of power, prowess in battle, disdain for foreigners and derision of all things intellectual. For instance, Iago calls Cassio 'this accounting book, this abacus' (Abadjieva 2005: 15). When the wannabe tribal leader announces his entitlement to a higher rank, the Bulgarian translation renders 'lieutenant' as 'second in command', connoting Iago's desire to become Othello's substitute. This Iago is an embodiment of male entitlement to the summit of power, regardless of knowledge, aptitude or moral principles. When, at the end of the scene, he starts waving the flag in a grossly exaggerated manner, he gives physical expression to the enormity of his ambition – a physical action recalling displays of street patriotism in electoral rallies and ultra-right marches.

Before long, Iago strategically appropriates the entire performance space, including the site of Othello and Desdemona's opening love scene and their 'bedroom' further upstage, against the back wall. He quickly scales the metal scaffolding framing these intimate spaces and, having climbed through violent contortions to the top, concocts his destructive plan. In the translation, his declaration of the plan to bring down Othello, 'It is engendered' (1.3.402), is rendered as 'I have conceived' – an explicitly gendered articulation amounting to a linguistic usurpation of the feminine. Iago thus enacts a demonic parthenogenesis, rendering the feminine superfluous and anticipating the physical destruction of the women in the final act.

As the play's action builds to its tragic climax, Iago's usurpation of privacy is re-enacted by an entire grotesque parade of uniformed men who invade the space of intimacy. Burlesque interpolations of the most inane type of barracks humour debase the romantic designation of this space. 'Who left this iron rod here?' asks a drunken Othello as he struts unsteadily in his undershorts, drooping cigarette in mouth. The mumbled nonsense is echoed down the chain of command as one clueless soldier follows another on the metal gangway framing what used to be the site of a love ritual. If, earlier, it was Iago who rendered the feminine superfluous, in this scene an entire army of men ridicules the romance. The masculine bastardization of the tragic genre reaches its climax in an interpolated scene involving a street cleaner. Also wearing a rumpled military uniform, his fly open, he summarizes the plot in macaronic Russo-Bulgarian. Here is a prologue-like character who pops up halfway into the dramatic action, his absurdist comedy reflecting the deliberate demotion of the tragic. This outrageously metatheatrical scene, openly directed to the audience, trivializes the tragedy of women as street gossip.

Against the onslaught of grotesque military tribalism, Abadjieva's production posits female characters of power, elegance and agency, which makes their violent destruction even more poignant. While the cross-casting of the parts estranges femininity, it effectively highlights and diversifies its performative markers. The actors tread a fine line between representation and presentation, identification and estrangement of their characters. The tall and attractive Desdemona and Emilia (Yulian Vergov) capture the audience's attention more powerfully than the diminutive Iago and the moody Othello. Desdemona moves with an exquisite elegance and emotional expressiveness, while Emilia, who towers over her husband, is capable of containing Iago's aggression and responding to it in kind. The women's actions, dramatic and affective, bridge the gap between the world of the play and that of the audience, tapping into experiences of women's trauma, often invisible in the local culture. Abadjieva's approach to these traumatic experiences alternates between the demotic and burlesque on the one hand, and the tragic on the other: her female characters navigate easily the divide between comedy and tragedy, arousing the spectators' sympathy in both registers.

A comic scene inserted in 4.2, and performed in the very space where Iago first appeared lording it over Roderigo, dramatizes the women's capacity to subvert Iago's malicious masculinity. As Emilia rails against the 'cogging, cozening slave' who has slandered Desdemona 'to get some office' (4.2.134), the actor performing Iago visibly shrinks in stature. When he attempts to regain the upper hand, demanding that Emilia produce her handkerchief, Desdemona raises her hand like a referee in a football match and in no uncertain terms forbids Iago to mention the handkerchief. Thus, the symbolic vehicle of the tragedy becomes a joke, while the following inverted comic sketch allows the women to fawn over Iago as if he is an infant. They lift the shrunken Iago on their laps, exclaiming: 'Look here, Emilia, how pitiable he is! Look: what a small hand, what a tiny shoulder piece; and this little man, too, wants to be a general' (Abadjieva 2005: 56). The comedy culminates in the infantilized Iago wetting their dresses. Though the women's comedic triumph is soon contained, this scene of female power provides a visual antidote to Iago's pervasive toxicity, as it invites the audience to laugh at his puniness along with Emilia and Desdemona. By turning the tables on the villain before the murderous resolution, by laying claim to the power of comedy, the women characters engage the audience in affective reciprocity.

The tragic endgame begins when the sophisticated satire of Iago's belittlement gives way to a slapstick scene of a violent football kick around. Othello's interrogation of Emilia about Desdemona's alleged unfaithfulness is also rendered in intensely physical terms. His questions come as a double onslaught of words and the tossing of a basketball at her, which she deftly heads back. In this ridiculous and violent mishmash of basketball and football, Emilia's headers function as striking back at Othello. When the tempo picks up dangerously, Desdemona enters to stop the violence, a moment of devastating gentleness, which brings to a halt the brutal tempo of the scene. The ensuing stasis acts as a reprieve of refined peacefulness at odds with the physical comedy. It recalls the fleeting harmony between Othello and Desdemona in the swing scene with which the play opened. Both women then join an absurd kickout, which leaves them smashed on the floor. In this ludic dramatization of tribal masculinity, their resistance is ultimately obliterated. The initially contained football game takes over the entire performance space; the stage is engulfed in smoke; the architectonics of the play world is blown apart by raging strobe lights.

In the end, it is the women who restore the stature of the tragic, shaken to the core by the burlesques of tribal masculinity. For the murder scene, Abadjieva develops a symphonic aesthetic, interweaving Shakespeare's language with music, movement and light. She juxtaposes musical cues from different periods, played as repetitive short phrases recalling the haunting repetitions of Philip Glass. Together with the music, the sinuous back-and-forth struggle of Othello and Desdemona along the entire length of the space where the opening scene was set conveys a sense of the tragic as fatally inexorable. Desdemona's death is choreographed in four movements within the tight space between the quasi-cinematic metal frame and the back wall. First, Othello ritualistically strangles her with his bare hands; a dance-chase across the stage follows; Desdemona is then smothered with the handkerchief in a visual echo of the movements that symbolized their marriage; finally, she is thrown around, like a rag doll, until she collapses against the stage wall in a pool of water, while Othello loses himself in a dervish-like trance. The counterpointing of exquisite balletic movement and the domestic terror it represents delivers a devastating affective punch on the audience.

In a production that has erased race from Shakespeare's tragedy and made gender its focus, Othello is denied both the story of his life with which he wooed Desdemona (1.3.129–46), and his self-epitaph and elevation in death (5.2.336–54). His final words amount to a self-curse:

Whip me, ye devils,
From the possession of this heavenly sight!
Blow me about in winds, roast me in sulphur,
Wash me in steep-down gulfs of liquid fire!
O Desdemon! dead, Desdemon!

(5.2.275–9)

Thus, Desdemona becomes the sole source of tragic affect. However, there is no resolution to the narrative. The production ends with two empty swings at the opposite ends of the stage, waiting for new re-enactments of the story, as if history were waiting to repeat itself, like a visualized Beckettian scream. Whether the intense 'now-ness' of performance may invite what Eugenie Brinkema has termed 'the unexpected and the unthought' to articulate itself as political action in the muddled gender discourses that have dogged recent Bulgarian politics (Brinkema 2014: xii–xiii), or whether a doomed circularity will prevail, is a question which remains open and for every member of the audience to resolve, as an intellectual stance or as an action.

Ivan Mladenov's *Othello* (2008): A tragedy of social exclusion[5]

The adaptation of *Othello*, written, directed and produced by documentary film-maker Ivan Mladenov, melds the life stories of men incarcerated in the Varna prison, for serious crimes, with scenes from Shakespeare's tragedy. Shot on a shoestring budget over a few weeks of a muggy seaside summer, Mladenov's *Othello* features people forgotten by society, rich in passions and poor of words, agents and victims of odious crimes, indifference and injustice. Alternating these life stories with performances by the inmates of brief scenes from Shakespeare's play, the film upends any preconceived notions of the barbarity of criminals and the civilization they have offended against. According to Tzvetan Todorov, 'barbarity' is an inalienable human quality, characterized by 'a sense of murderous rivalry that makes us refuse to grant others the right of access to the same joys and the same goods that we ourselves hope to enjoy'. He defines 'civilization' as 'the ability to see others as others and yet to accept . . . that they [are] as human as ourselves' (Todorov 2010: 21, 195). Social theorist Maffesoli sees little hope for the awakening of such abilities, and points to the triumph of 'barbarian' neo-tribes that have usurped social spaces previously marked as contractually civilized (2004: 134). Mladenov's cinematic storytelling taps into both sentiments. On the one hand, he encloses stories and images of the socially and personally 'barbarous' within a narrative revealing the neo-tribal barbarity of the post-communist state. On the other hand, his aesthetic elicits a compassionate, civilized response to the humanity of the Other and an understanding of the barbarous social mechanisms that have modelled and enabled him. In an overview of Mladenov's work, film critic Ivo Draganov underscores its civic pathos: 'Today, in the era of material success, when the heroes of our time are yuppies, thugs, models, when money rules supreme, [Mladenov] has dedicated . . . years of his life to persuade [forgotten] people that he can portray them compassionately [and] in their own environment; people authentic, genuinely suffering, and unheard of before'. His films are documents, Draganov continues, 'that accuse the governing class of incompetence, apathy, and misanthropy' (Draganov 2007).

The film opens with a medium-close shot of a heavily tattooed Othello (Alexander Stoyanov), wistfully declaring to the camera, '[Desdemona]! perdition catch my soul / But I do love thee! and when I love thee not / Chaos is come again' (3.3.90–2). It is followed by a long take of the barbed wire top of the prison wall and pale sun beyond. A prison guard (Staiko Dimitrov) lists horrific events witnessed on the job, the dry bureaucratese of his enunciation undercut by his facial expression of broken resignation. The prison is thus established as both setting and character. Predominantly low-angle, deep-field shots, blown up details (shredded plastic caught in the barbed wire, the black bolt of a cell door, etc.) create the sense of a distorted environment. At the same time, the guard's grotesque horror stories about prisoners setting themselves on fire, attempting to hang themselves, sewing up their mouths with copper wire, establish the prison as a monstrous materialization of a system's barbarity.

Contrasted to the representational palette of the opening sequence, the scenes with the prisoner-actors are predominantly presentational. Their self-narratives and most of the scenes from Shakespeare's tragedy are rendered through extreme close-ups of the faces against a blue or black background, the camera painstakingly documenting each emotional nuance. The cinematography commands complete attention to the stories told and an emotional proximity to the characters. At the time of the film's production, Alexander Stoyanov, who played Othello, was serving a sixteen-year sentence for the murder of his fiancée; Krassimir Iliev, in the role of Iago, was sentenced to a twenty-year term for over 100 counts of international fraud; Zhivko Terziev, as Cassio, was in prison for aggravated murder, committed under the influence of alcohol; Maxim Dimitrov, Brabantio, was serving a second term for armed robbery after an initial fifteen-year sentence for the same crime; Nikolai Nikolaev, cast as Desdemona, was a first-time offender serving a six-year prison sentence for fraud; Konstantin Drumev, performing Roderigo, was a repeat offender serving a fifteen-year sentence for robbery.[6] However, as tellers of their own stories and as Shakespearean performers, none of these men appear irrevocably barbarian; they come across as both vicious and vulnerable, aggressive and resigned, treacherous and betrayed. Without rendering them sentimentalized or heroic, Mladenov connects the convicts' self-narratives with Shakespearean scenes, intersecting the classical tragedy with contemporary Bulgarian histories.

'I don't believe there is an evil person', declares Mladenov in a reflection on his movie-making principles, 'for me it is important to see in one's character their own inimitable world'. He uncovers these worlds through a quiet, almost static cinematic approach that derives its energy, in the filmmaker's own words, from 'the passions of the characters – their rage, love, and hatred' (Mariyanska 2009). 'Valiant Othello' is appropriately dignified as he relates, straight to Desdemona's father, how Desdemona chose him: 'She loved me for the dangers I had passed / And I loved her that she did pity them' (1.3.168–9). Stoyanov's self-narrative following this declaration connects the emotional refuge that Othello sought in Desdemona to a new improbable love which had flourished during his prison term. As he confides to the camera with a mixture of self-deprecation and contentment, there is 'at least one person from the seven or eight million in Bulgaria today who love[s] me'. A full twelve-second pause ensues before he packs an emotional punch: 'And I won't be a black sheep. She knows full well about my sentence . . . if I was the monster that the papers describe, who would be with me or trust me?' (*Othello* 2008: 15.60–17.04). The amazement of Shakespeare's ex-slave and racial Other at being loved by Desdemona is here translated into the desire of a convict and a 'black sheep' to be trusted and loved, if only by one person.

Though a small character in Shakespeare's tragedy, Brabantio acquires a rich personality through the intertextual connections with the life story of Maxim Dimitrov, cast in this part. He offers an animated recollection of the movie-like 'adventures' that first landed him in prison. They started with robbing a Second World War Resistance museum in order to secure guns and grenades for his first armed robbery. The museum exhibits were used as props in an attack intended to secure 500 levs (at the time, the equivalent of about £30) for a year's supply of formula for his lactose-intolerant infant son. For these pathetic theatrics used to secure a sum unaffordable to a working-class Bulgarian family in the destitute 1990s, he was slapped with an inordinately long sentence. After fifteen years inside, Dimitrov threw himself into work seven days a week to save up for a visit to Moscow, where he hoped to reconnect with his children who had moved there with their Russian mother. He was, however, unable to make enough to pay his bills and those of his ailing mother, and soon ended up in prison again for two other armed robberies. During his second prison term, like Brabantio, he thought he had lost his daughter forever. Playing Brabantio's part was an occasion for much soul-searching. Intersected with Dimitrov's story of losing connection with his children, Brabantio's paternal possessiveness takes on a tender dimension. Among the participants in the film, Dimitrov is exceptional in experiencing acting as catharsis. Working on the film, he says, takes you to 'a point, when you start talking, and you can no longer stop; it's like pouring water out of a jug. You talk and talk, and it's like you get cleansed and a burden lifts off'.[7]

Perhaps the strongest condemnation of post-communist lawlessness and the concomitant abuse of the have-nots in the film is the story of Zhivko Terziev (Cassio). No 'great arithmetician' (1.1.18), he is a simple man, who used to rent municipal land to raise sheep and grow corn and wheat. He was powerless, however, against the members of the local hunting club who ruined his crops and tried to force him off the grazing field by shooting their guns at night in the glaring headlights of their SUVs. When one of the hunters, parading the entitlement of Bulgaria's new business class, threatened Terziev's father and shot two of the guard dogs to drive his point home, the shepherd was pushed beyond his limits. 'Full of quarrel and offence', like Othello's intoxicated lieutenant (2.3.47), he beat up the hunter and left him unconscious. The man died before the ambulance arrived hours later, as there was no cellular coverage in the area. Telling his story to the camera, Terziev initially appears as sorrowful as Cassio about his 'mistake', but remorse quickly gives way to bitterness:

> Everyone walks over the poor. You stand no chance. The way things are, there is no justice. No one acknowledges truth and law, nor that one is in his right because he's working his ass off. They come, buy lambs, eat and drink, shoot around . . . to whom shall I complain . . . when those to whom you should be complaining are the people doing it?
> (*Othello* 2008: 21.19–37)

Though spoken by an incarcerated man, it is impossible to dismiss this condemnation of a society in which justice is meted out so selectively, where lawlessness and violence are normalized.

Just as in Shakespeare's play, Iago, that true barbarian, is the system's spokesperson and its most outspoken critic. A despicably duplicitous character, he embodies the very values he criticizes. In the film, Krassimir Iliev, who performs Iago, has been sentenced for acts of large-scale fraud, a crime endemic to the post-communist transition. Like Iago, he manages to deflect interest from his own person to develop an aggressive discourse about justice, serving his 'peculiar end' (*Oth* 1.1.58). To the camera, he reveals the bare minimum of his life story: the length of his sentence, his crime and the years he has served. The rest of his on-screen time he dedicates to a precisely worded accusation:

> I believe that when one is sentenced for whatever crime, above all, the concept of justice should be present, as well as the understanding of the purpose of punishment. At this point in time, punishment pursues and achieves a single goal: to destroy the individual. Like many others, I think

that we have no chance . . . to re-join society like normal people because the state is denying us this chance.

(*Othello* 2008: 28.58–30.03)

As he explained in an interview, his main incentive to participate in the film was to reveal what happens after incarceration, not only to domestic TV audiences, but potentially to the world, since he was aware that the film would participate in international festivals.[8] While the irony of having one sentenced for heavy fraud expose the failings of the penal system is not lost upon the viewers, his denunciation is compelling. We believe him even as we realize that he has offered us an agenda instead of a confession, in the same way that we recognize the truth in Iago's equivocation to Othello, 'O monstrous world! Take note, take note, O world: / To be direct and honest is not safe!' (3.3.380–1).

In his study of cultural resentment and fear of otherness, Tzvetan Todorov maps a route to resolving this plague of our times: 'Two stages have to be crossed before anyone can become civilized: in the first stage, you discover that others live in a way different from you; in the second, you agree to see them as bearers of the same humanity as yourself' (Todorov 2010: 21–2). Mladenov's film dares its spectators to take both steps. He sensitively uncovers the discomforting humanity of 'barbarians' and creates time and space for them to tell their own stories, enabling an affective connection between the film's viewers and the invisible and reprehensible people on the screen. At the same time, the film sheds unforgiving light upon the barbarity of post-communist 'civilization', its institutions and practices.

* * *

The two appropriations of Shakespeare's *Othello* analysed in this chapter continue a local tradition, introduced by Lyuben Grois, of refracting race to shed light on contemporary social traumas in a racially homogeneous society. Audiences entering Abadjieva's and Mladenov's claustrophobic worlds become witnesses of normalized violence against women, of tribalism, masculine toxicity and the thwarted masculinity of those who have become collateral damage of post-communism. While the two twenty-first-century directors are ambivalent about the attainability of resolutions, their aesthetic forges powerful affective connections with the Other-within. In the process, their spectators are given a space to take the civilizing step of recognizing the humanity of the Other, even in conditions exacerbated by the economic, political, gender and cultural-identity crises of post-communism.

Notes

1 In Grois's production, Othello was performed by Yordan Spirov; the scene design was by Dobromir Petrov.

2 On Bulgaria's post-communist transition to a façade economy and its effect on the cultural sphere, see Sokolova and Stavreva (2017: 1–14).

3 This section builds on the authors' conference paper, 'Gender and the Space of Tragedy in Liliya Abadjieva's *Othello* (2005)', for the seminar on 'Gender(s) Elsewhere in Contemporary Performances of Shakespeare', organized by Francesca Rayner and Kirilka Stavreva for the 2019 Congress of the European Shakespeare Research Association in Rome, Italy. We are grateful to the seminar participants for their supportive and insightful feedback.

4 Abadjieva first staged *Othello* in 1995 while still a student at the National Academy for Theatre and Cinema Art; she revisited the play with American actors in 2008 at the Lit Moon World Shakespeare Festival in Santa Barbara, California. Her 2005 production garnered the highest theatre awards for the year.

5 This section develops ideas introduced in Stavreva (2018).

6 In an omission with symbolic connotations, likely necessitated by the conditions of film production, the performers of the Duke

and Emilia – the two characters associated with justice in the play – remain uncredited and never tell the stories of their lives.
7   Maxim Dimitrov in discussion with Stavreva, Varna Prison, Bulgaria, 15 January 2014.
8   Krassimir Iliev in discussion with Stavreva, Varna, Bulgaria, 19 January 2014.

References

Abadjieva, L. (2005), *Otelo: Stsenichna versiya* [*Othello: A Scenic Version*], trans. L. Ognyanov, unpublished manuscript, Sofia: National Theatre 'Ivan Vazov' Archive.

Brinkema, E. (2014), *The Forms of the Affects*, Durham: Duke University Press.

Dimova, B. (2018), 'Sas srebro v kosite: Hrisan Tsankov, Boyan Danovski i Lyuben Grois v spomenite na Nikola Petkov' [Silver in the hair: Hrisan Tsankov, Boyan Danovski and Lyuben Grois in Nikola Petkov's memories], *Obache*, 15 October. Available online: https://obache.bg/9721/sas-srebro-v-kosite-hrisan-tsankov -boyan-danovski-i-lyuben-groys-v-spomenite-na-nikola-petkov/ (accessed 2 April 2021).

Directorate General for Regional and Urban Policy (2013), *Analysis Unit B1, European Commission Country Sheet: Bulgaria*. Available online: https://ec.europa.eu/regional_policy/sources/ docgener/informat/country2012/country_bg_en.pdf (accessed 2 April 2021).

Draganov, I. (2007), 'Chovetzite na Ivan Mladenov' [The People of Ivan Mladenov], *Kultura*, 7, 23 February. Available online: http:// www.kultura.bg/bg/article/view/12646 (accessed 2 April 2021).

Grois, L. (1986), *Director's Notebooks*, compiled by G. Kofardjieva, B; Urumov and S. Baichinska, Sofia: Nauka i izkustvo.

Maffesoli, M. (2004), 'The Return of the Tragic in Postmodern Societies', trans. R. Felski, A. Megill, and M. Gaddis Rose, *New Literary History*, 35: 133–49.

Manchev, B. (2004–6), 'Violence and Political Representation: The Post-Communist Case', in A. Vacheva, Y. Eftimov, and

G. Chobanov (eds), *Kultura i Kritika, Chast IV: Ideologiyata – nachin na upotreba* [*Culture and Criticism, Part IV: Ideology: A Means of Consumption*], Varna: Liternet. Available online: http://liternet.bg/publish2/bmanchev/violence_en.htm (accessed 2 April 2021).

Mariyanska, E. (2009), 'Rezhisyorat Ivan Mladenov: Maika mi umrya na 30 ot bolno surtze' [Director Ivan Mladenov: My Mother Died at 30 from Heart Disease], interview, *Blitz*, 21 August. Available online: http://www.blitz.bg/article/13450 (accessed 2 April 2021).

Nikolov, K. (2019), 'Drastichen rast na ubijstvata na zheni pri domashno nasilie' [A Drastic Increase in Domestic Murders of Women], *Mediapool*, 4 February. Available online: https://www.mediapool.bg/drastichen-rast-na-ubiystvata-na-zheni-pri-domashno-nasilie-news289376.html (accessed 2 April 2021).

Othello (2008), [Film] Dir. Ivan Mladenov, Sofia: Bulgarian National Film Centre.

Shakespeare, W. ([1997] 2016), *Othello*, ed. E. A. J. Honigmann, rev. edn, intr. A. Thompson, The Arden Shakespeare, third series, London: Bloomsbury.

Shurbanov, A. and B. Sokolova (2001), *Painting Shakespeare Red: An East-European Appropriation*, Newark: University of Delaware Press.

Sokolova, B. and K. Stavreva (2017), '"The Readiness is All", or the Politics of Art in Post-Communist Bulgaria', *Bulgarian Shakespeares, Toronto Slavic Quarterly*, 60: 1–17. Available online: http://sites.utoronto.ca/tsq/60/SokolovaStavreva0_60.pdf (accessed 2 April 2021).

Stavreva, K. (2018), 'Tales of Strangers/Strangers' Tales: Performing Barbarity as Anti-Spectacle in *Othello*', *Cahiers Élisabéthains*, Special Issue: *Europe's Shakespeare(s)*, 96 (1): 201–13.

Tenev, L. (1968), 'Otelo sreshtu Otelo [Othello against Othello]', *Narodna kultura*, 41, 12 October.

Todorov, Tz. (2010), *The Fear of Barbarians: Beyond the Clash of Civilizations*, trans. Andrew Brown, Chicago: The University of Chicago Press.

3

Estranged strangers

Krzysztof Warlikowski's Shylock and Othello in *African Tales after Shakespeare* (2011)

Aleksandra Sakowska

Krzysztof Warlikowski's *Opowieści Afrykańskie według Szekspira* (*African Tales after Shakespeare*),[1] based on *King Lear*, *The Merchant of Venice* and *Othello*, is characterized by misdirection and fluidity. This has led to confused reception by audiences and critics, all the more so since the production appears not to engage sympathetically with the otherness of its principal characters. Furthermore, Warlikowski's theatre effectively 'foreignizes' Shakespeare by employing different estrangement strategies such as the complex and intrusive process of collating the plays with other texts and a relentless use of intermediality. All this affects audiences' understanding and perception of the performed classical playtext, by making for a fragmentary and disjointed spectating experience.

Warlikowski's story-telling centres on the identities of his Strangers, but his gaze remains multi-directional, never focused on a single identity, story or social issue. This may seem problematic when it comes to staging strangeness, since it leaves Shakespearean Strangers more estranged than ever. Nonetheless, this approach, which Warlikowski pioneered and uses in all his adaptations of the classics, is not alien to Poland's mainstream theatre, which often plays on conflation of identities to challenge traditional Polish values.

My bi-focal analysis of *African Tales* puts a spotlight on this production's post-textual and post-historical portrayals of Shylock and Othello. I first discuss Warlikowski's purposeful stereotypical treatment of ethnicity in *The Merchant of Venice*, questioning the extent to which, by exaggerating racial stereotypes in post-Holocaust Poland, he actually deconstructs them. I then turn to characterization in *Othello*, with its politically incorrect depiction of race in the use of blackface. So doing, I also consider the links between Warlikowski's work, its internationalization and the current state of mainstream Polish theatre to which he belongs.

Theatre practitioners in twenty-first-century Poland are intent on obscuring 'Shakespeareness' – a canonical Shakespeare established by Polish translations that has become part of everyday language. Directors achieve this by modernizing the language, through the use of new translations, actor improvisation and digital technologies. In this way, layers of meaning are added to the plays which are already palimpsest-like. Albeit in an antagonistic way, Shakespeare's text remains the most important element in all productions, often used as a sparring partner. Such creative, even cannibalistic, adaptations remain a strong trend on the twenty-first-century Polish stage. Described as a 'burglar's strategy' (Burzyńska 2008: 41), this kind of approach would be considered post-dramatic in Western theatre. In the case of

Polish theatre, however, modernism is a traditionally strong influence, which has led to the emergence of a national avant-garde theatre practice.[2]

Over the past two decades, Poland has seen eight stagings of *The Merchant of Venice* and six of *Othello*, which have explored the plays mostly through the concept of the Other: this includes homosexuality and the marginalization of women as well as attitudes towards old age and disability. Anti-Semitism and racism have not been a central focus. Directors seem to have been unwilling to use post-colonial theory in the depiction of race and ethnicity, thus perpetuating certain stereotypes even while treating them with irony or humour. Polish theatre practitioners are focused on finding new meanings and readings, sometimes relevant to the here and now, sometimes used as springboards for their own creative journeys. More recently this has tended to revolve predominantly around the blended identities we all perform in our societies. That is why it is relevant to consider *African Tales* from a phenomenological perspective, an approach whereby insights may be gained into artistic intentionality. I am referring here specifically to Roman Ingarden's concept of 'flash pictures', 'suddenly illuminated and just as suddenly extinguished', which 'have great illuminating power and, simultaneously, the great power of revealing the objects that appear in them' (Ingarden 1973: 283). When watching non-traditional performances of Shakespeare, this approach may productively open up some key aspects of identity politics.

Since *African Tales* is an adaptation, the notion of 'author' and 'authorship' needs to be considered and it is closely connected to intentionality. This is because phenomenology gives credence to the 'I', the first-person perspective, unlike literary theory which treats it as a highly subjective and unreliable voice. The chapter will therefore attempt to capture moments of authorial recognition and assertion – for example in theatre reviews or interviews with the director and dramaturge – and show how they may shape our understanding of the performance. The Husserlian brand of intentionality is particularly important here, 'what it means for something to be a perceived object, a remembered event, a judged state of affairs, if we ignore the intentional states (the perception, the remembering, the judging) that reveal these objects to us' (Gallagher and Zahavi 2012: 129). In this way, phenomenology links an experience and an object and may help us understand that adaptation is a conscious act that constitutes object-directed intentionality.

Warlikowski's multi-focal explorations of identities: A 'saturation of experience'

Warlikowski is one of the most prolific and innovative Shakespearean adaptors, with thirteen stage productions under his belt (Sakowska 2011: 336). His work is multi-lingual, created regularly in France, Germany and Belgium, and at his Nowy Teatr (New Theatre) in Warsaw. He represents a well-established neo-modernist trend, which he blends with German post-dramatic practices.[3] His Shakespeare productions of the 1990s, *The Taming of the Shrew* and *Hamlet*,[4] opened up a serious debate on human sexuality and otherness.

The director is fascinated by threshold identities, and interested in what Marjorie Garber calls the 'third term',[5] which questions the traditional binary categories of 'male' and 'female', not as yet another category but as 'a mode of articulation, a way of describing a space of possibility' (Garber 1992: 11). According to his dramaturge, Piotr Gruszczyński, Warlikowski believes that Shakespeare was a homosexual, and recognizes that the Other in the Renaissance must have 'suffered in solitude and silence . . . homosexuals, women, blacks, Jews, people condemned to defeat' (Gruszczyński 2007: 108).[6] Warlikowski has always been interested in flipping or destabilizing stereotypes:

[T]he black Othello should be white so that it is the white person who is the object of the experiment, so that he can see and feel for himself what it means to be verbally abused. . . . The white should play the black, and the black the Jews, only then will we be able to understand the weight of those insults. (Gruszczyński 2007: 210)[7]

This liberal, progressive view of blended identities, and perception of exclusion as universal and post-historical, runs through all of Warlikowski's productions. Yet, social thinkers such as Zygmunt Bauman have warned against indifference caused by merging inclusion and universality, which is a primary trait of globalization.[8] And indeed, Warlikowski's approach does not always work, nor is it sufficiently transparent when it comes to the depiction of ethnicity in otherness.

What is also characteristic of Warlikowski's work is the intense 'saturation of experience' (Sakowska 2018): spectators are exposed to intermedial performance using a mixture of multiple – traditional and new – media on stage. Jerzy Limon describes this effect as a 'text installation' (Limon 2006: 101–11), where the artistic vision of the director and dramaturge often leaves Shakespeare's text barely visible. In *African Tales*, Warlikowski departs from Shakespeare because his aesthetics is interested in fragmented narratives with significant shifts in points of view. His radical reduction of the three plays, supplemented with a number of other texts, leads to the creation of a new dramatic work, with a new title. His interest in blending identities and obscuring the authorial intention is evident in his creative decisions at all levels, down to the much-debated poster, designed by the controversial Polish artist Zbigniew Libera.[9] Initially, the production was advertised as the 'trilogy of Others' (Urbaniak 2011) – Lear (the old man), Shylock (the Jew) and Othello (the black man). The final result highlights all possible racial and ethnic stereotypes and does not engage sympathetically with the otherness of the main characters. Played by the same (acclaimed Polish theatre and film) actor, Andrzej Ferency, who was sixty when the production premiered, Shylock, Othello and Lear represent three Others, patriarchal figures who destroy the lives of their daughters and wives. The five-hour performance is roughly divided into four parts, with two intervals.

Shylock is a Jew and Portia is a Jew: Blending otherness in *The Merchant of Venice*

The Merchant of Venice section of *African Tales* is preceded by one short scene from *King Lear*, the encounter of three daughters and their father, which introduces the theme of age and sickness. This opening scene ends with Cordelia's rebellious 'nothing' (*KL* 1.1.87) and Lear's ensuing rage, which reveals that he is seriously ill.[10]

The lights fade out. When they come on again, the play has shifted to 1.1 of *Merchant*. Warlikowski stages a lovers' tryst, in which a rather old[11] and dapper Antonio pleasures a young and handsome, but rather aloof, Bassanio. In despair, Antonio offers him money in the hope of obtaining a response, but to no avail. The well-known storyline follows in fairly linear format, continuing with Shakespeare's 1.3, in which Shylock, Bassanio and Antonio make a deal in the menacing setting of a butcher's shop, with the Jewish merchant wielding two sharp knives and slicing meat on the counter. Some lines are significantly modernized for a stronger impact. Antonio's 'But lend it rather to thine enemy, / Who, if he break, thou mayst with better face / Exact the penalty' (*MV* 1.3.130–2)[12] becomes a vulgar 'you will be able to fuck your enemy'. This confrontation of two Others, a privileged Christian homosexual and a bloodthirsty despised Jew, is morally ambiguous. It becomes distasteful when Antonio spits in Shylock's face, while Bassanio leaves with a mocking 'Oy vey, oy vey'.[13] Then follows Jessica's story, reduced to just one line: 'Dad, I'm leaving'.

The next key scene brings on the characters from Art Spiegelman's *Maus*,[14] a controversial graphic novel which depicts Jews as mice, Poles as pigs and Nazis as predatory cats. Warlikowski makes use of *Maus* in a visually stunning, but highly ambivalent way. Tubal enters wearing a mouse's head and traditional Jewish religious attire. He informs Shylock that Antonio's ships have been lost at sea. Soon afterwards, two pig-headed figures appear, forcing him to hide under the table. Initially, the pigs seem to be a blend of various characters. They tease Shylock about Jessica's elopement and simulate sex on the table, one pig crooning to the other, 'we'll make a Christian woman out of you yet'. Atrocious anti-Semitic insults are uttered on the stage. Even Shylock joins in, suggesting that they 'make soap of the Jew'.

Warlikowski's depiction of otherness often involves mockery and chimes with Jerzy Grotowski's use of profanation. For Warlikowski this is a way to deal not only with myths and stereotypes, but also with unacknowledged Polish guilt for anti-Semitic acts during the Second World War. However, the possibility of multiple readings of the *Maus* scene makes any cathartic resolution difficult. The scene is hardly therapeutic for Poles who are depicted as fornicating pigs abusing a Jew. And any Jewish members of the audience would question Shylock's self-mockery, while the Nazis, the joint tormentors of Poles and Jews, are not represented at all. Sympathetic critics have described this misleading dramaturgical strategy as a 'poetics of fragment', which offers an interpretation that is 'incomplete, abandoned, so that you can go back to it' because it is always 'open, unfinished, never-ending' (Wojciechowska 2011: 25). Furthermore, Warlikowski shows that atonement is impossible and no therapeutic solution available. The male characters in his play, Othello, Shylock, but also homosexual Bassanio, Antonio and Iago, are all implicated in violence or betrayal against those we might term the true Others of *Merchant* and *Othello*: Portia and Desdemona. Thus, the director exorcizes the past wrongs of men against women, offering his own vision of the plays by rewriting their stories and giving them a strong new voice to speak of their traumas through soliloquies by Wajdi Mouawad, commissioned by Warlikowski (Mouawad 2011).

Portia's motivations and actions as shown on stage are rather clear and easy to relate to. She is an ageing, confident and clever woman who knows what she wants, even if her financial situation is controlled by her father's bizarre will. Realizing the nature of Bassanio and Antonio's relationship, she confronts her object of desire and prospective husband by putting in front of him three laptops showing photographs of the love triangle of Bassanio–Antonio–Portia. Next, she forces Bassanio to make a choice: 'if you want me you must choose'. Bassanio's and Portia's body language and stage movements suggest a power struggle. At first, Bassiano refuses to be forced into any decision and leaves, but soon returns, approaches the laptop showing Portia and slams down the screens of the two other laptops. Even a hastily written cheque, almost thrown into his face, does not appease him. When Portia, after finalizing the transaction, wants to pleasure him, thus mirroring the earlier scene between Bassanio and Antonio, the young man ignores her advances. Nevertheless, she continues to undress him but when his genitalia are exposed, Portia, infuriated and disappointed, exclaims: 'you could not even get it up!'

This Portia's story then unfolds in a similar way to Shakespeare's: she attends the trial dressed as a man and gets Antonio off the hook; at the same time, she learns how deeply Bassanio is committed to his friend. However, she delivers more than just learned legal advice. Like an ancient Greek chorus, Portia also comments on the finale of *Merchant*, both physically and verbally. After Shylock's trial, she sits down on the couch to eat and subsequently vomit a pound of minced meat from a plastic tray. Next, she recites her long metaphorical soliloquy, on the subject of 'Portia's gender', in which she seems to compare her situation with that of the Jew:

> We need to feed the gods with our flesh; but today our gods must be fed with kilograms of flesh and a pound is not enough

> ... the Jew has long disappeared, but we keep creating him so we can hate him anew. ... it is like a bottomless hole, everything that goes through it comes out at the other end. Did a Jew fall in love with a Christian? To devour out of love, why not, it is beautiful, desire is a question without an answer ... No man will be satisfied with less than everything.[15]

This soliloquy becomes intelligible only in the context of the next scene, where Warlikowski and Gruszczyński juxtapose Mouawad's text with a fragment of Jonathan Littell's historical novel, *The Most Kindly*.[16] Before their wedding Portia tells Bassanio Littell's tale about a king's daughter and her uncurbed sexual desire, which leads to the deaths of her lovers. Littell's princess is unable to attain satisfaction with mere humans and she decides to make love to the sea, which finally brings her fulfilment but also destroys her and her city. This is Portia's way of telling Bassanio that she will not settle for an arranged marriage with a man who does not love her. In an act of rebellion, she rejects Bassanio on hearing his wedding vow, in which he promises her eternal love and fidelity, and kneels down to promise herself to God instead. She takes the Catholic vow for novices, offering her human flesh to God: 'I promise to live in celibacy, obedience, without property, devoted to the celestial Father, to achieve consummate love in the service of God'. This act connects with her earlier soliloquy in which she recognized the right of the gods to human mortal bodies and the need to accept sacrifice to attain love, as suggested in Littell's story.

Othello in blackface: We should be mortified and that's the point

Blackface on Polish stages belongs to a wider European tradition, where it was used to enable white actors to play 'foreign' characters. In post-1989 Poland, Othello became white. While blackface has become unacceptable, there are as yet almost no black professional actors in Poland. Since the production was co-funded by several European theatres, Warlikowski could have invited a guest black actor from abroad or perhaps chosen a Polish actor of Middle Eastern origin.[17] Instead, he chose to work again with Ferency, whom he had cast, to great acclaim, as Petruchio and Prospero in 1997 and 2003 respectively.

The *Othello* section opens with the Catholic nuptials of Ferency's blackfaced Othello, who has just stepped out of the part of Jewish Shylock. His young white bride can hardly contain herself and keeps giggling, while her much older fiancé,[18] dressed in a modern military uniform, looks at her with paternalistic indulgence. The playscript for this section, which is based on Shakespeare's *Othello*, is perhaps the most ambiguous directorial and dramaturgical intervention, reducing the Other's heroic story to a white man's envy for a black man's sexual prowess. The wedding ceremony is followed by an animation film flashback of their relationship, which shows Desdemona performing oral sex in the bathroom of a night club.[19] This leads to their arrest and public humiliation. More importantly, this incident later becomes the butt of jokes among Othello's entourage and a way to shame Desdemona.

Desdemona is an ethnically ambivalent character, wearing colourful African dresses, with her golden locks piled up and kept in place with a bright headdress. Where Portia's gender identity is fluid, Desdemona has a fluid ethnic identity. She did not feel comfortable among her trendy Venetian friends who despised her. Warlikowski seems to be analysing the impossibility to translate oneself wholly into an Other's identity. 'Behaving black'[20] does not change Desdemona's ethnicity, something she does not understand. At one point, she imitates an African tribal dance, which degenerates to animal-like movements. Through Desdemona, Warlikowski brings to the fore the issue of racial stereotypes, which may spring to life when one attempts to cross thresholds of race – racial stereotypes are still very much present in modern societies.

A final soliloquy, 'The arm of Desdemona', shows her descent into madness and utter desperation: 'love walks on the edge of an abyss, with no helping hand . . . there is more and more desert and less and less garden'. In contrast to Portia's tale about the lustful princess whose desire could not be satisfied by a mortal, Desdemona recites a list of sexual acts as if they are part of her disgrace. She delivers her lines half-crying, clearly embarrassed. Her soliloquy leaves spectators with the powerful impression that disgrace is a major aspect of the production. According to Adam Radecki, Warlikowski's play 'remains in the power of the discourse of disgrace: it conveys the unspoken, most difficult, unbearable, profane, incestuous [contexts] . . . *African Tales* is suffused with disgrace' (Radecki 2012).

Desdemona's 'disgrace' strengthens the stereotype of the fallen woman and makes her characterization conventional, albeit truer to Shakespeare's story. At the last hour of her life, Desdemona's only companion is a stuffed dog she hears yapping and howling, sounds which match her own state of mind, as she prepares to 'give herself to death as she gave herself to love'.[21] From this point on, the impossibility of finding fulfilment in love becomes the theme explored by way of J. M. Coetzee's *Summertime* and a thoroughly re-envisioned fragment of *King Lear*. According to Warlikowski, these act as additional lenses refracting the issues already raised in the production (Kędzierski 2012).

Coda: It's all about the audience

Theatre never provides universal messages. Touring productions such as *African Tales* are read differently depending on the space and time of the performance, and on a number of extra-theatrical factors. Most of all, the reception of such a production is culturally determined. For many Western reviewers, the *Othello* segment was impossible to process without seeing it as an unintentional,[22] or indeed intentional, promulgation of racism.[23] For more conservative, religious audiences, for example in Romania, the depiction of sexuality and nudity (especially male nudity) was unacceptable and this resulted in walkouts during the 2018 International Shakespeare Festival in Craiova (Cazacu et al. 2019: 78).

For audiences in Poland, *African Tales* 'also entered another debate: the national soul-searching related to Poland's relationship to the Holocaust, a debate fuelled by a 2001 book, entitled *Neighbours*' (Sokolova 2018: 99).[24] Viewed from this angle, the *Merchant* segments remain as vital as at the time of the production's premiere in 2011. In the ensuing decade, Poland's right-wing government has passed laws forbidding any suggestion that Poles were complicit in the Holocaust.[25] While this does not apply to artists or scientists, it exposes productions such as *African Tales* to protests from spectators who do not want to hear about Polish involvement, even if incidental, in the Second World War extermination of Jews.[26] *African Tales* has preserved this part of Polish history which students cannot learn in schools, introducing a wider historical context of crimes committed in Nazi-occupied Poland.

In his productions, Warlikowski most effectively analyses Polish culture itself. While theatrical performance is an ephemeral event, Warlikowski's productions have remained topical in Poland long after they premiered. The late 2010s and the change of decade have seen Poland riding on the wave of dangerous nostalgia (like many other European countries), and this has been giving rise to hatred targeting all forms of otherness and to xenophobia, in the context of the migrant crisis. Nationalism, supported (covertly) by the Polish government, permits behaviours which should have no place in contemporary Europe. *African Tales* remains an important statement on the multiple forms of exclusion of the Other.

Wherever it has been performed, *African Tales*, with its post-textual and post-historical representations of Shylock and Othello, tells the story of 'estranged strangers'. Shylock remains painfully linked to Polish history, however radically changed on the narrative level through various post-textual strategies. Othello, on the other hand, becomes post-historical and to a certain degree post-racial. As Bryce Lease observes:

> Unlike Warlikowski's important work in the establishment of gay and queer counterpublics that establish historical trajectories of gay identities, new modes of feminism and the opening out of constrained and fragmented Polish/Jewish relations, race is dehistoricised in *African Tales* and used as a means to express a universal social marginalisation of otherness that required more nuanced adjustments to notions of positionality. (Lease 2016: 191)

Indeed, Warlikowski's Shylock and Othello may easily come across as diminished and stereotyped, to open up space for the female characters whose stories can be developed to expose patriarchy and the failure of love. Love, which Warlikowski views with pessimism, does not heal in *African Tales*. Portia and Desdemona are the truly excluded ones in their societies. In the end, their only escapes from the men who betray them are either the Church or death.

Warlikowski's 'widening of interpretation' is achieved at the cost of Shakespeare, through the radical and intrusive process of 'infusing [his] plays with other texts' (Wojciechowska 2011: 26). Warlikowski makes his intentions clear: he wants to connect with his spectators, whom he considers 'desensitized individuals'.[27] Here lies a strong phenomenological link between Warlikowski's raison d'être and his adaptation:

> My aim is to wake them [the audience] up from a nap, and sensitize them anew. I do not know if this is a provocation, maybe just [a way of] loosening up, arousing, activating and raising awareness. *The Merchant of Venice* is familiar . . . Shakespeare is familiar. . . . I want to say [to the audience] that they are much mistaken.[28]

It is important to observe that Warlikowski often quotes Coetzee as the key to many of his productions:

> I need the stranger that he gives me. The subversiveness which is in all his books ... Unfortunately, theatre is a finite world, while all of Coetzee's books are infinite ... Literature teases the theatre with its freedom. (Gruszczyński 2012: 62)

Polish critics consider that Warlikowski uses Coetzee's *Summertime* in *African Tales* to ridicule male weakness and egoism: 'thanks to this [dramaturgical device] Shakespeare's male worlds are bruised by the female voices rejecting a patriarchal model for love and family' (Drewniak 2012). Yet this suggests a neo-modernist sensibility that also comes from Warlikowski's exposure to Polish literature, particularly Witold Gombrowicz (Gruszczyński 2007: 135).[29] Warlikowski understands that a country as traditional in the treatment of female rights as Poland is so intent on marginalizing and even criminalizing women's lives and acts that women are the real Strangers.[30] While elsewhere in Europe and further afield, women continue to hammer away at the glass ceiling, Polish women remain gaslit and powerless in the face of regressively conservative laws.[31]

In the end, *African Tales* is multi-directional, never focused on a single identity. Its chief features are the 'anti-story' storytelling and 'out-of-character' characterization which make the portrayal of otherness often ambiguous. The questions raised by Warlikowski's productions are numerous, but they remain unanswered. Questioning itself is of importance. And there, in his method, lies the role of theatre, and of Shakespeare.

Notes

1 Created by Warlikowski's Nowy Teatr ensemble in Warsaw and co-funded by Les Théâtres de la Ville de Luxembourg, Théâtre National de Chaillot and Prospero European Theatre Network.

2 This should be ascribed to Stanislaw Wyspiański's *Study of Hamlet* (1905), which argues that any appropriation of Shakespeare needs to be carried out in the form of a new relationship between the artist and Shakespeare's text/s (Wyspiański 2019).

3 Although Hans Thies Lehmann coined the label 'postdramatic theatre' (Lehmann 2006), he admits to post-dramatic practices being an extension of modernist and post-modern practices, including 1960s Polish avant-garde directors such as Jerzy Grotowski and Tadeusz Kantor.

4 Both productions have been extensively analysed from the Lacanian, Freudian and Kristevian standpoints and are of particular interest to pioneers of Polish Queer Studies.

5 Marjorie Garber's concept (Garber 1992).

6 Agnieszka Graff notes that equating gays with Jews preceded recent Polish discourses: in *Nationalism and Sexuality: Respectability and Abnormal Sexuality in Modern Europe* (1985), George L. Mosse traces how the image of the Jew and the homosexual overlapped in German nationalist discourse in the late nineteenth century (Graff 2006).

7 My translation throughout, unless specified otherwise.

8 'Bauman notes that tolerance . . . becomes a tool that makes it easier for us to hide our SENSE OF SUPERIORITY, our AVERSION TO THE OTHER eagerly concealed under the cloak of political correctness. Bauman warns that INDIFFERENCE TO DIVERSITY and ELIMINATION of the subject of OTHERNESS from the public discourse . . . means that our culture loses what should matter most to it: interest in and sensitivity to UNCOMMONNESS. Tolerance ossifies stereotypes, Uncommonness incapacitates them' (Meissner 2011).

9 The posters placed on the billboards in Warsaw drew several complaints from the local residents, which were later picked up by the media and escalated into a row that reached the Mayor's office. Interestingly, it is the exposed genitalia of men that caused public outrage but nobody criticized the dubious handling of a post-colonial theme.

10 References are to R. A. Foakes's edition (Shakespeare 1997).

11 In this case the actor is aged with make-up.

12 I am quoting from John Drakakis's edition (Shakespeare [2010] 2014). All references to Shakespeare's *Merchant of Venice* are to this edition.

13 A Jewish expression showing exasperation, often used (jocularly) by non-Jewish speakers in an anti-Semitic context.

14 Warlikowski's use of *Maus* is also subversive because no publisher in Poland was prepared to publish the book initially. There were many protests from right-wing circles who considered the work anti-Polish, since it suggested that Poles were complicit in anti-Jewish atrocities. On 25 May 2001, a Polish news site reported protests by dozens of activists outside the offices of a magazine, *Przekrój*, while Piotr Bikont, who translated the book, looked through the window wearing a pig mask, fuelling violent outbursts from the crowd (Pstrągowski 2016).

15 Lines transcribed from a DVD provided by Teatr Nowy; my translation.

16 'Air' (Littell 2009: 878–9).

17 Piotr Borowski, of Iraqi descent, played Othello in Poznań in 2013, in the production directed by Paweł Szkotak. Borowski is a young actor, however, and Warlikowski wanted to cast an aged actor.

18 This strategy is used either as a form of grotesque to distance the character from race or as a conflated metaphor to depict otherness. I have not seen it used realistically on stage to portray, specifically, ethnicity, apart from Warlikowski's production.

19 According to Bauman, 'the individual, public space is not much more than a giant screen on which private worries are projected ... public space is where public confession of private secrets and intimacies is made' (Bauman 2000: 39–40). Polish theatre developed this liquid trait into one of its dominant aesthetics, reflecting seminal changes to the private vs. public sphere of modern societies in a globalized world, with 'colonization of the public sphere by issues previously classified as private and unsuitable for public venting' (Bauman 2000: 69–70).

20 Perhaps it is a subtle critique of such cases as Rachel Dolezal, a white woman who pretended that she was African American. It could also be a more general critique of misguided cultural appropriation.

21 These are Desdemona's words in the performance.
22 Lease writes: 'Warlikowski attempted to produce equivalences of exclusion without properly attending to the ethics of representation produced by the particularities of ethnicity, race and gender in the Polish cultural context. Employing an actor of colour, for instance, might have actually challenged facile or easily won arguments for postcolonial equivalences in postcommunist Europe and the Global South' (Lease 2016: 196).
23 Using Eldridge Cleaver's 1968 *Soul on Ice* was particularly problematic for some members of the audience. A convicted rapist, Black Panther activist and self-proclaimed revolutionary, Cleaver traces in this series of essays his own development from a 'supermasculine menial' to a radical black liberationist. Using Cleaver as a mouthpiece to discuss race rang disingenuous, all the more so since in his later years he turned a conservative republican. His text is uttered on stage by the white Venetian court (Iago) in order to shame the relationship of Desdemona and Othello.
24 *Neighbours*, by the American historian Jan T. Gross, investigates the massacre of the Jewish community at Jedwabne. Poland's unresolved post-Holocaust legacy underpins much of Warlikowski's work and thinking about Polish history.
25 'Poland's Institute of National Remembrance (IPN) law states: "Whoever accuses, publicly and against the facts, the Polish nation, or the Polish state, of being responsible or complicit in the Nazi crimes committed by the Third German Reich . . . shall be subject to a fine or a penalty of imprisonment of up to three years"' (BBC 2018).
26 Polish theatres funded by local councils dominated by the right-wing party (PIS) have been quietly working towards replacing those artistic directors who allow any critique of Polish traditions, history, heterosexual normativity and Catholic religion.
27 Warlikowski in Kędzierski (2012).
28 Warlikowski in Kędzierski (2012).
29 Gombrowicz's character in *Ferdydurke* (1937) is made to adopt, and experiments with, different 'faces' (read: 'identities') on a

journey of self-discovery. The novel strongly associates violence and the assignation of 'faces'/'identities'.

30 Poland has the most restrictive abortion law in Europe. Despite this, there are repeated efforts by Catholic right-wing circles to instil further restrictions and punishments, including jailing women who undergo abortion. There is practically no sex education in schools, since teachers follow Catholic Church guidelines on anticonception. Many Polish doctors including gynaecologists have signed declarations of conscience to state that they adhere to Catholic teachings which do not allow them to advise women on abortion or prenatal tests. More and more Catholic-managed pharmacies refuse to sell condoms.

31 European Union regulations on domestic violence against women were introduced in Poland under a more liberal government, but they are criticized by the Catholic Church, which claims that such laws are aimed at the destruction of the family unit. Women are increasingly pressured to stay at home to look after their children and give birth to more, encouraged by a 'family-friendly' monthly allowance of PLN 500 (circa £100) for married couples with at least two children.

References

Bauman, Z. (2000), *Liquid Modernity*, Cambridge: Polity Press.

BBC (2018), 'Poland Holocaust Law: Government U-turn on Jail Threat', 28 June, *BBC News*. Available online: www.bbc.co.uk/news/world-europe-44627129 (accessed 2 April 2021).

Burzyńska, A. (2008), *The Classics and the Troublemakers*, Warszawa: Instytut Teatralny im. Zbigniewa Raszewskiego.

Cazacu, S., N. Galland, M. Harbuziuk and A. Sakowska (2019), '*African Tales after Shakespeare*, directed by Krzysztof Warlikowski for Nowy Teatr, Warsaw; Amza Pellea Main Auditorium of Marin Sorescu National Theatre, Craiova, 23 and 24 April 2018' (review), *Cahiers Élisabéthains*, 100 (1): 75–9.

Drewniak, Ł. (2012), 'Trzy pogłoski i Warlikowski' [Three rumours and Warlikowski], *Bluszcz*, 1 (1), 11 January. Available online: http://nowyteat.pro-linuxpl.com/download/bluszcz_drewniak.pdf (accessed 2 April 2021).

Gallagher, S. and D. Zahavi (2012), *The Phenomenological Mind*, London: Routledge.
Garber, M. (1992), *Vested Interests: Cross-Dressing and Cultural Anxiety*, London: Routledge.
Graff, A. (2006), 'Gej, czyli Żyd' [Gay means Jew], *Lewica.pl*. Available online: http://lewica.pl/index.php?id=10994&tytul=Graff:-Gej,-czyli-%AFyd (accessed 2 April 2021).
Gruszczyński, P. (2002), 'Próby korekcyjne. Dopisywanie' [Correctional Attempts. Adding Text], *Dialog*, 1–2: 222–5.
Gruszczyński, P. (ed.) (2007), *Szekspir i uzurpator* [Shakespeare and usurper], Warszawa: Wydawnictwo W.A.B.
Gruszczyński, P. (2012), 'Life Below the Equator: An Interview with Krzysztof Warlikowski', trans. N. Durkalec, *werkwinkel*, 7 (2). Available online: http://wa.amu.edu.pl/werkwinkel/interview_Warlikowski.pdf (accessed 2 April 2021).
Ingarden, R. (1973), *The Literary Work of Art: An Investigation on the Borderlines of Ontology, Logic, and Theory of Literature, with an Appendix on the Functions of Language in the Theater*, trans. G. G. Grabowicz, Evanston: Northwestern University Press.
Kędzierski, M. (2012), 'Czarna Pustynia' [Black Desert], *Teatr*, 2. Available online: https://teatr-pismo.pl/4078-czarna-pustynia-rozmowa-z-krzysztofem-warlikowskim (accessed 2 April 2021).
Lease, B. (2016), *After 89: Polish Theatre and the Political*, Manchester: Manchester University Press.
Lehmann, H. T. (2006), *Postdramatic Theatre*, London: Routledge.
Limon, J. (2006), 'Kto trzyma kalejdoskop' [Who holds the kaleidoscope?], *Dialog*, 10 (October): 100–11.
Littell, J. (2009), *The Kindly Ones*, London: Vintage.
Meissner, K. (2011), 'International DIALOG-WROCŁAW Theatre Festival Oct 7th–Oct 15th 2011', *Culture.pl*. Available online: https://culture.pl/en/event/international-dialog-wroclaw-theatre-festival-2011 (accessed 2 April 2021).
Mouawad, W. (2011), 'Płeć Desdemony' [Portia's Gender], 'Ramię Desdemony' [The Arm of Desdemona] and 'Kordelia' [Cordelia], commissioned by K. Warlikowski, trans. M. Ochab for *African Tales*. Available online: http://old.e-teatr.pl/pl/programy/2015_02/65261/opowiesci_afrykanskie_nowy_teatr_warszawa_2011.pdf (accessed 2 April 2021).

Pstrągowski, T. (2016), 'Człowiek za "Mausem". Sylwetka Arta Spiegelmana' [The man behind the Maus: on Art Spiegelman], *Książki*, 5 December. Available online: https://ksiazki.wp.pl/czowiek-za-mausem-sylwetka-arta-spiegelmana-6145960752220289a (accessed 2 April 2021).

Radecki, A. (2012), 'Oddalić wielki powrót ojców' [Averting the great return of fathers], *Dwutygodnik*, 70. Available online: https://www.dwutygodnik.com/artykul/2869-backstage-oddalic-wielki-powrot-ojcow.html (accessed 2 April 2021).

Sakowska, A. (2011), 'No "Happy Wrecks" – Pessimism and Suffering in Krzysztof Warlikowski's Adaptation of *The Tempest* by William Shakespeare', *Shakespeare Bulletin*, 29 (3): 327–38.

Sakowska, A. (2018), 'Feminist Shakespeare and Saturation of Experience in Monika Pęcikiewicz's Intermedial Adaptations', *Cahiers Élisabéthains*, 96 (1): 59–74.

Shakespeare, W. (1997), *King Lear*, ed. R. A. Foakes, The Arden Shakespeare, third series, London: Bloomsbury.

Shakespeare, W. ([2010] 2014), *The Merchant of Venice*, ed. J. Drakakis, The Arden Shakespeare, third series, London: Bloomsbury.

Sokolova, B. (2018), '"Mingled Yarn": *The Merchant of Venice* East of Berlin and the Legacy of "Eastern Europe"', *Shakespeare Survey*, 71: 88–103.

Urbaniak, M. (2011), 'Szekspir według Warlikowskiego' [Warlikowski's Shakespeare], *Wprost Weekly*, 42 (17.10). Available online: http://www.e-teatr.pl/pl/artykuly/125589.html (accessed 2 April 2021).

Wojciechowska, A. (2011), 'Ojcobójczynie' [Father-murderesses], *Notatnik Teatralny*, 62/63, Special Issue, 'Warlikowski': 24–33.

Wyspiański, S. (2007), *Hamlet*, ed. M. Prussak, Warsaw: Ossolineum.

Wyspiański, S. (2019), *The Hamlet Study and The Death of Ophelia*, trans. B. Bogoczek and T. Howard, London: Shakespeare's Globe.

4

Drags, dyes and death in Venice

The Merchant of Venice (2004) and *Othello* (2012) in Belgrade, Serbia

Zorica Bečanović Nikolić

The ontological importance of interpretation, famously emphasized by Martin Heidegger and his interpreter Hans-Georg Gadamer, is vividly expressed by Wolfgang Iser as 'We interpret, therefore we are' (Iser 2000: 1). Understanding is an essential part of being. By interpreting, we conduct our existence and our interpretations are inevitably conditioned by our own hermeneutic situation. As clarified by Gadamer in *Truth and Method* (2004: 291–9), the hermeneutic situation implies historically, therefore socially and culturally conditioned understanding of a meaning. Acts of interpretation are at the core of many Shakespeare's works, but the two Venetian plays, *The Merchant of Venice* and *Othello*, with their disturbing intercultural encounters and confrontations, contain provocative instances of (mis)interpretation and (de)construction of existentially significant meanings. As such, they offer active resonance to the globally relevant current experience of otherness, whether in the subjective mode of being the Other, or in the receptive mode of meeting/accepting/integrating/rejecting/manipulating . . . the Other. At the beginning of the twenty-first century, Serbian theatre audiences have seen two thought-provoking productions of the two plays, proposed as starting points for their own comprehension of Shakespeare's texts, self-understanding and grasp of otherness. *The Merchant of Venice*, directed by Egon Savin in 2004, and *Othello*, directed by Miloš Lolić 2012, were both staged at the Yugoslav Drama Theatre.[1] Both Savin and Lolić are known for daring interpretations of the classics contextualized in contemporary cultural and political circumstances. These two productions embody their responses to the otherness of another culture, race, faith, gender, and probe inter-personal, social and political manipulation.

The two Venetian plays are structured around intricate webs of interpretation. In *The Merchant of Venice*, Portia interprets her suitors, all representatives of different cultures, and in the trial scene, disguised as a learned doctor, she interprets Venetian law; the suitors interpret Portia's father's posthumous, life-determining brainteaser, by means of which they can win Portia. If they choose the wrong casket, they must give up marriage to any other woman. Antonio interprets his antagonist Shylock, as a Jew and proto-banker; Shylock interprets the Venetians, their Christian religion, laws and customs. In *Othello*, Brabantio and the Duke of Venice interpret Desdemona and Othello's inter-racial marriage; Desdemona interprets her love for Othello; Iago (mis)interprets Desdemona's behaviour, and Othello, misled by Iago, misinterprets his wife's character and their marriage. All these interpretations are conditioned by the corresponding hermeneutical situations of the characters' mind-sets, enabling them to reach out, estimate, accept, reject, use or abuse the Other.

If we cautiously introduce Gadamer's theory of interpretation, keeping in mind that he travelled the wide distance from the philological, theological and judicial hermeneutics to the general hermeneutics he developed, we can discern, in these dramatic instances of interpretation, quasi-equivalents of the basic hermeneutical steps: *subtilitas intelligendi* (understanding), *subtilitas explicandi* (explanation) and *subtilitas applicandi* (application) (Gadamer 2004: 306–10). As meaning is achieved by way of the mental tools provided by language, culture, religion, social customs and prejudices, the first two stages turn out to be culturally (linguistically and historically) conditioned, while the last one, the application of the acquired meaning, affects life itself. Portia gets the desired husband thanks to Bassanio's successful interpretation; failing to interpret her father's enigma, the princes of Morocco and Arragon should remain unmarried forever; the application proceeding from the hermeneutic manoeuvre at the court leaves Shylock condemned and without an alternative to the required religious conversion; Iago's fragmentary hints of inconclusive interpretation produce paranoid jealousy, a murder and a suicide. In all these instances, the final stage of interpretation – the application – concerns not only the subject of interpretation, but also the Other, who is the object of interpretation, like Desdemona, or a constitutive part of the meaning sought after in the process of interpretation, like Othello or Shylock.

In *The Merchant of Venice*, there are several foreigners who are degraded to stereotypes. Portia is disdainful towards her suitors and ridicules them. She mocks their behaviour, physical appearances, national manners and fashions. Here we find the working of prejudices particular European people have against other European people, an intra-European disdain for otherness, or in Freud's words, the 'narcissism in respect of minor differences' (Freud 1957: 90). From Portia's 'Italian' perspective, the French lord Monsieur Le Bon is so frivolous that she considers him a nonentity: 'God made him, and therefore let him pass for a man' (*MV* 1.2.53–4); Baron Falconbridge is an Anglophone, ignorant of any other language, and a bizarre compendium of foreign fashions and customs (1.2.64–71); the Scottish lord inspires an allusion to the constant tensions at the Scottish border and to uncertain offers of support against the English from the French (1.2.74–8); the young German is a drunkard (1.2.81–94). Arragon is another European, presumably Catholic, with his own scene in the play. Although his arguments are consistent, sensible, based on honourable moral values, the mirror image he gets from the chosen casket is that of a 'blinking idiot' (2.9.53). Dumbfounded, he asks 'Is that my prize? Are my deserts no better?' (59). The major differences of race and religion are represented by the Prince of Morocco and Shylock, both of whom invoke the basic human bodily sameness, as if to excuse themselves for being Others, or to remind their collocutors that 'the body is not in the first place a physical object but a form of relationship, a principle of unity with others', as Terry Eagleton puts it (1986: 43):

MOROCCO

Mislike me not for my complexion,
The shadowed livery of the burnish'd sun,
To whom I am a neighbour, and near bred.
Bring me the fairest creature northward born,
Where Phoebus' fire scarce thaws the icicles,
And let us make incision for your love,
To prove whose blood is reddest, his or mine.

(*MV* 2.1.1–7)

SHYLOCK

I am a Jew. Hath not a Jew eyes? hath not a Jew hands, organs, dimensions, senses, affections, passions? fed with the same food, hurt with the same weapons, subject to the same diseases, healed by the same means, warmed and cooled by the same winter and summer as a Christian is?

– if you prick us, do we not bleed? If you tickle us, do we not laugh? if you poison us, do we not die?

(*MV* 3.1.53–60)

In *Othello*, Iago's and Brabantio's culturally conditioned interpretations of dark skin colour as reasons for fear, rejection and contempt leave the spectator in no doubt that Othello is not a desirable husband for any Venetian girl, let alone a senator's daughter. The web of interpretations is complicated by the fact that Othello is a valiant Christian commander to whom the state is hugely indebted for its military success. Not unlike Shylock, Othello is needed in Venice, but unlike Shylock, Othello is Christian. The scene of his suicide throws into relief the Christian allegiance of his hybrid identity which he values above his abandoned Muslim roots:

And say besides that in Aleppo once,
Where a malignant and turban'd Turk
Beat a Venetian and traduc'd the state,
I took by the throat the circumcised dog,
And smote him thus!

(*Oth* 5.2.350–4)

Correspondingly, Iago uses his manifold guile and instrumental empathy, as Stephen Greenblatt has convincingly argued in *Renaissance Self-Fashioning* (1980), to detect in Othello's complex hybrid identity the vulnerable otherness that leads the Moor to his own fatal (mis)interpretation.

For Helga Geyer-Ryan, Venice is 'above all its significations, the arche-topos of the uncanny' (Geyer-Ryan 1996: 157). Shakespeare's Venetian plays are suffused with, and magnify, this uncanniness: 'neither land nor water' (Geyer-Ryan 1996: 157), at the borderline between Occident and Orient, Venice seems to invite deconstruction as a strategy of interpretation. Constituted as a geo-topical double-bind, culturally and religiously European, economically and politically inclining towards the East, very liberal in many ways, in others very conservative, not unlike the Europe of today, seemingly multicultural Venice is ambiguity itself. Thus, Shylock and Othello are at the same time citizens of Venice and aliens, partly integrated but deficient, with an inherent lack, which the psychoanalytic hermeneutics of suspicion recognizes as Venice's own:

> Money can no more complete the Jew Shylock than military success can perfect the Moor Othello. The meaning of their Jewishness and Blackness, around which the dramatic action revolves, must be read not only as the apparition of the ethnic other but also as the revelation of the lack at the core of the Venetian existence, a lack which they have sutured in themselves by projecting it onto the Jew and the Moor. (Geyer-Ryan 1996: 159)

It has often been said that Shakespeare was a deconstructionist *avant la lettre* (Eagleton 1986: 1; Waller 1991: 21; Bečanović Nikolić 2007: 245). His dramatic enactments of Renaissance rhetorical competence, known as *ad utrumque paratus* ('Ready for any alternative') have made many of his plays appear as the rabbit-or-duck enigmas (Rabkin 1981: 43–4). Shylock's rigid legalism seems callous, but at the same time he 'is triumphantly vindicated even though he loses the case: he has forced the Christians into outdoing his own "inhuman" legalism' (Eagleton 1986: 37). The guile of Portia's interpretation of the bond leads to the condemnation of Shylock, but at the same time reveals the 'charade of the system', 'the genuine illusions at its heart' (Eagleton 1986: 38), 'all delusions of security' (Geyer-Ryan 1996: 160) and opens a deconstructive *mise-en-abyme* of undermined meanings. The claim of Antonio's flesh, as an instance of potential perverse aggression, can also be read as an exposure of a fundamental sameness, and 'a grotesque parody of Eucharistic fellowship' (Eagleton 1986: 83).

The unaffected, the undone seems to be part of the uncanniness of Shakespeare's Venice. Portia interprets the unwritten and Iago induces Othello to interpret the unconsummated. The inexistent adultery, featured only as a fiction in Iago's insinuations (Parker 1991: 54–7), deconstructs Othello's sanity, destroys Desdemona's and his own lives. Iago's 'I am not what I am' is a formulaic image of deconstruction. The narrative core of Othello's identity, fatally attractive to Desdemona, proves susceptible to the deconstructive scheming of Iago, who 'knows that an identity that has been fashioned as a story can be unfashioned, refashioned, inscribed anew in a different narrative; it is the fate of stories to be consumed or, as we say more politely, interpreted' (Greenblatt 1980: 238).

Let us now behold 'through the looking glass' of the productions the two Serbian directors created as twenty-first-century responses to Shakespeare's own deconstructive strategies in the Venetian plays. As post-modernist interpretations, both productions take post-humanist or anti-humanist standpoints, calling into question the traditional humanist perspective of universal human nature. The uniqueness of every particular social and existential stance makes everyone Other to the other Other. Nevertheless, otherness does not necessarily imply only difference but sameness as well. The dialectics of otherness and sameness relativizes binary oppositions like male/female, white/black, Christian/Jewish, Christian/Muslim, truth/fiction, suggesting that one often underlies or is part of the other. Ambivalent and polyvalent meanings and internal contradictions thus come to the fore. By building upon such vacillation of binary oppositions, both directors astutely lead their interpretations in the direction of political representations. The result in each case is a 'double exposure' of Shakespeare's text and of Serbia's cultural, social and political context. The presumed multicultural character of post-Yugoslav societies is implicitly targeted in *The Merchant of Venice*. In *Othello*, Shakespearean fiction is projected on the Serbian reality of aggressive populist culture and deceitful political discourse. These political aspects include subversive tendencies and invite disillusioned audience responses.

Post-Yugoslav post-humanism in Egon Savin's *The Merchant of Venice* (2004)

Savin's *Merchant* (2004) stressed difference and otherness, in all its guises: sexual, racial, national, religious. The elegant decadence of the lagoon city in the scenography of Miodrag Tabački served as a backdrop to the stylish gay atmosphere of the opening conversations of Antonio with the young Salerio, Solanio, Lorenzo, Gratiano and Bassanio, all gay in gestures, intonation and outfit. Irfan Mensur's Antonio was a distinguished, melancholy homosexual. The air of light playful homoeroticism, mainly suggested by movement and gesture, flowed into a rapturous second scene, with Portia played as a virtuoso drag queen. The male super-star of Serbian theatre, Dragan Mićanović, fashioned his role with a sophisticated seduction, which made him/her attractive in both feminine and male homoerotic manner. The line separating and/or uniting femininity and male homoeroticism was hardly discernible, and thus produced a deconstruction of gender binary oppositions. The hilarious in-joke legible to Serbian audiences was Mićanović's fashioning of his beautiful young character after his then wife and equally famous actress and singer, Ana Sofrenović.

The production was post-humanist insofar as it didn't imply anything like a universal human nature; there was nothing suggestive of Human-as-such condition; every existential situation was made as particular as possible: Shylock's, Antonio's, Portia's, Jessica's, Lancelot's ... Shylock was played by the late Predrag Ejdus, an actor with great charisma. The initial tradition of producing *The Merchant of Venice* in Belgrade (1869, 1893, 1905, 1923, 1928) implied the tragedy of the persecuted Jew. In 1928, between the two World Wars, Dobrica Milutinović is said to have fashioned this role with warmth after the real Belgrade Jews. The famous 1953 production, directed by Hugo Klajn, psychoanalyst, translator, theatre director, and author of a most influential collection of essays *Shakespeare and*

Humaneness (1964), lessened the sympathy the Belgrade public had been used to feel for Shylock. In his Marxist interpretation he emphasized the cruelty of banking and finance capitalism. The Shylock of 2004 was an endangered and ghettoized Other. The intended and achieved sympathies of the spectators were more balanced than in the past tradition, due to the relativizing effect of post-modern irony. Minimal but still discernible *Verfremdungseffekt* was present in most roles. Nevertheless, Shylock's Jewishness was accentuated; in the 'Hath not a Jew eyes' speech, it was disturbing. Equally stressed was his shrewd understanding of the legal matters, including the dependence of Venetian prosperity on the international business-friendly and banking-friendly legal prerogatives. The Jew may not have been genuinely welcome in Venice, as the arrogant and humiliating attitude of Mensur's *grand seigneur* Antonio towards Shylock was affirming, but the importance of foreign money for Venetian investments was the air this particular Venice was breathing. 'Which is the merchant here, and which the Jew?' (4.1.170) could, then, in this production, be understood as a symbolic equivalence of international banking and trade.

More naïve, utterly ingenuous, simple-minded and proud, glaring in its African exhibition of personal prestige was the otherness of the Prince of Morocco. His culturally conditioned understanding of gold as the only acceptable way of praising Portia, and his consequent choice of the (wrong) gold casket, which Geraldo de Sousa saw as Morocco's mapping 'his way through the labyrinth of material culture and ethnographic interpretation' (Sousa 1999: 75) was another ironic but still sympathetic representation of the Stranger in Venice. In the otherwise sophisticated setting, the appearance of Morocco, with Portia who was this time more bewildered than disdainful, reminded one of an ethnographic interlude.

The inherent ambiguity of the two most prominent Others was a hallmark of this production. Along with his arrogant proto-capitalist and anti-Semitic attitudes, Antonio emanated melancholy and grief. His gesturally signalled but frustrated and virtually impossible love for the younger man, and the resulting willingness to sacrifice himself for love, coupled with his melancholy, made the arrogant part seem somewhat softer. On the other hand, 'legal connoisseur' Shylock's near-tragic defeat and consequent condemnation, requiring conversion to Christianity, brought in an almost palpable sense of humiliation and alienation, all the more uncanny by not being tragic *sensu stricto*.

Shylock's Jewishness and citizenship of Venice, Morocco's cultural incompatibility with the desired Western matrimonial tie, based on the logic of inverted values, Antonio's unfulfilled homosexuality underneath his social distinction and wealth, converted Jessica's Jewish origin all implied the convoluted nature of identity which is more often than not hybrid in some way. Savin's production embodied the problem of the minority Other in the religiously, racially and nationally unified community, or in the community with a dominant religion, with clearly dominant cultural, economic and gender policies. In a region which experienced the tragic consequences of the conflicts that led to the disintegration of the federal republic of Yugoslavia, the situation of individuals belonging to national minorities in a nominally multicultural society, which *was* and *was not* truly multicultural, was very much like Venice in this play (Geyer-Ryan 1996: 159–61). This similarity was inevitably evoked by the production. The implication of such an analogy was an important part of the particular post-1990s hermeneutic situation of the authors of this production. However, the parallels were not blatantly obvious nor didactic, but artistically implied. The scenography represented the chronotope of Venice in the 1920s, with, as we saw in the very last scene, the Italian fascists organized in 'fascios'. Jews and homosexuals, in that context, were equally endangered. Director Savin rewrote Shakespeare at the very end of Act 5: Portia's servants appeared in black fascist shirts and took Antonio away. By this deconstructive coup de théâtre the merchant and the Jew ended up being on the same endangered side: 'Which is the merchant here, and which the Jew?'

Colour-washed panopticon in Miloš Lolić's *Othello* (2012)

Otherness, alterity and foreignness were in the focus of Miloš Lolić's interpretation of *Othello* in 2012. This production will be remembered for abundant quasi-expressionist pouring of colours on stage and on actors, for their individual and mutual dyeing of bodies in yellow, black, green, blue. Yellow seeped into the minds of audiences, as a lasting memory of this theatrical provocation.

The Venetian first act was staged in front of a solid dark grey metal backdrop, which created a stern and austere visual context, implying the gravity of Venetian politics and interests. There was nothing frivolous or lavish about this background. The design (Jasmina Holbus) suggested that the game of living in Venice seemed to be cynical, hard and cruel. Desdemona appeared in a light turquoise dress made up of metal mosaic particles which looked like chainmail (costume design by Marija Jelesijević) and made us infer the audacious bravery of a woman both gentle and courageous. Othello's face was at first painted black, in the old-fashioned manner, plainly denoting his racial otherness. The otherness of an African is hardly an issue in contemporary Serbian society, there being so few of them visible at all, except for diplomats, a few students or a scarce tourist. There are no actors of African origin. So, the obviously conventional black make-up was both part of the theatrical tradition and of the semiotic function of colours in this production. The accomplished and needed, as well as callously manipulated, Othe(r)llo can be anyone with a different identity. In the Balkan circumstances, you name them: every representative of any ex-Yugoslav nation in any of the ex-Yugoslav republics and now separate states, is the Other, in a way, in the respective contexts; the Romani people are Others; even a cosmopolitan citizen with no racial, national or religious difference can be such an Other. Vojin Ćetković made Othello an uncouth and raucous soldier, brave and aware of his own military merit, but also in love and naïve. In telling his story, he was plain and truthful, as opposed to the conceited Brabantio and the grandiose, calm and calculating Duke.

Except for Desdemona, the characters at the military outpost in Cyprus were conventionally Venetian in dress, but closer to the rowdy behaviour of the contemporary international consumer, including Emilia and Bianca. In addition to this presentist aspect, Nikola Đuričko's savvy Iago seemed to have stepped out of Giuseppe Verdi's famous letter to Domenico Morelli, in which he discusses the character: with 'an absent-minded air, nonchalant, indifferent to everything, sceptical, a cutting manner, speaking of good and evil lightly' (Bassi 2016: 22; Verdi 1971: 227) A distinctive feature of this production was that all the characters were present throughout the action: when Cassio was spoken about, the actor playing Cassio was somewhere on stage, though 'absent', and the spectators could see him. This permanent visibility implied the ominous eeriness of what Michel Foucault calls 'panopticism', a system of social control and distribution of power-knowledge (Foucault 1995: 200–4). The panoptic format of reality TV programmes, which are very popular in Serbia as elsewhere, could be inferred as well – the master-observer and the master-interpreter being, of course, Iago. Like Richard III and Edmund, Iago provides the audience with the privilege of dramatic irony – we know as much as the Machiavellian villain, and more than his victims. In this production, the mute and uninformed presence of all the characters on stage all the time uncannily embodied a 'panopticon' with its inherent dramatic irony and sinister dialectic involving both the lack and surplus of knowledge in the play.

The stage design for Cyprus was dominated by the yellow floor upon which the action was developing. This could suggest the yellowness of bile, of the lies of the gutter press, the 'yellow-media' worldview. Contemporary politics in the so-called countries of 'transition' is often enhanced and mediated by the banal, vulgar and offensive media, home-made or franchised from the global media-market. Like Iago, they pour all kinds of poisons into the raw, unsophisticated and paranoid ears of their consumers. Like manipulation, lies are a mental poison. This production was presentist in the way all characters behaved like contemporary Serbs, or, for that matter, like many other contemporary people, regardless of their ethnicity, without the artful gloss of Venetian human dignity and courtesy. This low-mimetic aspect was underlined by the globalized, uniform, populist entertainment of the dances during the celebrations in Cyprus. At moments, Iago stuck his tongue out. Cassio and Othello kept pronouncing 'honest' when talking about 'honest Iago' so quickly that it could not be properly heard or understood. The result was a smudgy 'hns' sound, a slurring of the Serbian 'čsni', as if the adjective 'honest' were disappearing from the contemporary vocabulary, fading away for good, equally hard to utter and to comprehend.

Desdemona's face was at times coloured by the black make-up from Othello's face and Emilia wiped it from time to time, as if to keep her on the Venetian/European side. As Iago advanced with his venomous manipulation of Othello's mind, Othello painted his face in green, and once he admitted to jealousy, he poured green paint all over himself. As if coloured by Iago's manipulative fiction, he revealed how a 'green-eyed monster' grew out of Iago's 'yellow' 'improvisation of power' (Greenblatt 1980: 222–54). The visual effect of the colour green was intertwined with the sound of Othello's powerful, echoing scream. Entirely drenched in green, he coloured Desdemona's 'moist hand' (*Oth* 3.4.36), and ordered Cassio's murder. The stage began to look like an abstract expressionist painting by Jackson Pollock. When Lodovico entered (4.1.212), Othello washed off the green, which washed off the black make-up as well, exposing the face of the white actor. Symbolically, this was perhaps a demonstration of deeply integrated whiteness, or rather, of the integrated values of European culture, including the strict Christian attitude towards passion in marriage, as discussed by Greenblatt (1980: 222–54). However, it could also be interpreted as the Other's urge not to be an Other, to integrate in his hybrid identity colours which were not initially his own.[2]

The inconsistency of colours replacing one another embodies the inconstancy of any existential situation, of any value in the world, of what is true and what is not. In Shakespeare's text, the interpretation, improvisation and mind-manipulation by Iago, who identifies himself through the antinomy 'I am not what I am', are all engaged in undoing the Other. Thus, love and faithfulness are forced into appearing as adultery, a trusting husband is turned into a jealous man, a devoted lover into a murderer. The changing colours added to the vertiginous, contradictory, deconstructive dynamics of setting truth and lie side by side.

The last dominant colour used in the production was blue. Othello painted himself blue before killing Desdemona, and by his deadly touch she too turned blue. The yellow of bile and lies, the green of jealousy, the black of Othello's otherness and the blueness of death, grief, sadness, melancholy and despair appeared against a background of gold, as the initially grey metal backdrop changed to gold. At the moment of murdering Desdemona, Othello's face turned white. The lighting and the position of the couple created a Caravaggio-like composition saturated with light against the suppressed glow of the golden background. Light emanated from the intertwining of the coldness and passion of Othello's murder with the tranquility of Desdemona's loyalty and the deep passion of her love. An agonizing African and a dead white woman who had rebelled against patriarchy composed an illuminated sculpture of excluded alterity (Callaghan 2000: 92–3). Although his face was no longer painted black, he obviously stood for the ultimate otherness against the rest of the Venetian world. Black, white, green or blue, Othello's skin pigmentation was different from the other skin hues in the cast, colouring through physical contact Desdemona's as well. Dympna Callaghan speaks of the capacity of blackness to absorb all aspects of otherness as a specifically Renaissance configuration of othering (Callaghan 2000: 78). Today, at a time when the goal of a multiracial, multicultural society is at once valued and problematic, all colours have the capacity to absorb otherness – which is why Lolić insisted on changing them. Even before the murder scene, Othello and Desdemona were most of the time spotlighted against the steel-grey, night-dark or dim-gold background. Compared to the other characters, in Venice or in Cyprus, they were both Others. Thus, after the kaleidoscopic colour transformations their bodies underwent during the performance, the audience were left with pure light, and with the symbolically mediated realization that 'both Africans and white women present the peculiar practical and conceptual obstacles inherent in the dramatic depiction of those categories of persons whose cultural alterity, for different reasons, requires their exclusion' (Callaghan 2000: 92). With his ultimately colourless face, exposed in Caravaggesque lighting, Othello seemed to embody a pale, solemn warning of tragic mindfulness against the existential blindness of both steel-grey and golden Venice, of individual or political scheming, or even mere frivolous lifestyles in both Venice and Cyprus.

Othello's several colours dyed Desdemona, who eventually died – dyed. His original (black and Muslim) colour had been permeated with the (Christian) 'colours' he championed as a Venetian general. Iago's manipulation added a specific yellow of indiscreet and scandalous inferences, and a specific green of jealousy, already identified as such in Shakespeare's text as the 'green-eyed monster' (*Oth* 3.3.168). This production seemed to suggest that Desdemona's death was caused by Othello's mental absorption of the colours of Venetian/Christian/European values, which, *pace* Greenblatt, once integrated into his mind, became a cultural construct susceptible to Iago's deadly deconstruction. Instead of the initial, austere metal background of Venice in the first act, the final background suggested a visually effective and obviously ironic distant golden skyline.

The only death which occurs in Venice is Brabantio's, yet Desdemona's, Othello's, Roderigo's and Emilia's deaths also belong to Venice. The protagonist of Thomas Mann's *Death in Venice*, the celebrated author Gustav von Aschenbach, experienced the gradual recognition of his ecstatic love for a foreign youth against the backdrop of the morbid appeal of a city whose 'obtrusive spell on the entrails' (Mann 2019: 48) drove him to death. The vicinity of *eros* and *thanatos* in Venice has, since Mann, become proverbial. Geyer-Ryan foregrounds the excessive force of the return of the repressed (Geyer-Ryan 1996: 157), both in the modernist narrative of *Death in Venice* and in the two early modern Venetian plays. 'What returns in the Venetian experience', Geyer-Ryan writes, 'as a spectre from the outside is the subject's repressed alterity, which is necessary for its symbolic position – the apparition that Lacan calls *jouissance*' (Geyer-Ryan 1996: 158). Further on, following Lacan, she directs us towards a psychological kernel relevant to Othello: the unifying (narcissistic) function of his 'mirror image', situated between *jouissance* and the symbolic order, is deprived of its optimal balance. Her argument is that 'where the *jouissance* of power is given free rein, a dialectics of destruction is triggered. In this respect, Venice appears as a purveyor of truth, but it is a truth which is fatal in the end for a subject imprisoned in the narcissistic mirages of its ego and deceived by the supposed stability of its social bonds' (Geyer-Ryan 1996: 158). Othello could have preserved a balance between the two types of narcissism, had not Iago interfered with his undermining mental incisions, which triggered the Moor's 'dialectics of destruction' (Geyer-Ryan 1996: 158). Iago recognized Othello as limited by his two narcissistic mirages: that of valiant warrior and Venetian general, and that of a Venetian husband. However, he is at the same time 'deceived by the supposed stability of social bonds' (Geyer-Ryan 1996: 158). When Iago confronts the personal constitution of the never-entirely-integrated Stranger with fragile balance between the mirror image and the symbolic identity, he seems to exult in the cynicism of deconstructing Othello's personal identity and confidence in the bond of marriage. Shakespeare expressed this convoluted dynamics of subjectivity and otherness, inner and outer, in his poetic drama. In the time of post-dramatic theatre, Lolić, in his 2012 *Othello*, played with the semiotic potential of colours to represent the complex dynamics of human subjectivity and the conflicting layers of hybrid identity. The text was present in all its strength, the characters and action slightly contemporized, but the most memorable aspect of the production was the non-verbal semiotic experiment of dyeing the bodies of Othello and Desdemona, and by consequence, their minds as well, along with the ambiguously multicultural Venetian background of their tragic deaths.

A circular concluding glance at the beginning of this essay and the ontological importance of interpretation in relation to the interpreters' hermeneutic situation can lead to the question of the presentist relatedness of the two productions to their own here-and-now. Neither of the directors was unaware of the specific chronotope of their productions, but they were not making obvious political or didactic appropriations of Shakespeare. Their artistic involvements were not directed towards the ideological translations or explanations of the issues of racial or sexual otherness, but rather towards the deep disturbance of the spectators, towards stirring the feelings of profound concern for the Other, face to face with the Other, face to face with death, as in the philosophy of Emmanuel Levinas, who reads in the face of the Other his or her very mortality: 'It is precisely in this reminder of the responsibility of the *I* by the face that summons it, that demands it, that claims it, that the other is my fellowman' (Levinas 2006: 160).

The interpretations of *The Merchant of Venice* and *Othello* created by directors and actors, taken further and developed by the spectators in their own interpretations, confirm the existential significance of experiencing these plays as theatrical events. In both of the productions discussed here, the encounter with the Other hurt the spectator through his/her suffering. In a world full of misunderstood, manipulated, ideologically constructed or deconstructed, integrated or disintegrated Others, the theatrically engendered feeling of pain may, like the terror and pity of the Aristotelian catharsis, lead to more responsible, (post)humanist encounters with the Other, similar to Shakespeare's Prospero's symbolic, as much as merely topical, identification of Caliban as the 'thing of darkness' which he acknowledged his own (*Tem* 5.1.275–6).

Notes

1 Yugoslav Drama Theatre was founded by Bojan Stupica in 1947 as the representative multinational theatre of the socialist Yugoslavia. It has been the venue of many productions which are regarded as artistic keystones of the Yugoslav and the Serbian theatre. Egon Savin (b. 1955) has directed plays by classical and contemporary authors of world literature as well as Serbian and Yugoslav authors. He has been awarded numerous prizes for his work and is considered as one of the most original theatre directors in the region of South Eastern Europe. Miloš Lolić (b. 1979) has directed plays by Robert Musil, Federico García Lorca, Shakespeare, Wolfgang Bauer and other playwrights, in Serbia, Germany and Austria. His productions have been awarded distinguished prizes and are recognized as breakthroughs in contemporary explorations of theatrical expression.

2 'In Othello's ecstatic words, the proper sentiments of a Christian husband sit alongside something else: a violent oscillation between heaven and hell, a momentary possession of the soul's absolute content, an archaic sense of monumental scale, a dark fear – equally archaic, perhaps – of "unknown fate". Nothing *conflicts* openly with Christian orthodoxy, but the erotic intensity that informs almost every word is experienced in tension with it. This tension is less a manifestation of some atavistic "blackness" specific to Othello than a manifestation of the colonial power of Christian doctrine over sexuality, a power visible at this point precisely in its inherent limitation' (Greenblatt 1980: 241–2).

References

Bassi, S. (2016), *Shakespeare's Italy and Italy's Shakespeare*, New York: Palgrave Macmillan.

Bečanović Nikolić, Z. (2007), *Šekspir iza ogledala*, Beograd: Geopoetika.

Callaghan, D. (2000), *Shakespeare Without Women*, London: Routledge.

Eagleton, T. (1986), *William Shakespeare*, Oxford: Blackwell.

Foucault, M. (1995), *Discipline and Punish: The Birth of the Prison*, trans. A. Sheridan, New York: Vintage Books.
Freud, S. (1957), *Civilization and Its Discontents*, trans. J. Riviere, London: The Hogarth Press.
Gadamer, H.-G. (2004), *Truth and Method*, trans. J. Weinsheimer and D. G. Marshall, London: Continuum.
Geyer-Ryan, H. (1996), 'Shakespeare after Derrida and Marx: Death in Venice and the Utopia of the Open Society', *Arcadia Band*, 31 (1/2): 155–64.
Greenblatt, S. (1980), *Renaissance Self-fashioning*, Chicago: University of Chicago Press.
Iser, W. (2000), *The Range of Interpretation*, New York: Columbia University Press.
Levinas, E. (2006), *Entre nous. Thinking-of-the-other*, trans. M. B. Smith and B. Harshav, London: Continuum.
Mann, T. (2019), *Death in Venice*, trans. M. C. Doege, New York: Barnes and Noble.
Parker, P. (1991), 'Shakespeare and Rhetoric: "Dilation" and "Delation" in *Othello*', in P. Parker and G. Hartman (eds), *Shakespeare and the Question of Theory*, 54–74, London: Routledge.
Rabkin, N. (1981), *Shakespeare and the Problem of Meaning*, Chicago: University of Chicago Press.
Shakespeare, W. (2010), *The Merchant of Venice*, ed. J. Drakakis, The Arden Shakespeare, third series, London: Bloomsbury.
Shakespeare, W. (2011), *The Tempest*, ed. A. T. Vaughan and V. Mason Vaughan, The Arden Shakespeare, third series, London: Bloomsbury.
Shakespeare, W. (2016), *Othello*, ed. E. A. J. Honigmann, rev. edn, intr. A. Thompson, The Arden Shakespeare, third series, London: Bloomsbury.
Sousa, G. U. de (1999), *Shakespeare's Cross-Cultural Encounters*, Houndmills: MacMillan.
Verdi, G. (1971), *Letters of Giuseppe Verdi*, ed. Charles Osborne, London: Victor Gollancz.
Waller, G. (1991), 'Decentering the Bard: The Dissemination of Shakespearean Text', in G. D. Atkins and D. M. Bergeron (eds), *Shakespeare and Deconstruction*, 21–45, New York: Peter Lang.

5

The Merchant of Venice in France (2001 and 2017)

Deconstructing a *malaise*

Janice Valls-Russell

When it premiered in Paris on 15 September 2001, Andrei Șerban's production of *The Merchant of Venice* was eventful in more ways than one.[1] It marked the end of the play's absence from the boards of the Comédie-Française, where it had been staged last in 1905 in Alfred de Vigny's adaptation.[2] The tragic serendipity of the play's opening four days after the 9/11 terrorist attack on New York's Twin Towers created a ripple of unease that might be summed up as follows: why did Șerban choose to set his *Merchant* in today's world of finance, in offices just like those that had been targeted by Al-Qaeda, thereby playing into the hands of those who equated capitalism with Jewishness? Surely Shakespeare's Shylock and Venetians belonged to the past.

In the light of subsequent events, Șerban's modernization, which would have come as no surprise to American and other

European audiences, can be viewed as prescient. It uncovered something lying underneath the surface – more easily done, perhaps, by a Romanian-born Other standing outside French mainstream culture. In 2006, Ilan Halimi, a young French Jew, was tortured and killed by an urban gang: later referred to in the media as 'le gang des barbares', they had kidnapped him on the assumption that, being Jewish, his family were bound to be rich. In January 2015, a terrorist claiming allegiance to ISIS attacked a kosher supermarket, leaving four dead, after two other terrorists decimated the editorial board of the satirical weekly *Charlie Hebdo*. During the presidential election campaign of 2017, Emmanuel Macron's career as a banker with Rothschild gave rise to rhetoric and caricatures reeking of anti-Semitism. So when, in 2017, Jacques Vincey staged his own version of the play as *Business in Venice*, setting it in the banality of a supermarket, he was using an ambience with an uneasy proximity to real violence. The hatred that can flare up between what the social theorist Michel Maffesoli calls urban *tribus* (neo-tribes) or, indeed, between rival businessmen thus acquired a very topical resonance.

An awareness of the world around the theatre underpins both Șerban's and Vincey's aesthetic choices. Through setting, re-scripting and casting, they enfold the fate meted out to Shylock in Venice within a wider, contemporary exploration of the mechanisms of othering and otherness. This aspect of their productions was mostly overlooked by reviewers who tended to focus on Shylock. So did some spectators, among them members of the Jewish community, who protested against Șerban's production by writing to the Administrator General of the Comédie-Française (Kuttner 2001); leaflets carrying the message 'Attention: danger' were distributed outside the theatre of Tours on the opening night of Vincey's production (Fischer 2018: 84). Whether regretting the staging of the play in what is considered the temple of French theatre, or calling for a boycott, such initiatives reflected genuine fears of resurgent anti-Semitism. They may also be viewed as a symptom of a deep-seated *malaise*, discernible in the very rarity of the play on French stages.

France is still finding it difficult to come to terms with the anti-Semitic passions that wrenched French society apart over the Dreyfus affair (1874–1906) and which erupted afresh under the pro-Nazi Vichy regime during the Second World War. Consequently, while the Comédie-Française opted to silence *The Merchant of Venice* by not including it in its repertoire, directors who chose to stage it tended to adopt a philo-Semitic approach, like Marguerite Jamois (1961), and/or keep it at a safe distance by setting it in Victorian England, like Guy Rétoré (1971), or the Renaissance, like Luca Ronconi (1987).[3] One exception was Jean Le Poulain, who staged the play in the vein of *commedia dell'arte*. His production, which was aired on a public television channel (France 3) in 1980, elicited complaints from an anti-racist organization and from the Chief Rabbi. On the academic front, meanwhile, French Shakespearean Pierre Spriet argued that staging *Merchant* in a post-Holocaust world should be 'abandoned' (Spriet 1988: 59).

Choosing, as Șerban and Vincey have done, to set the play in the audience's here and now marks a break with the French tradition of moving the action elsewhere. It also creates unease. What happens on stage is no longer something that is safely locked in the past – neither the attacks on Shylock, nor the mocking of Morocco and Arragon.[4] This was made explicit in both productions through a play on stereotypes, and the presence or absence of visual markers to indicate (supposed) otherness. The productions also probed the uncomfortable issue of the relative status, in the scale of discrimination and othering, of anti-Semitism and racism, through a twofold exploration: of the othering processes at work and of the banality of such processes.

In tracing the ways otherness is mapped onto the individual who is targeted, constructed and consequently cast out as an Other, Șerban and Vincey transposed the workings of anti-Semitism to the level of the community. Their approach recalls, while adapting it to a social group, the deconstruction of the anti-Semite which is the subject of Jean-Paul Sartre's essay,

Réflexions sur la question juive (translated into English as *Anti-Semite and Jew*). Written in 1944 before the full horror of the death camps hit the world, and published in 1946, this essay is a landmark contribution to French intellectual introspection into the Dreyfus affair and the anti-Jewish laws of the Vichy government. While much of the terminology may appear dated and some generalizations may seem downright embarrassing, Sartre's theory about 'man . . . as a being "in a situation"' remains hermeneutically valid (Sartre 1976: 42).[5] Well before Maffesoli theorized the breaking apart of the French republican social contract under the pressure of urban neo-tribalism and the spread of archaic mental patterns on the internet, Sartre was drawing attention, through anti-Semitism, to the survival of 'a regressive social force and a conception deriving from the prelogical world' (103). It is this post-modern resurgence of archaism that is staged in these two productions – and thrown at the audience which thus cannot evade Sartre's warning that 'anti-Semitism . . . affects us all directly' (109).

Andrei Șerban's *Merchant of Venice* (2001): 'Étrangers en France'[6]

Set in the languorous, steamy atmosphere of a gym-cum-sauna, the opening scene revealed a male hedonist community.[7] Theirs was a way of life far removed from Shylock's world as seen in the following scene – a no-frills hi-tech office in reds and blues, with a restless man sitting at a desk and talking in several languages to invisible contacts over the telephone and via his computer. The overall design (Marielle Bancou and Dominique Schmitt) matched the structuring of the production as a series of tableaux linked by extradiegetic music (Elisabeth Swados) and movement that hinted at a potential fluidity between the different worlds. Folding screens in pastel shades and a golden glow – which changed to a moonlit blue wash in Act 5 – conveyed the *farniente* prosperity of Belmont, where a triangular swing served as a reminder of the play's emotional triangulations. In contrast, the dark, oppressive world of Shylock's home was closed off by the (ghetto?) wall, above which Jessica first appeared; circulation within the house was impeded by chests and screens. The courtroom had an uncompromising symmetrical red and black décor. Continuity between the different worlds was provided by striped mooring poles that served as columns, streetlamps and flaming torches. Depth and perspective were created – or impeded – by see-through hangings that peeled away different layers of perception or created a succession of filters, signalling the play's threshold-crossings and impossibilities. Characters moved between these hangings, or under them, as when Jessica crawled through after the money chests to join Lorenzo; sometimes they remained outside them, excluded. The layout of the courtroom suggested both constraint and the remoteness of the law: the judge sat on an elevated pedestal up stage, while members of the jury and court audiences stood behind high desks. Nobody stirred when Shylock was thrown to the ground and kicked by the Venetians centre stage, an act all the more terrifying as it took place in a courtroom.

Shylock, played by the Polish-born Andrzej Seweryn, passionately sought to negotiate a margin of agency and control over his life, by exercising forms of power – be it over his financial partners, or his daughter. At least one reviewer chose to underplay the complexity Seweryn gave his character, preferring to dwell on what he considered a 'clumsy' casting. Seweryn's Polish accent, he wrote, recalled the Yiddish accent of Jewish jokes (Nerson 2001: 93), indirectly implying that his non-native-French accent ruled him out for the part. Focusing on moments when Seweryn allowed his impeccable French to slide into Eastern-European cadences, this same reviewer chose to criticize this, impervious to what it revealed of the character's emotional disarray and the vulnerability of the Other.

Seweryn's Shylock's business suit was identical to Antonio's, his hat similar, but when he removed it to greet other Venetians, with a (self-)mocking obsequiousness, he revealed a kippah. His was a Shylock as a 'type', in the vein French audiences expect of Molière's Harpagon – Şerban had staged *L'Avare* for the Comédie-Française a year earlier. But there was much more to the performance than that: as he left the house, Shylock moved into the audience, glanced back at Jessica, then walked on, tossing her a bag of coins over his shoulder. He knew, she knew, the audience knew, that she was leaving him. Henceforth both, irremediably, would be outcasts – he without, she within the community she aspired to. Shylock's response, after Tubal's report (Christian Blanc), was to play to another stereotype well known of French audiences to this day, the Jew in Gérard Oury's film *Rabbi Jacob* (1973).[8] This highly popular comedy ridicules xenophobia through the character of an irascible businessman (Louis de Funès) who finds himself taking on the disguise of a rabbi. Performed immediately after the interval in front of the closed red curtain 'turned "Wailing Wall"' (Fischer 2009: 318), Seweryn's impersonation of Funès impersonating a Hasidic rabbi, stamping, half-dancing and chanting revenge against Jessica and Antonio, provided a grating comic interlude that threw back at the audience its passive endorsement of stereotypes.

As the play progressed, and Shylock was mocked, hounded and finally beaten to the ground in the courtroom scene, Seweryn seemed to collapse. However, his body remained on the stage throughout Act 5, a dark shapeless mass. Portia (Clotilde de Bayser) and Nerissa (Johan Daisme) sidestepped him, vaguely glancing down as at a vagrant sleeping in a doorway, and moved on. Lorenzo (Jérôme Pouly) did not even acknowledge his humanity: stretching on the ground, he leaned against his prone body, using him as the moonlit bank.

Whatever vulnerability Antonio and his friends may have shown in the opening scene through their nakedness, it held no empathy for Shylock's life. Antonio kicked Shylock off the stage before accepting the bond; aggression and hatred were the cohesive glue of the Venetians' collective persona. Their interchangeability was suggested by identical garb (street-gang outfits, followed by dark suits, white shirts and black hats in the business and courtroom scenes) and by their choreographed movement. The penitents' robes and cowls they wore in the carnival scene, which was performed as a dance with flaming torches, tapped into the Sartrian 'prelogical' archaisms. Pointing back to the medieval tradition of Good Friday processions, as well as to its more recent Ku Klux Klan manifestations, the dance collapsed anti-Judaism and anti-Semitism, past and present, European and global. Even as it seeks to brand those who are being othered with visual markers, the semiology of othering erases the individuality of the otherer: anyone could be under those cowls – including members of the audience. Hence it was all the more shocking when, after that disturbing choreography, Lancelet[9] (Nicolas Lormeau) suddenly brandished a cowl – his? – streaked with blood and shook it at Shylock inside the house. Hatred, at that moment, had the frightful face of a jester and shockingly intruded in the domestic sphere. The bloodstained cowl and the prayer shawl, which Shylock had left behind on departing, remained lying on the stage in close proximity.

Jessica (Céline Samie) picked up the shawl and draped it over a chair after briefly clasping it to her heart. She pulled out a cross, held it over the shawl, then hung it around her neck. Inevitably, her construction of the Christians was at odds with what the audience already knew of them, which was confirmed by the glee with which Lorenzo welcomed the boxes of gold rather than Jessica. Ultimately, her otherness proved to be not so much religious as social: her clothing and behaviour indicated that she did not belong to the world of Belmont, any more than her father belonged to Venice, even though she had by then changed into the outfit of a 1960s American tourist on the Côte d'Azur, with overlarge sunglasses and flowing clothes that were stridently out of place in Belmont. She was ignored by Portia and Nerissa, yet tried to fit in by tossing rice during the wedding and hovering with a big eager smile. The money she had brought Lorenzo did her no more favours than the ducats Shylock had lent Bassanio, just as the trial imposed on

Portia's suitors by her father merely served to raise false hopes in those other Others, the princes of Morocco and Arragon.

Staged in succession, Morocco's and Arragon's scenes were designed like tableaux, viewed through a scrim, with Antonio and Bassanio, Lorenzo and Jessica, watching. A kind of Asian martial-arts ritual for Morocco, a toreador dance for Arragon: Otherness was made visible by reducing its rituals to mockery. Morocco collapsed into unconsciousness after he chose the wrong casket and had to be carried out. Arragon, too, collapsed, but managed to stagger out through the audience. Such dramatic exits are traditionally used for Shylock and their presence in the production showed how much wider Venetian xenophobia extended.

Unusually, these scenes introduced an onlooker, an unobtrusive dark-skinned servant in a dark dress (D'Jazzy). Given no lines, no name, she was reduced to her lowly social status, without a story of her own. Yet, in the cold world of the play, she was the only human who showed some of the sensitivity to the condition of the Other Emmanuel Levinas calls for (1991). She looked at Morocco with compassion and crouched at his side before he was taken away. Sharply calling her to attention, Portia instructed her to pick up the scimitar and commented disparagingly on 'tous ceux . . . de sa peau' ('all of his complexion', 2.7.79).[10] The servant repeated 'sa peau' ('his complexion'): 'oui', snapped Portia, and the girl ran off stage. When she returned for Arragon, she looked keenly at him, as if trying to see the man behind the part. Later, she danced with Lancelet (in a bright blouse and jeans), then slipped away with him. She was the 'negro' Lancelet was accused of impregnating (3.5.35), an exchange Șerban moved to the beginning of Act 5 to underscore the unbalance of the Jessica/Lorenzo 'romance'. This was also a moment that reminded the audiences of something else as well: when the servant girl appeared, Jessica, who was seated on the swing, did not even look at her, repeating the gesture of class and ethnic othering to which she was herself subjected.

At the end of the play, Morocco and Arragon appeared rear stage, stripped to the waist, just as Lorenzo learned of his changed fortune. As he and Jessica read the letter, the two Others moved forward, held out their hats, begging Portia for money. Disconcerted, she gave them some coins and they ran off. The moment was so fleeting that the audience barely had time to identify them in the greyish dawn. Like Shylock, still lying on the ground, they were ghosts of Portia's past, and of the collective past of the audience. They were the nomads and migrants one tries, or even chooses, not to see, the spectral Strangers-without or within in a land made strange by its alienating gaze, bringing to mind lines from a poem Louis Aragon wrote during the Nazi occupation of France, *La rose de Noël*:

> Quand nous étions étrangers en France
> Des mendiants sur nos propres chemins
> Quand nous tendions aux spectres d'espérance
> La nudité honteuse de nos mains
> [When we were strangers in France / Beggars on our own lanes / When we held up to the spectres of hope / The guilty nakedness of our hands]
>
> (Aragon 2007: 1020)

The Salle Richelieu of the Comédie-Française, with its proscenium stage, does not encourage interactions between performers and audience. When they do occur, they tend to be significant. Such were the moments when Antonio kicked Shylock who then descended into the audience, as if seeking protection; and when, on Antonio saying 'prête comme à un ennemi' ('lend it rather to thine enemy', 1.3.130), Shylock turned to look at the spectators, as if calling them to witness. The effect was reversed when, after mocking Shylock's grief over the loss of his daughter, Salerio (Christian Cloarec) sat down among the spectators.[11] Shylock pointed his stick at them when he called for vengeance, and again during his speech on slaves, as if exposing society's sham and hypocrisy. At the end of the court scene, Șerban built up the sense of a crowd indifferently witnessing the humiliation of an individual who could be among them, but was not one of them. To achieve this, he let his actor move through the audience from stage left, up round the back of the house, and down stage right, in a journey of social degradation, in the midst of audience silence.

Jacques Vincey's *Business in Venice* (2017): Creating the Jew

This production, which premiered at the Théâtre Olympia in Tours in September 2017, moved Venice to the familiar if nondescript location of a supermarket, with its rows of shelves laden with groceries, cleaning products and drinks. Harsh neon lighting exposed characters and wares alike to scrutiny. A low stainless-steel freezer (that later transformed into a butcher's slab) occupied the centre of the stage. The upstage area was screened off by a translucent storehouse curtain of vertical plastic strips. This setting (designed by Mathieu Lorry-Dupuy) gave no clue as to the identity of its owner or manager: it acted as a Venetian street, Shylock's office and even his home, reducing his existence to its social utility.

Just as Shylock's store could be any shop around the corner of any city street in the world, there was nothing to set him apart: no religious, ethnic or cultural marker. Jacques Vincey's Shylock wore no kippah and bore no trace of an accent. He and Antonio (Jean-René Lemoine) resembled each other in build, height and appearance, which lent credence to Portia's 'Which is the merchant here, and which the Jew?' (4.1.170). They faced each other across the stage, occasionally moving into each other's performance spaces, signalling that this was a confrontation about territory and influence, mainly economic – nothing more, on the face of it, than the usual 'Business in Venice', until Bassanio turned to Antonio for a loan that disrupted the precarious equilibrium.

The potential for nastiness was evident, however, already in 1.1, when the Venetians crowded into the store to the sound of loud disco music. Judging by their appearance, the carnival had already started. Antonio was Superman, incongruously sporting an Elizabethan ruff. A pink-Ganesh-headed figure in white T-shirt turned out to be Solanio (Théophile Dubus). Gratiano (Anthony Jeanne) seemed to compensate for his short stature by wearing oversized ram's horns. A carnival-goer in a long fur coat, hat, black beard and long side-locks turned out to be Bassanio (Thomas Gonzalez). Under his open coat he wore a white Lycra leotard with a face crudely painted on his stomach; a thick beard hung around his crotch. The discomfort the costume was intended to create intensified as the Venetians, helping themselves to drinks off the shelves, started trading anti-Semitic banter: 'Comment dit-on vache folle en Israel?' 'Vashkenazi' (How do you say mad cow in Israel? Vashkenazi).[12] The medley of their costumes signalled a haphazard aggregate of put-on identities, some of them half-human, half-animal, with Bassanio's easily the most repulsive of the lot. This urban tribe seemed to have stepped out of Maffesoli's definition of tribalism as 'a certain ambience, a state of mind . . . expressed through lifestyles that favour appearance and "form"' (1996: 98). Spectators may have recalled the 'gang des barbares' when the group later raided the store, emptying the shelves while Jessica made off with the cash-drawer, in a luminous skeleton disguise.

Shylock returned to find the store deserted and stripped bare, the word 'Juif' (Jew) sprayed in large letters on the plastic curtain. Silently, he started wiping it before cleaning the floor and walls, to the sound of a slow, intermittent throbbing. Targeted as the Other by a bunch of youths who were themselves devoid of recognizable identifiers – they could be Christian, Muslim, non-believer, left-wing, right-wing, non-political – Shylock steadfastly remained a secular Jew. Even under stress, he displayed no signs of otherness, whether in appearance or accent. He remained faithful to the long upheld French republican ideal of the 'integrated', secular Jew, an ideal which defined figures like

Alfred Dreyfus and the philosopher Raymond Aron who liked to recall that it was Nazi anti-Semitism that made him turn to his Jewishness (Bensussan 2011: note 3). Clearly, the process Vincey was mapping out was similar to the one described by Sartre: 'it is the anti-Semite who creates the Jew' (1976: 103).

The gang's hostility was all the more powerful in that it took over Shylock's territory – his business and the home it stood for. Not only was he targeted, he was also isolated: there was no Tubal, no reference to fellow Jews, nor to the synagogue, nothing to establish whether he really was Jewish. What did emerge was that the othering process triggered off an aggression that broke through his controlled manner, as it had done earlier when Antonio struck him after accepting the bond. Shylock's determination was clear in the way he chose his knife from a butcher's case and sharpened it with deliberation.

Shylock was the only character who did not wear a disguise or take on a feigned identity. In contrast, Morocco and Arragon's otherness was exoticized to the point of caricature, almost as if they too were part of a carnival. Morocco was a dark-skinned Prince of Zanzibar, and Arragon an Asian Prince of Siam: both were played by Gonzalez who was also Bassanio. In this unusual tripling of Portia's suitors transpired a trick to get the right casket. Make-up, wigs and costumes ensured that these two suitors were far removed from Bassanio's appearance. Their faces were projected onto a screen at the back of the stage, and Gonzalez's strongly accented delivery (in total contrast to Shylock's) was distorted by loudspeakers. Crude ethnic and linguistic othering turned out to be the mask of a racist's pursuit of wealth, the anti-Semite using the perfidy of stereotyped codes to play up to Portia's prejudiced attitude to 'foreignness'. The overall design intensified the distancing effect, since the choice of caskets was staged as a play-within, in the form of a live-TV lottery, hosted by Portia (Océane Mozas), a stereotypical blonde in a long shimmery dress. Her face, framed by wavy hair, was projected onto the screen, the Golden Fleece beckoning in the breeze which, of course, was an illusion. Once the show was over and Bassanio had finally chosen the right casket, she discarded her blonde wig, lace dress and shrill manner to emerge as a sophisticated dark-haired young woman in white blouse and stylish slacks, before recasting herself temporarily as a young male lawyer. It was left to the audience to decide who Portia actually was.

The return to Belmont seemed to consolidate the established allegiances and power dynamics. Generationally, Jessica, who in the earlier scenes was clearly bored with a life of running a store and keen to escape it by joining 'the tribe', belonged with the Venetians. Her transgression was a teenage rebellion, after which she cavorted with Lorenzo on a showy pink bed in Belmont in Act 5.

But for the bed, Belmont was an austere, uncluttered space in the same tones as the green baize of the courtroom. This was Portia's territory, in which Bassanio, vulnerably bare-chested, with the ruff still around his neck, did not belong; his hollowness was exposed as the carnivalesque veneer of urban loucheness was peeled away. Similarly, Antonio's place, like his world of trade, was elsewhere. Belmont remained beyond his reach and though he had gained control over Shylock's territory, his tribe had regrouped and moved on. Left alone at the end, as in many productions, incongruous in his Superman top under a jacket, he, and his business interests, seemed to have been ill served by his immature, opportunistic hangers-on. Ultimately, there was no more substance to the merchant Antonio than to Bassanio/Morocco-Zanzibar/Arragon-Siam.

Fakeness prevailed, a lack of authenticity, except where Shylock was concerned, most evident in the deep sense of personal bereavement with which he responded to Jessica's elopement. References to the turquoise ring, the monkey and the two thousand ducats were cut. Standing on the edge of the stage, he spoke quietly, as if sharing his thoughts with the audience, and the unemphatic way in which he imagined her 'dead at [his] foot' (3.1.80) suggested that with his daughter gone, prosperity was meaningless. Hence, perhaps, his indifference to Bassanio's efforts to buy his mercy and his cold drive for revenge, which spectators could sympathize with insofar as the Venetians were a primal bunch, an aggregate of dangerously unstable identities bonded by nastiness and bent on trapping Others in assigned roles. During the trial, Gratiano stood among the audience to hurl insults at Shylock, and this jolted spectators back into the discomfort on which the play had opened. The offensive behaviour they had witnessed earlier on stage had now shifted within their midst, pressing them to decide whether they belonged to the tribe of otherers, or not. The intention was evident: 'Vincey stated that the cast had an obligation to approach the issue head on and not elude or stifle [anti-Semitism's] present-day manifestations, insofar as we are all implicated to a greater or lesser degree' (Fischer 2018: 84).

The pressure on the audience had in fact been exerted from the outset by an added prologue written by the translator, Vanasay Khamphommala. It was spoken by Pierre-François Doireau, who appeared under his own name, in the list of characters and in the script. Dressed in an orange polo shirt and matching ginger hair, bow-legged, he entered carrying a tray loaded with packs of meat. Complaining that more had been spent on the set than on the actors – especially members of the cast like himself who held three (other) roles (Lancelet, Salarino and the Duke) – and recalling that the Shakespeare industry itself was 'gros business' (big business), he asked spectators to toss him a few euros, accusing them, when no one responded, of being a tight-fisted bunch of . . . The unspoken reference to 'Jews' was unmistakable, all the more so since he went on to remind any 'cathos' (Catholics) in the audience of the generosity they are expected to show during church collection. Throughout the play, Doireau periodically punctured the dramatic illusion by telling the audience when he changed roles.

Conclusion: Perspectives from the margins

The disturbing otherness of *The Merchant of Venice* in the French repertoire transpired in theatre reviews. Those who objected to Şerban's contemporary setting overlooked the fact that he had opted for similar aesthetics the previous year for *L'Avare*, a production also designed by Bancou. While those choices had been welcomed as ways of 'rejuvenating' and 'dusting off' Molière,[13] they were criticized in the case of *Merchant* for bringing anti-Semitism into today's world. Yet, a few months after Vincey's production opened, three years to the day after the January 2015 attack, a kosher supermarket was set on fire, and the word 'Juif' sprayed on the façade – though owned by a Jew, the shop had a Muslim manager. In February 2020, as information began to circulate about Covid-19, a regional daily headlined fears about the 'péril jaune' (yellow peril); high-street comments on France's Asian community seemed to echo Portia's contempt for the 'Prince of Siam'.[14]

In their design, tone and the issues they chose to address, Şerban's and Vincey's productions moved beyond the post-Holocaust debate on the ethics of staging or not *The Merchant of Venice*. Without eluding the hatred that targets Shylock, Şerban and Vincey explored other forms of othering, addressing the dangers of the post-modern juggling with identities at a time when French society seems to be losing faith in the Republican ideal of a social contract that helped to paper over divisions after the Second World War.

Both, Şerban and Vincey, used Shakespeare as a tool to explore French society, in spite of choosing different translations and aesthetic approaches. At the centre of their respective approaches was the world of high-tech and fast finance, and a bleakly anonymous supermarket. Circling around were ever re-configuring neo-tribes in search of territorial advantage and financial gain.

Vincey's Shylock was a secular, isolated figure, unattached to a wider community, who believed he was so integrated as to have achieved near-invisibility. Şerban's character seemed to belong to a diasporic network, and could turn to it for support, even at the expense of impersonating, in garb, appearance and manner, what a mainstream audience could have seen in films like *Rabbi Jacob*.

Both directors' choices enacted what Sartre does in his essay, which is to describe eidetically, and with metadramatic flair, situations, things or people (Bensussan 2011: 139).[15] They put their audiences in a position from which they could not 'escape', as when the actors sat or stood among the spectators, or performed in front of the curtain, employing techniques of cutting out the stage world of illusion. While anatomizing the workings of those 'mobs or those instantaneous societies which come into being at a lynching or during a scandal' (Sartre 1976: 20–1), the two directors also offered a critique of the action and the characters from the inside, by introducing perspectives from the margins. These were mediated through servants, thereby appropriating and extending Shakespeare's own dramatic technique with the use of the clown in his plays. The fragile potentialities of métissage were suggested through figures major and minor: Shylock and Jessica, Lancelet and the black servant (in Şerban's production). The productions dwelled on the timeless, nomadic status that threatens all those who are othered, epitomized in 'this quintessence of man, disgraced, uprooted, destined from the start to either inauthenticity or martyrdom' (Sartre 1976: 98), and the cut-throat egoism of tribalism.

At the end of Şerban's production, Antonio stepped forward and addressed the audience: 'nous ne sommes pas pleinement satisfaits, posez-nous des questions' (we are not wholly satisfied, ask us questions). No one did, of course. And when he added, 'nous répondrons à tout', did he mean 'we shall answer them all' or 'we shall account for everything'? And did that 'we' also embrace the audience and, beyond it, the community? Unanswered questions are the stuff this play is made of, perhaps because they remain unanswerable.

Acknowledgements

I should like to thank the following: Jacques Vincey and Vanasay Khamphommala, who provided me with a video and the typescript of their production; Susan L. Fischer for our conversations on *Business in Venice* and exchanges during the Covid-19 lockdown; the staff at the Comédie-Française library and archives; and, last but not least, my dear friend Boika Sokolova.

Notes

1 This was a reprise of the production Şerban directed for the American Repertory Theatre in the winter of 1998–9, with the same designer, Marielle Bancou, and composer, Elizabeth Swados, but a different cast, and a number of directorial inflexions. This discussion focuses on the Paris production.

2 This was the first staging of Shakespeare's play, and of Vigny's adaptation, which he wrote in 1829–30.

3 For a history of French stagings see Déprats (2001: 122–6).

4 The spelling used here follows John Drakakis's edition (Shakespeare [2010] 2014). All references to *The Merchant of Venice* are to this edition.

5 Nicolas Weill considers Sartre's essay to be acutely relevant (Weill 2008): 'C'est cette redoutable capacité de survie et d'adaptation [de l'antisémitisme] que reflète l'appel final à considérer que cet "archaïsme prélogique" "n'est pas un problème juif: c'est *notre* problème"' (It is that fearsome capacity for survival and adaptation [of anti-Semitism] which is reflected in [Sartre's] final plea to consider that this 'prelogical archaism' 'is not a Jewish problem: it is *our* problem'). All unacknowledged translations are mine. For a re-examination of Sartre's essay, see the collection of essays in *October* 1999.

6 'Strangers in France', a line by Louis Aragon, from his poem *La rose de Noël*, published in *La Diane française*, a collection of verse written during the Nazi occupation of France (Aragon 2007: 1019–20, 1020).

7 I worked from the photo archives of the Comédie-Française and a video recording of the production (*Le Marchand de Venise* 2002).

8 On this comedic film's success in the 1970s, and its enduring intergenerational appeal, see Mulvey (2017) and the introduction to this volume, note 4.

9 The spelling of the name used here follows Drakakis's edition (Shakespeare [2010] 2014).
10 The words spoken by Portia are not quite those of the translation Șerban used (Déprats 2001), which prefers 'teint' (hue, complexion) to 'peau' (skin).
11 This production conflated a number of roles, doing away with Salanio, Salarino and cutting the scenes with Lancelet's father.
12 This does not appear in the typescript kindly provided by the translator, Vanasay Khamphommala (Khamphommala 2001).
13 The quotations are from a review published in *Paris Normandie*, 15 March 2000, unsigned, no page ref.
14 Members of Asian communities (or people perceived as such) were also targeted in the United States and Britain during the Covid-19 pandemic.
15 The full quotation is: 'Tous ceux qui ont connu Sartre ont raconté cet extraordinaire talent qui était le sien de décrire éidétiquement les situations, les choses ou les gens qu'il rencontrait' (All those who have known Sartre have reported that extraordinary talent of his to describe eidetically situations, things or people).

References

Aragon, L. (2007), *Œuvres poétiques complètes*, vol. 1, ed. O. Barbarant, Bibliothèque de la Pléiade, Paris: Gallimard.
Les Aventures de Rabbi Jacob (1973), [Film] Dir. Gérard Oury, France: Films Pomereu and Horse Films.
Bensussan, G. (2011), 'Sartre, Levinas et les Juifs: Phénoménologie de l'antisémitisme et ontologie du judaïsme' [Sartre, Levinas and Jews: The Phenomenology of Antisemitism and Ontology of Judaism], *Les Temps modernes*, 664: 137–50.
Déprats, J.-M. (trans.) (2001), *Le Marchand de Venise*, Paris: Théâtrales.
Fischer, S. L. (2009), *Reading Performance: Spanish Golden Age Theatre and Shakespeare on the Modern Stage*, Woodbridge: Tamesis.

Fischer, S. L. (2018), 'Jacques Vincey's "Business in Venice" in a French supermarket: Shakespeare's *Merchant* and perceptions of antisemitism', *Cahiers Élisabéthains*, 97 (1): 84–94.

Hollier, D. (ed.) (1999), *Jean-Paul Sartre's Anti-Semite and Jew*, special issue of *October*, 87 (Winter).

Khamphommala, V. (trans. and adap.) (2001), *Le Marchand de Venise (Business in Venice)*, typescript kindly provided by the translator.

Kuttner, H. (2001), 'Le Français diabolise le juif Shylock' [The Comédie-Française diabolizes Shylock the Jew], *Paris Match*, 20 November: np.

Le Marchand de Venise (2002), [VHS film] Dir. Andrei Şerban and Gérard Lafont, France: La Comédie-Française.

Levinas, E. ([1969] 1991), *Totality and Infinity: An Essay on Exteriority*, trans. A. Lingis, Pittsburgh: Duquesne University Press.

Maffesoli, M. (1996), *The Time of the Tribes: The Decline of Individualism in Mass Society*, trans. D. Smith, London: Sage.

Mulvey, M. (2017), 'What Was So Funny about *Les Aventures de Rabbi Jacob* (1973)? A Comedic Film between History and Memory', *French Politics, Culture & Society*, 35 (3): 24–43.

Nerson, J. (2001), 'Shylock ou le Juif Süss?' [Shylock or Süss the Jew?], *L'Avant-Scène*, November: 92–3.

Sartre, J.-P. ([1946] 1976), *Anti-Semite and Jew*, trans. G. J. Becker, with a preface by Michael Walzer, New York: Shocken Books.

Shakespeare, W. ([2010] 2014), *The Merchant of Venice*, ed. J. Drakakis, The Arden Shakespeare, third series, London: Bloomsbury.

Spriet, P. (1988), 'The Merchant's Doom', *Cahiers Élisabéthains*, 34 (1): 53–60.

Weill, N. (2008), 'Réflexions sur la question juive' [Reflections on the Jewish Question], *Le Monde*, 14 July. Available online: www.lemonde.fr/idees/article/2008/07/14/reflexions-sur-la-question-juive_1073182_3232.html (accessed 2 April 2021).

PART TWO

New nationalisms, migrants

Imperfect resolutions

Induction 2

Lawrence Guntner

Part Two (New nationalisms, migrants: Imperfect resolutions) considers nations which are not 'new' in a historical sense, but are currently undergoing processes of redefining themselves in terms of shared history, language and cultural heritage, categories still operative in defining inclusion, or exclusion, within Europe's national communities. For three of the countries under discussion – Romania, Hungary and Germany – these processes intensified with the fall of the Berlin Wall in 1989 and the ensuing collapse of the Soviet Bloc. Fifteen years earlier, Portugal had also seen the end of four decades of hard dictatorship and the rise of a similar national debate. In the Netherlands, an 'old' democracy and a country perceived as tolerant, debates on nationhood took a new direction after 11 September 2001 and the attack on New York's Twin Towers. These processes were accelerated throughout Europe from 2015 onwards, by the influx of refugees and migrants from the Middle East and Africa. The ongoing redefinition of nationhood based on ethnicity has led to a rise in xenophobia, racism, anti-Semitism and homophobia.

In her discussion of *The Merchant of Venice* in Romania, Nicoleta Cinpoeș draws attention to the country's polyglot ethnic make-up and to the tensions over the linguistic possession of Shakespeare's narrative. For Romanians living under Russian and Ottoman occupation in the nineteenth century, Shylock was not a Jewish usurer, but a Romanian who felt a stranger in his own country. Under the communist regime

(1945–89), as in other Eastern Bloc countries, Shylock made rare appearances, if any. Twenty-first-century productions and adaptations have also been 'steeped in civic debates and contemporary politics', especially in a society rife with anti-Semitism, patriarchal gender attitudes and homophobia.

In communist Hungary too, Shylock was long absent from the stage. The word 'Jew' was taboo in common parlance, and Hungarian complicity in the Holocaust remained unmentionable in public. Since 2010, intolerance, in particular anti-Semitism, has been again on the rise, exacerbated by the influx of migrants and refugees who entered the European Union via Hungary in 2015. Natália Pikli investigates how two productions reacted, or not, to the radical political developments which took place between 2013 and 2016 – a short span of time that enables her to see the shift towards more conservative theatrical representations.

In contrast with former communist countries, the Netherlands regularly staged *The Merchant of Venice* and *Othello* after 1945. Performances, typically in the philo-Semitic post-Holocaust tradition, portrayed Shylock as a dignified but vulnerable outsider, and Othello as a noble but naive African mercenary, side-stepping issues of anti-Semitism and racism. After 9/11, and the murders of a right-wing populist politician in 2002 and the controversial film-maker Theo van Gogh in 2004, the political climate in the Netherlands changed radically. Coen Heijes investigates how these events had an effect on performances of *Othello* and *Merchant* and how the polarization of Dutch politics was not addressed in either of these productions.

Francesca Rayner takes Stephen Greenblatt's idea that any empathy Shakespeare may have felt for Othello is mediated by Iago, and asks whether the performative act itself can create a 'radical empathy', understood as an act of political solidarity that would question nationalist norms – white, male, heterosexual, Christian – embodied by Iago. She studies two productions of the play to conclude that Portuguese directors and spectators seem unwilling to challenge social norms and traditional Shakespeare narrative, or to engage in a radical empathy with the play's racially discriminated Other and its victims of domestic violence.

The Merchant of Venice has been performed regularly in Germany since 1945, at times controversially. This was not the case with *Othello*. After 9/11 and especially after the influx of refugees in 2015–16, *Othello* appeared frequently on the stages, either in radical adaptations, or in productions strategically defamiliarizing Shakespeare's text. Bettina Boecker discusses two productions from the 2015–16 season, which were planned and rehearsed before the actual refugee crisis. The first is a radical tradaptation, entitled *Othello after Shakespeare* – 'after' suggesting both chronology and 'according to' Shakespeare. The second, a production of *Merchant*, had the translated text projected on video screens as the performance developed into a rehearsal by six actors who shared their roles. While in the first, Othello remained the visually un-othered centre, in the second, there was no centre at all.

What connects the essays in this section is the lingering sense of missed opportunities to grapple with the question of the Other, on and off stage. What Cinpoeş notes about Shylock in Romania seems to be true of the other productions of *Merchant* discussed here, and of *Othello* as well: 'the distance between talking the talk and walking the walk is one yet to be travelled before . . . the wandering stranger, is "give[n] welcome" (*Hamlet* 1.5.164)'.

6

'Barbarous temper', 'hideous violence' and 'mountainish inhumanity'

Stage encounters with *The Merchant of Venice* in Romania

Nicoleta Cinpoeș

Discussing previous interpretations of Shakespeare's *The Merchant of Venice* in Romania, Louise Biber bemoans that

> many young people of the new generation make the same mistakes and display the same provocative and disreputable practices. . . . Considerate relations should replace hostility, barbaric practices, persecution, and the force of the strongest . . . for humanity's common good. (2009: 262)

Both Biber's review and her method – re-viewing the play against its mainstream interpretations – apply as much to the object of her 1899 critique, Bogdan Petricescu Hasdeu's *Three Jews: Master Shylock by Shakespeare, Mr Gobseck by Balzac, and Master Moses by Alexandri* (1865), as to the two stage productions this chapter focuses on.

Like the play's first stage productions in the two Romanian Principalities – Iași, Moldavia, 1850, and Bucharest, Wallachia, 1854 – Laszlo Bocsárdi's *Merchant* for 'Tamási Áron' Hungarian Theatre in Sfântu Gheorghe (2010) and Horațiu Mălăele's *Shylock* for the Comedy Theatre in Bucharest (2017) were steeped in civic debates and contemporary politics. When re-viewing these productions, my method posits that Romanian stage encounters with *The Merchant* – both early and recent – occur 'outside [the play's] moment of origin'; like any Shakespeare play, *Merchant* has 'meaning because . . . [its] very otherness is a challenge to our own thinking, feeling and values' (Di Pietro and Grady 2012: 51). It also takes on board John Drakakis's warning vis-à-vis the pitfalls of such presentist approach, namely not to 'elid[e] the text's own "presentist" investments, and what we then make of them when *we* invest their particularities with *our* meanings' (2013: 179). However, as with any exploration of staged Shakespeare in languages other than English, my pursuit adds the caveat that the 'presentist investments' of the 'text' refer to a Shakespeare playtext that is already linguistically and culturally mediated, and genre hybridized, a process which more often than not has estranged, if not ignored, the Elizabethan play and its investments. Therefore, unpacking these layers of investments is interested in voicing the dialogue between the mediated text and *its* 'present', when either or both have been muted by the 'barbarous temper', 'hideous violence' and 'mountainish inhumanity' of past political regimes. Seeing staged *Merchants* in Romania as instances of presentist dramatic practice in their own right, I am also interested in how they continue to negotiate 'confronting' and 'bypassing' (Ackermann 2013: 143) local history as well as aim to transfigure the future –

a trait/fate shared, as Boika Sokolova argued (2018), with other European countries, especially those from the former Eastern Bloc.

Enter Shylock

As Michael Dobson argued (2017: 20), 'of all Shakespeare's comedies, *Merchant* seems to have been the first to be taken abroad', as early as 1611. Having reached Transylvania – then part of the Austrian-Hungarian Empire – via Franz Xaver Felder's tour with five Shakespeare productions, the adaptation of *Merchant* performed in Hungarian theatres in Sibiu and Brașov in 1794 and 1795[1] spoke of the dispossessed status of the non-citizens of the Empire.

Shakespeare spoke Romanian first in George Bariț's translation of the mercy speech in 1840.[2] The first Shakespeare staged in Romanian was an adaptation entitled *Shylock or the Usurer of Venice* put on by the National Theatre of Iași in 1851, on a script (from French) by Alecu Vasiliu, and successfully received. Three years later, M. Millo's Bucharest company produced *Shylock the Jew or the Blood-bargain* 'adapted' from Mr D. Alboaz and 'translated by Mr. Teulescu' (Duțu 1964: 15).[3] The Hungarian National Theatre in Cluj, Transylvania, also staged the play in 1853 and again in 1865, using Lajos Lukács's 1840 translation of Friedrich Schlegel's German version in productions which interpreted Shylock as 'a victim of legal and political manoeuvres' and Portia's court speech as 'social resistance' (Bartha 2014: 93).

Back in the mid-nineteenth century, *Shylock or the Blood Bond* may have been a re-mediated French melodrama adaptation that guaranteed box-office success, but it appealed to Romanian directors and audiences for its civic and human rights potential – a French import readily relevant to the local 'drame social'. In the years following the failed 1848 Revolution, Shylock's plight and challenge of the law were not the Jews' but the oppressed Romanians', who were themselves Strangers in their own country – under Russian occupation in the northern Principality and in the southern one, under Ottoman rule. During the Russo-Turkish War, Romania gained its independence, in 1877; however, as a young country just tasting its freedom, it promptly showed that 'the quality of mercy' was 'strained' (*MV* 4.1.180).[4] Only when the recognition of the country's own identity (borders and independence) was conditioned, at the Congress of Berlin (1878), by amending the Romanian constitution to grant civil rights to all its inhabitants, regardless of their ethnic or religious appurtenance, did it finally concede.

Merchant continued to be of interest to Romanian theatre, with six translations between 1885 and 1955, several print adaptations and many stage productions. Like the play, the country's policies – as it went from territorial unification with Transylvania in 1918, to authoritarian monarchy, military dictatorship, popular republic and communist tyranny – remained inextricably bound with the status of the Stranger. Within this, anti-Semitism raised its ugly head during the pogroms led by General Antonescu's military dictatorship (responsible for over 270,000 deaths) and the communist period, whose anti-minorities policies literally put a price on the lives of all those perceived as Strangers.[5] Too close for comfort, Shakespeare's play almost disappeared from the Romanian stage, recording two productions both away from mainstream stages. *Merchant* remained a stark absence on Romanian stages even after the fall of the Berlin Wall, which ensued the historic reconfiguration of Europe. Post-1989, Romanian staged Shakespeare moved from doing dissident work to exorcizing the communist past and navigating the uncharted territory of the country's new democracy. Confronting its history found some place in the general euphoria of the newly acquired freedoms (Cinpoeş 2010: 187–222).

The first post-1989 *Merchant* was an adaptation staged by the State Jewish Theatre, Bucharest – the first Jewish professional company with an uninterrupted history of performance since 1876.[6] The play's three plots and many of its characters ghosted Grigore Gonţa's production of Arnold Wesker's *The*

Merchant, retitled *Shylock* (in I. Kara and George Volceanov's translation) for its Romanian premiere on 6 July 2000. The same year, another *Shylock* opened at Teatrul Mic, Bucharest, in Tudor Chirilă's production in which Shylock's enemy was not (Mihai Dinvale's) Antonio – a 'detached, malleable' character (Lipan 2001: 74) – but Shylock himself. Trapped in old stage conventions of 'othering', Dan Condurache's Shylock 'avoid[ed] head on engagement with his character' and 'lapse[d] into overzealous priggishness'; the stereotyping – through 'nasal voice' and 'forced clowning' – was not only awkward but 'froze' the text's potential (Lipan 2001: 74). Carmencita Brojboiu's set and costumes matched the production's black-and-white interpretation of the play's main conflict, whose binary palette was disrupted only by the colourful band of suitors.

'Which is the merchant here? And which the Jew?' (*MV* 4.1.174): Laszlo Bocsárdi's 2010 *Merchant*

Though diversity was enshrined in law, with the changes in the country's constitution and new legislation adopting the framework of the *acquis communautaire* conditional to Romania's accession to the European Union (EU) in 2007, the fate of the Stranger in everyday life reconfirmed that 'enthusiasm for democracy co-existed ... with extremism and intolerance' (Cinpoeş 2016: 289).

How we respond towards people different from us was the challenge director Laszlo Bocsárdi's 2010 production of *Merchant* posed right from the beginning. Its prologue extended the Stranger's case beyond the Jew's. Delivered as an aside by László Mátray's Antonio, it 'help[ed] to avoid potential misunderstandings' rooted 'in antisemitism-phobia' (Ady 2012). Its 'didactic' ring was better suited to exchanges with 'extremists' outside but superfluous in the theatre (Lucaciu 2011); for Ady (2012), it was hard to separate from

'Antonio's leather-clad figure, rejected in his unspoken and unrequited homosexual attraction'. Coming from Tamási Áron Hungarian Theatre, Sfântu Gheorghe, whose existence and work had been, pre-1989, an act of survival for Hungarian-born citizens in Romania,[7] the prologue, like the production, was 'a warning about the misleading identity of the other, the Stranger, the neighbour who is different, perceived as a threat to the supposed homogeneity of "our" community' (Georgescu 2011). Three more questions rounded up this approach to *Merchant*: 'Can we trust the law?', 'Should we fear women?' and 'Where does money come from and what is its use?'

Designed by Jozsef Bartha, Bocsárdi's long-term collaborator, the spare and bare set worked *with* the venue specifics: the exposed walls of the theatre, dusty and stained, enclosed a decaying Venice; a few scaffolding ladders stood against the walls and a small red curtain kept from view the three caskets throughout; Judit Dobre Kóthay's nondescript costumes deliberately disrupted space and temporal location. Placing the audience on raked seating on the stage was more than typical 'Romanian provincial theatre fashion' (Andronescu 2011): it pushed the action back stage and left the auditorium an empty space. Its immediate effect was to distance further the love stories and any comedy, and to emphasize the presentist investments and priorities of this production. Each character climbing up and down the ladder steps reflected the individual's evolution on the scale of moral values (Lucaciu 2011). Within the three hours, the role of the Stranger as the 'disruptor of order, traditions and habits' (Georgescu 2011) was occupied, in turn, by Shylock, the usurer Jew, by Portia, the intelligent woman who was heard only when disguised in a man's world, and by Antonio, whose love for Bassanio excluded him from both Belmont's heterosexuality and Venice's heterosociality.

Invited by the time and place non-specificity of the setting and costumes, all traces of detached spectating were removed: the 'fools with varnished faces' (*MV* 2.5.32) – actors sporting simplified Venetian masks – popped up from among 'us', the audience. That 'we' were this Venice rife with xenophobia, homophobia, anti-Semitism and anti-feminism became even more self-evident in the second half. After the interval, the spectators returned to find the tables literally turned: they still sat on the stage but faced the auditorium. No red curtain obstructed the play's action and the remainder of the production held 'the mirror up to Nature to show Virtue her feature, Scorn her own image, and the very age and body of the time his form and pressure' (*Ham* 3.2.22–4).[8] When Portia, disguised as the lawyer, made her plea from the edge of the small impromptu platform-stage (wooden planks on top of a few front row seats), she represented the spectators, not the young Venetians spread across the stalls and gallery. That the play's action extended to the real world was doubly uncanny at the matinee performance (in the National Theatre Festival, Bucharest, 2011) when the auditorium doors of the Bulandra venue left open by the actors literally brought in the daylight and the hustle and bustle of the street.

This Venice was a world devoid of emotions: Shylock, an old man, 'despise[d] the clownish, love games of youth' – both the Christians' and his daughter's. The Venetian 'golden boys' openly mocked Shylock's principles and conduit (Barabás 2010). The tension between the two life-styles was palpable; so was 'the clash between the powerful visuality [and physicality] of the Romanian theatre and the more rational, realistic Hungarian theatre' (Barabás 2010) that has defined the company's artistic identity, since Bocsárdi's arrival as artistic director in 1995. The eclectic approach enhanced the production's focus on diversity and difference, with fleeting symbols of specific times disturbing its non-specificity. While Morocco's and Arragon's identities as Strangers were conflated by having Tibor Pálffy play both in a costume uncannily resembling a suicide bomber, the Duke stood out in his period dress, representing the old, abstract 'state authority that does not interfere with the act of justice' (Andronescu 2010). The fluidity of Antonio escaped pinning down only to be held, at knifepoint, in the ultimate act of Stranger-phobia. Stripped of his black shirt, Antonio was literally pinned to the table by Shylock's weight; his naked torso and white gag clashed with his leather trousers and studded belt. The violent image, at once invoking and punishing (sexual) difference, embodied persecution – new as much as old, given the choice of rusty scales and weights used in every food store in communist Romania.

The production's live soundscape, too, hybridized styles and interventions: Szabolcs Boldizsár's flute-playing was sometimes nostalgic, at other ominous; Zsolt Szilágyi was the voice that accompanied vocally the entire production. The choice of an aria from Tchaikovsky's *Onegin* which the tenor came on stage to deliver in Russian was this production's intriguing embodiment of the play's unconvincing happy ending which denied any closure – save for the moral that 'justice and money making are fickle games' (Zlotea 2012).

The impact of Bocsárdi's *Merchant* went beyond its home venue and audience: it played in Hungarian-speaking Romanian cities, at the National Theatre Festival, Bucharest, toured in Hungary, and was nominated for Best Theatre Production at the UNITER (National Theatre Union) Awards in 2011. That year, another *Merchant* claimed the attention and a UNITER award: Gareth Armstrong's one-man-show *Shylock*, a bespoke theatrical event, translated by theatre critic and academic Marian Popescu, adapted for the radio by Răzvan Popa, and performed by Ion Caramitru (Kipper 2012).

'By indirections find directions out' (*Hamlet* 2.1.63): Horațiu Mălăele's 2017 *Shylock*

Hopes that a new Romanian translation of *Merchant* – part of Volceanov's *Complete Works* project – would attract theatre practitioners' attention and elicit new stage productions were running high in 2012. Launched at the International Shakespeare Festival, Craiova, that year, Horia Gârbea's translation offered a modernized, stage- and reader-friendly text. It did not break the silence or manage to challenge the interpretive legacy of Shakespeare's play and character Shylock on Romanian stages. The Festival's rich biennial programme, too, maintained radio silence on this Shakespeare play, save for Piotr Kondrat's one-man *Shylock* in 2014.

As elsewhere, 2016 was a year of intense celebrations in Romania, where it marked a double anniversary: 400 years of Shakespeare heritage, and 140 years of Jewish theatre. The Jewish State Theatre, Bucharest, was making history by launching the first edition of the International Festival of Theatre in Yiddish (2016); Jewish history, too, was the focus of a joint-venture between the Comedy Theatre and the Capital's Mayor's Office. The project, which opened in the 2017–18 theatre season, proposed a live exercise in confronting Jewish history and engaged with Shakespeare's *Merchant* at one removed via Armstrong's one-man show. I caught up with this *Shylock* at the International Shakespeare Festival, Craiova, in 2018, in an edition where Shakespeare's play and Jewish history were also disputed in Krzysztof Warlikowski's *African Tales by Shakespeare* for Novy Teatr, Warsaw.[9]

Once again, *Merchant* reached Romanian and international audiences at the Festival in a mediated approach which shared with the play's first Romanian incarnation in the mid-nineteenth century both its civic agenda and genre hybridity. A half-way house between Armstrong's 1999 play and Shakespeare's *Merchant*, this *Shylock* recast its source one-man-show as a play for eight characters, a disembodied voice and eight Venetian masks. The production programme openly announced *Shylock* after Armstrong as an adaptation, packaged it as a one-man concept by signalling Horațiu Mălăele's double role – as Shylock and director[10] – and was not shy about the project's double patronage – the City Council's financial sponsorship and the Comedy Theatre's creative input. A man of many parts (as the illustration on the front page intimated), Mălăele's cartoons captioned each section of the programme. Once credit was given where due (casting page and Armstrong's short biography), the programme proceeded to montage the history of the Jews, of Shakespeare's play and of its reception – as per Armstrong's script – in nine narrative tableaux using black-and-white photographs from the production as visual codas (*Shylock* – Production Programme 2016). The Festival advertised the production as 'a journey into the history of Jewishness and anti-Semitism, a sad history of intolerance, hatred and ample suffering, told with a bitter smile by Tubal, the only friend Shakespeare gives to the Jew in *The Merchant of Venice*' (*Planeta Shakespeare* 2018: 64), acknowledging the project's entwined histories, educational stance and anti-discrimination agenda. All this was 'ripe stuff for Colibri, Craiova's venue for children and youth theatre' (Carson, Cinpoeş and Foulquie 2019: 107) that gave the production exposure to a public of a different age range (recommended for 14+) and spectating experience (Calinescu 2019).

Like any adaptation, this entailed negotiation: 'inevitable' cuts, 'reattributions' and 'changes . . . mostly in the cause of clarity and brevity' but also 'to strengthen' its 'case' (Armstrong 1999: 63). As Julie Sanders argues, 'it is at the very point of infidelity or departure that the most creative acts of adaptation take place' (2015: 25). Ingenious 'creative infidelity' streamlined and reprioritized the source script to a seventy-minute performance, with no interval, which fleshed out seven of Shakespeare's characters Armstrong's Tubal impersonates, divvied up its historical commentary between projected visuals (designed by Dilmana Yordanova) and the programme, where it relegated the great Shylocks of the English stage and the play's recent film history.

The resulting show played to full houses, both in Bucharest and Craiova; press responses were mixed. Alina Epingeac (2017) saw it as an unconvincing didactic attempt, which in spite of the great expense (on cast, set, costumes) amounted to 'an ostentatious and whining finger shoved into our eye' worthy of one star, a view echoed in spectators' comments: 'a disappointing . . . cliché conflict between "the good afflicted Jews" and "the bad racist Christians"' (Epingeac 2017, 'Dan' 2018). Reproaches from the theatre buffs' camp ranged from gratuitousness theatrics (projections, *commedia dell' arte*, oversized puppets, playback song, voiceover, overt contemporary referencing, visual cultural citation turned into the butt of jokes) that gave the actors a decorative role and reduced their performance to embarrassed pantomime, to 'the playscript's loss of dramatic force' when recast for eight (Lucaciu 2017). At the other end of the spectrum, reviews saw the show as engaging with the audience precisely through the centrality of its narrator/Tubal (George Mihăiță) on and off stage, and Shylock, who re-experienced the Stranger's journey through times and places, while the other characters were live arguments and spectators were the true protagonists of this – Brechtian – epic exploration.[11]

This proposed approach was overtly made from the start, when Mihăiță announced, alone on stage, 'Shylock! I am Shylock!' and proceeded with 'The pound of flesh which I demand of him / Is dearly bought; 'tis mine, and I will have it. / If you deny me, fie upon your law' (*MV* 4.1.98–100). On stage, this was 'a challenge to the fundamentally racist and segregationist institutions of Venice' (Carson, Cinpoeș and Foulquie 2019: 107), but when 'the stage light brighten[ed] as the figure turn[ed] to address the audience' – not as Shylock, not even as Tubal, but as an actor playing Tubal – the provocation 'I stand for judgement: answer, shall I have it?' (4.1.101) addressed every spectator and the here and now. Stepping into the audience, Mihăiță handed the story to the production's visuals (by Dilmana Yordanova) and supplied a live commentary to the video-projected history of anti-Semitism from the Roman Empire to the Renaissance and since, explaining 'Shakespeare's creative process, his sources' and how 'his imagination complet[ed] and/or edit[ed] existing narratives' (Carson, Cinpoeș and Foulquie 2019: 107). This guided confrontation with history was tense and intense, far from a PowerPoint historicist lesson, especially as Mihăiță delivered Armstrong's text with an extra dose of 'Romanian history of anti-Semitism for good measure' (Carson, Cinpoeș and Foulquie 2019: 107). It was not in the accent (as in Caramitru's radio performance) but in the intonation and stresses that words conveyed the interplay between the individual moments' and this production's presentist investments: when explaining the history of the badge, the pronunciation of the very name made Pope Innocent III anything but that and compared his Papal decision to a European directive.

Briefly sighted in the fast video montage, two images, 'the yellow pointed hat and the [Venetian] ghetto box[-sized room]', became the 'key identifiers of [both] Jewishness and anti-Semitic stances' (Carson, Cinpoeş and Foulquie 2019: 107) the production cited in its live stage action which was as enthralling visually in Iuliana Vîlsan's stage design. When proposed as an experience in which alienation hindered simple acceptance or rejection, 'the vision of a black-and-white world of right and wrong, inside or outside Venetian society' gained weight beyond what visually may have come across as animated tableaux 'from a pop-up book fit for illustrating the fight between good and evil in children's story' (Lucaciu 2017). Through estrangement, the familiar 'clown-like costumes [which] reflected the Commedia dell'arte theatrical tradition' simultaneously 'suggested a world of stereotypes and visual humour'; similarly, 'the masks worn by the Venetian characters resembled both the enduring image of the Venice Festival and the heads of birds with elongated fierce black beaks, ideally suited to pecking their prey' (Carson, Cinpoeş and Foulquie 2019: 107). Compared to the in-yer-face extravagance of the young Venetians, Tubal and Shylock appeared old and old-fashioned: their plain garb, 'the natural tones of their voices and their everyday demeanour ... acted as a comment on the exuberant youngsters' and on the new world 'of wealth and excess' (Carson, Cinpoeş and Foulquie 2019: 107) – both on and off stage. There were also overt comments on current stage practices: when Tubal stepped out of the action and off the stage to engage with the spectators, he turned the effect on its head by calling it out as forced entertainment and blamed the director for the idea.

The more Tubal negotiated his freedom – of space, time, speech, theatrics – the more imprisoned Shylock appeared.

From their first interaction, Shylock embodied every stereotype of the Stranger part history cast him in. Even without his yellow pointed hat, the lower voice, the accent, the shuffled walk, the slightly hunched gait, the repeated words and repetitive gestures showcased, Tubal explained, 'what was expected of Jews on stage – comedy and villainy', which made 'good box-office . . . not because we told jokes . . . but because people enjoyed laughing at us' (Armstrong 1999: 23–4) – not only in Shakespeare's time, the occasional laughter from the audience to this production suggested. As the Shakespeare plot thickened, Shylock – in words, silences, actions, stage position and acting style – stood in stark contrast to Antonio and his entourage, their gregariousness more jarring when juxtaposed to his quiet voice. Visually, too, they were an 'embarrassment of riches': their physical presence took up the stage; their flashy movement and gesturing resembled an ominous gathering of ravenous birds chasing Shylock, their prey. Leading the flock of Christians clad in black and gold, Bogdan Mălăele's 'Antonio was king of bling, a flamboyant gangster of poor taste, dressed in fur adorned with gold chains; all others' masks supplied an anonymity reminiscent of the impunity of internet bullying and trolling' (Carson, Cinpoeș and Foulquie 2019: 108), a generational divide enhanced by casting father and son as archenemies. As their boyish banter descended into verbal slurs soon matched by physical violence, the spectators' discomfort was palpable: pushed and kicked, Shylock was reduced to a heap (with just the white masked, mute Gondolier on his side) and the audience to silent accomplices.

In this Venice, physical isolation and imprisonment defined Jessica's life, all the more disturbing when in plain sight. Her confinement to the family home, a transparent box the size of a small room packed from floor to ceiling with belongings, was an uncanny reminder of both the Venetian Ghetto and ghettoizing practices past and present. Her loneliness (with no Lancelet for company) and desire to break free from imprisonment fuelled her elopement with Lorenzo.[12] Like the blame, which she 'misdirected at her father rather than the ghetto as an institution' (Carson, Cinpoeş and Foulquie 2019: 109), her action was misguided. Her Lorenzo (Lucian Ionescu) had nothing of Cristian Iacob's touching honesty and sincere love (at Teatrul Mic, 2001). What took Ruxanda Grecu's Jessica long to realize, the audience saw instantly: not only had she traded, literally, one box for another when entering this marriage, but she mistook for desire the tight grip of Lorenzo who was 'dexterously counting (aloud!) the notes stolen from Shylock *while* making love to Jessica' (Carson, Cinpoeş and Foulquie 2019: 107). Shylock, on the other hand, understood immediately the meaning of Jessica's absence and the ransacked home, losses he processed as distinct and in this order, as per Armstrong's text: harrowing sadness for the loss of his daughter turned into anger at the theft. For both, the Christians were to blame, Tubal explained: 'Bassanio had planned it, to get him out of the way! It was a conspiracy!' (Armstrong 1999: 36).

What marked the shift in Armstrong's play to Act 2 in this production was a marked departure both in terms of 'depth of introspections and plot delivery' (Carson, Cinpoeş and Foulquie 2019: 108). With Armstrong's history of British stage Shylocks excised, the faster pace and disjointed manner in which the string of cameos succeeded one another was distinctly Brechtian. Nowhere in the production was it clearer that Shylock was both the Jew and someone 'affected by exile within a society willing to accept his money, but not his friendship and human relationships' (Lucaciu 2017) than in his delivery of Shakespeare's 'I am a Jew' speech (*MV* 3.1.53–66). With no 'wig and nose' to shed half-way through (Armstrong 1999: 41), it was performed by Mălăele 'in front of a broken mirror – a metaphor for a fractured sense of self as a result of racist abuse. By this point Shylock had lost everything: he was no longer a father, his daughter had rejected their religion and defrauded him, so where was he supposed to find his identity?' (Carson, Cinpoeş and Foulquie 2019: 108). Opening the trial scene with Shylock's soliloquy and opting for a voiceover Duke[13] 'from large speakers at the back of the auditorium', the production automatically expanded the court to include the audience – with different means, the same idea Bocsárdi used in 2010. Disguised Portia – on stilts and draped in a red cloak – was more Ariel's harpy than learnéd Doctor Balthazar, and enhanced 'the impression of an unattainable authority, impossible to challenge, change or question' in this corrupt Venice. The mockery of justice was a grotesque display of double standards and hypocrisy delivered in quick succession: 'when Shylock changed his mind and asked for the money, Portia (Mirela Zeţa) laughed cunningly; when Shylock kneeled for the Duke's mercy, Tubal repeated Portia's mercy speech' (Carson, Cinpoeş and Foulquie 2019: 108).

The peak of the production's creative infidelity came in its ending, which departed from both Shakespeare's play and Armstrong's script. With the 'words "I am content" spliced together with "Please let me go, I am not well"' and 'delivered as one line', Shylock meant 'the opposite' (Carson, Cinpoeş and Foulquie 2019: 109). So did the production's finale: juxtaposing, in real time, Shakespeare's Acts 4 and 5, it brought into focus once again the blatant contrast between the loud, bright, frivolous and superficial Christians who sent Shylock, suitcases and all, into grim exile. The dance and celebrations in Belmont (stage fore) could not entirely erase from view Shylock sitting on his piled-up belongings; their loud singing and merrymaking could not drown the Jewish violin tune either. No words needed, indeed. The lights faded and the audience clapped eagerly. Too soon, the production chided; as 'the lights returned, the Christian characters now the actors bowing down at the front of the stage revealed the tableau of Shylock's emigration starkly' (Carson, Cinpoeş and Foulquie 2019: 109). The discrepancy – 'forcing the audience to clap while Shylock was still suffering' – brought right home the production's concept that the story was of here and now; 'the laughter that greeted the performance was laced with irony and sadness' (Carson, Cinpoeş and Foulquie 2019: 109) and the discomfort of complicity to hate, racism and discrimination.

'I stand for judgement' (*MV* 4.1.101)

On the quatercentenary of Shakespeare's death and *Merchant*'s life, Dobson spoke of this play as 'Shakespeare's comedy [that] has given the world a model for social harmony which also reckons the cost of that harmony to the excluded and the dispossessed' (2017: 26). As this chapter has argued, *Merchants* in Romania have always been about 'confronting the history' of its exclusion *and* 'bypassing' the history of those it dispossessed in the process.

In Bocsárdi's vision, *The Merchant of Venice* had some reckoning to do: neither the merchant nor the Jew were its heroes. Giving stage, instead, to ordinary people – the woman, the gay, the religious, the ethnically diverse – the production put the power straight into the audience's hands. When being cast, the spectators had the moral and civic responsibility to engage head on with those who, in the world outside the theatre, continued to remain outcasts. A wishful thought when in real life Romania '[t]he widespread presence of "casual intolerance" in public discourse – the day-to-day use of deliberate or unintended discriminatory and intolerant speech practices that reproduce and reinforce prejudices – reflects a state of cultural morphostasis, whereby radical right, intolerant and exclusionary ideas and attitudes are' not only perpetuated but 'strengthened' (Cinpoeş 2016: 291).

As in recent *Merchants* east of Berlin, in Bocsárdi's production 'homophobic, xenophobic, and gender issues come to the fore' (Sokolova 2018: 91) as means of thinking through broader issues of identity within the European context Romania has formally joined in 2007, but also in response to the spike in the indigenous nationalism that reignites political tensions between Romanians and Hungarians in Romania. While the history of anti-Semitism is being confronted in *Merchant* around Europe, Shakespeare's play continues to bypass it when staged in Romania. It still takes a mediated text and a hybrid approach to breach the subject and offer a civic lesson. Mălăele's

Shylock after Armstrong's did so by casting Tubal as the commentator on the presentist investments of Shakespeare's early modern play, as 'an agent of disambiguation of the play' and as a friendly guide through a compact history of European anti-Semitism. Through a 'necessary exercise for such a problematic topic, the systematic nature of prejudice emerged, with the hypocrisy of the Christian characters and of the laws of Venice, highlighting the institutional dimension of hate' (Carson, Cinpoeş and Foulquie 2019: 109). The fact that it did so at one remove – by borrowing the trope from Armstrong, by offering a half-way-house between his play and Shakespeare's, and by recycling the European history supplied by the one-man-show – indicates that the jury is still out on *Merchant* confronting Romania's history of anti-Semitism. Granted, this has moved on from the nineteenth-century's 'various offensively racial anthropological accounts of human evolution' (Drakakis in Shakespeare [2010] 2014: 119), but it resurfaces regularly in conspiracy theories that continue to demonize the Stranger. The fact that Armstrong's Tubal was *not* Shylock as well in this production, but remained just his 'Jewish friend' who commented from the comfort of critical distance, and that in Mălăele's adaptation, the onstage observer (the masked Gondolier) was mute, signalled that the distance between talking the talk and walking the walk is one yet to be travelled before Shylock, the wandering Stranger, is 'give[n] . . . welcome' (*Ham* 1.5.164).

Notes

1 Felder's tour also included *The Taming of the Shrew*, *King Lear*, *Hamlet* and *Romeo and Juliet* (Duţu 1964: 7).

2 A journalist and political leader of the Romanians in Transylvania, Bariţ was a keen liberal, in the Western European tradition. His '*Mercy,* after Shakespeare' (the 4.1 'mercy speech') appeared in Braşov, in *Foaie pentru minte, inimă şi literatură* (118).

3 On the Alboaz 'mystery', which conflated the names of French translators M. Du Lac and Jules-Edouard Alboize, and the appeal of this version to Romanian audiences, see Nicolaescu (2017: 129–48).

4 All references from *The Merchant of Venice* are to Shakespeare ([2010] 2014).

5 Between 1959 and 1989, the State's programme of 'repatriation' (read: ethnic cleansing) sold 200,000 Romanian Jews for 3,000 to 9,000 dollars per person (depending on their education). German- and Hungarian-born Romanians were also 'repatriated', via similar agreements.

6 After a successful debut in Iași, Avram Goldfaden's company moved to Bucharest, performing in towns along the way. During its uninterrupted stage activity, even through the Nazi-type military dictatorship during the Second World War, which banned Jewish actors from the stage and performing in Yiddish, and its successive transformations ultimately into the State Jewish Theatre, in 1948, this theatre has promoted Yiddish culture and given Jewish voices to drama classics.

7 This theatre's history is closely linked to its mission and '[t]he many names this institution received [over the decades] indicate a whole struggling past, with its hidden and open efforts of cultural policy, self determination, mission and artistic aim' (Tamási Áron Színház, www.tasz.ro/en/about, accessed 2 April 2021).

8 All references from *Hamlet* are to Shakespeare ([2006] 2016).

9 Aleksandra Sakowska discusses Warlikowski's production in Chapter 3.

10 Horațiu Mălăele is a well-known actor, cartoonist, writer and recently, director.

11 My analysis of this production is indebted to collaborative reviewing with Christie Carson and Guillaume Foulquie (Carson, Cinpoeș and Foulquie 2019: 106–9).

12 The spelling of the name used here follows Drakakis's edition (Shakespeare [2010] 2014).

13 The voice choice was symbolic as it cited directly another Duke denied the stage – Constantin Codreanu's for the 1974 radio *Merchant*.

References

Ackermann, Z. (2013), 'At the Threshold – Remembrance and Topicality in Recent Productions of *The Merchant of Venice* in Germany', in S. Brown, R. Lublin and L. McCulloch (eds), *Reinventing the Renaissance – Shakespeare and His Contemporaries in Adaptation and Performance*, 143–61, London: Palgrave Macmillan.

Ady, M. (2012), 'Mindennapi hiányaink' [Our Everyday Shortcomings], *Szinhaz*, 31 July. Available online: http://szinhaz.net/2012/07/31/ady-maria-mindennapi-hianyaink/ (accessed 2 April 2021).

Andronescu, M. (2011), 'Între Veneţia şi lumea ideilor' [Between Venice and the world of ideas], *Yorick. Revista Online de Teatru*, 14 November. Available online: https://yorick.ro/intre-venetia-si-lumea-ideilor/ (accessed 2 April 2021).

Armstrong, G. (1999), *Shylock*, London: The Players' Account.

Barabás, Z. (2010), 'Uzsora, irgalom, szerelem, igazság' [Usury, mercy, love, truth], *Kultúra*, 13 November. Available online: www.3szek.ro/load/cikk/34170/Uzsora (accessed 2 April 2021).

Bartha, K. Á. (2014), '*The Merchant of Venice* in Pest and Cluj (Kolozsvár) During the Habsburg Neo-Absolutism', in K. Gregor (ed.), *Shakespeare and Tyranny*, 77–104, Newcastle-upon-Tyne: Cambridge Scholars Publishing.

Biber, L. (2009), 'Shylock and Mr. Hasdeu's Comments, 1899', in M. Matei Chesnoiu (ed. and trans.), *Shakespeare în România. Texte 1836–1916*, 262–79, Bucureşti: Editura Academiei Române.

Calinescu, E. (2019), '*Shylock* după Gareth Armstrong – Teatrul de Comedie' [*Shylock* after Gareth Armstrong – Teatrul de Comedie], 30 March. Available online: https://lateatru.eu/shylock-dupa-gareth-armstrong-teatrul-de-comedie/ (accessed 2 April 2021).

Carson, C., N. Cinpoeş and G. Foulquie (2019), '*Shylock*, written by Gareth Armstrong and translated by Marian Popescu, adapted and directed by Horaţiu Mălăele for Teatrul de Comedie, Bucharest; Colibri Theatre for Children and Young Adults, Craiova, 2 May 2018' (review), *Cahiers Élisabéthains*, 100 (1): 106–9.

Cinpoeş, N. (2010), *Shakespeare's* Hamlet *in Romania: 1778–2008*, Lampeter: Mellen Press.

Cinpoeş, R. (2016), 'Righting it up: An Interplay-based Model for Analyzing Extreme Right Dynamics in Romania', in M. Minkenberg (ed.), *Transforming the Transformation?: The East European Political Right in the Political Process*, 278–98, London: Routledge.

Dobson, M. (2017), 'Shakespeare 400, Shylock 400', in I. Cristescu and G. Volceanov (eds), *Shakespeare in Romania: Shakespeare in the World*, 17–26, Bucureşti: Editura Muzeul Literaturii Române.

Drakakis, J. (2013), 'Shakespeare as Presentist', *Shakespeare Survey*, 66: 177–87.

Duţu, A. (1964), *Shakespeare in Rumania*, Bucharest: Meridiane.

Epingeac, A. (2017), 'Horaţiu Mălăele nu e Shylock' [Horaţiu Mălăele is not Shylock], *Yorick*, 10 October. Available online: https://yorick.ro/horatiu-malaele-nu-e-shylock/ (accessed 2 April 2021).

Georgescu, A. (2011), 'Unul, altul, celălalt, acelaşi' [One, another, the other, the same one], *Dilema Veche*, 23 February–3 March. Available online: https://dilemaveche.ro/sectiune/arte-performa tive/articol/unul-altul-celalalt-acelasi (accessed 2 April 2021).

Kipper, L. (2012), '*Shylock* de Gareth Armstrong', *PRWave*, 4 May. Available online: https://www.prwave.ro/shylock-de-gareth-armst rong-2/ (accessed 2 April 2021).

Lipan, C. (2001), 'Shylock versus Shylock', *Teatrul azi*, 1–2: 74.

Lucaciu, I. (2011), 'Neguţătorul din Veneţia – teatrul "Tamasi Áron" din Sfântu Gheorghe' [*The Merchant of Venice* – "Tamasi Áron" Theatre, Sfântu Gheorghe], 14 November. Available online: http://ileanalucaciu.blogspot.com/2011/11/negutatorul-din-venetia-teat rul-tamasi.html (accessed 2 April 2021).

Lucaciu, I. (2017), 'Imagini semnificative ale unei istorii amare' [Significant snippets from a bitter history], *Spectator*, 9 October. Available online: http://ileanalucaciu.blogspot.com/2017/10/shy lock-teatrul-de-comedie-sala-radu.html (accessed 2 April 2021).

Nicolaescu, M. (2017), 'Introducing Shakespeare to the Fringes of Europe: The First Romanian Performance of *The Merchant of Venice*', *SEDERI*, 27: 129–48.

Pietro, C. di and H. Grady (2012), 'Presentism, Anachronism and the Case of *Titus Andronicus*', *Shakespeare*, 8 (1): 44–73.

Planeta Shakespeare – Programul Festivalului Internaţional Shakespeare (2018), Craiova, Romania.

Sanders, J. (2015), *Adaptation and Appropriation*, 2nd edn, London: Routledge.
Shakespeare, W. ([2006] 2016), *Hamlet*, ed. A. Thompson and N. Taylor, The Arden Shakespeare, third series, London: Bloomsbury.
Shakespeare, W. ([2010] 2014), *The Merchant of Venice*, ed. J. Drakakis, The Arden Shakespeare, third series, London: Bloomsbury.
Shylock – Production Programme (2016), Teatrul de Comedie, București.
Sokolova, B. (2018), '"Mingled yarn: *The Merchant of Venice* East of Berlin and the Legacy of Eastern Europe', *Shakespeare Survey*, 71: 88–102.
Zlotea, I. (2012), 'Negustorii de dreptate' [The merchants of justice], *REFLEX 2 – Bienala Internațională de Teatru*, 25 March. Available online: www.reflexfest.ro/2/index.php?option=com_content&view=category&layout=blog&id=27&Itemid=61&lang=ro (accessed 2 April 2021).

7

Staging *The Merchant of Venice* in Hungary

Politics, prejudice and languages of hatred

Natália Pikli

It serves right this building is misshapen,
the nation is no better in its mould.
Thank you, 'tis good: refurbishing's mistaken;
The picture hurts but truth is being told.

(Ádám Nádasdy, 'Thoughts in the theatre')[1]

The Jew on the Hungarian stage and in Hungarian cultural memory

Hungarian Shylocks have enjoyed a curious history: after more than a century of unquestioned popularity on stage between 1836 and 1940, they were silenced and banned from the stage for political reasons until 1986 (Imre 2018), as in other countries behind the Iron Curtain (Sokolova 2018). The fall of the communist regime brought an end to theatrical censorship, and Shakespeare's famous Jew could and did return in fifteen different productions by permanent theatres between 1989 and 2019.[2] However, staging *The Merchant of Venice* in Hungary is still a sensitive issue for several reasons: besides the theatrical hiatus of forty-six years and the concomitant tabooing of the word 'Jew' in common *parlance* during the communist era, the lack of an honest confrontation with a national trauma exerts an influence on staging and directorial choices.

Hungarian state officials and citizens played a significant role in eagerly sending Hungarian Jews to their deaths in 1944–5: more than 400,000 of them – over 50 per cent of the prewar Jewish population – perished in Auschwitz, in ghettos, or were killed by Hungarian fascists (Stark 1993). Those few who returned (and did not later emigrate to Israel or other countries) were often treated with suspicion, their stories hushed up for a long time. For instance, in Székesfehérvár, a major city, 8,000 Jews were exterminated, the two destroyed synagogues were never rebuilt and a monument commemorating this was only erected in 2004. This national trauma was largely ignored in mainstream cultural and theatrical memory until the 2010s, when Pál Závada's novels and János Mohácsi's theatre productions (starting with *Ghetto Sheriff* in 2012) started successfully to animate relevant discussions.

The introduction of a communist regime in 1947 created a curious form of anti-Semitism: though Socialism's anti-racism was the officially sanctioned attitude, 'Jew' became a taboo word, and issues related to the Holocaust were referred to as events unconnected with Hungary, stripped of any Hungarian responsibility. After 1989, the lifting of such taboos seemed to open new possibilities for discussion; however, this did not always mean a change for the better. Especially since the conservative, anti-liberal political takeover in 2010, anti-Semitic, racist and otherwise intolerant attitudes have been on the rise, fuelled by party and government propaganda. The situation worsened in 2015, when the government quarantined Syrian refugees for days in rather inhuman circumstances in one of the main railway stations of Budapest, to serve its anti-migration propaganda, hoping to incite anti-racist sentiment among Hungarians. As a corollary, George Soros, a Hungarian-born Jewish-American businessman, became the government's favourite scapegoat, for, as they were still claiming at the time of writing, financing the refugees' migration to Hungary.

In such a social-political context, recent productions of *The Merchant of Venice* offer inspiring instances of de- or re-constructions of the Stranger on the Hungarian stage. This chapter discusses a highly successful and politically prescient production at the National Theatre, Budapest, by the Mohácsi brothers (2013), which highlighted profound anti-Semitic and intolerant attitudes in Hungarian society. As a counterpoint, after the refugee crisis in 2015, Bertalan Bagó's production in Vörösmarty Theatre, Székesfehérvár (2016), remained surprisingly apolitical. As Dennis Kennedy points out, fresh and innovative 'foreign Shakespeares', often in new translations or rewritings, may provide new and inspiring takes on the original plays, since they are shaped by their immediate cultural and political context (Kennedy 1996: 136–7). The two productions under discussion offer distinct examples of theatrical experience, where audiences and theatre professionals were influenced by both aesthetic and socio-political concerns (Shevtsova 2001: 130). The Mohácsi brothers' avowedly anti-racist production, re-constructing the figure of the Jew in what purported to be a nonchalantly racist *mise-en-scène*, had a huge impact in a politically charged context, when the National Theatre and its artistic and managing director, Róbert Alföldi, were attacked and accused of being 'anti-nationalist, gay and Jewish', by extremist right-wing politicians and their 'culture lackeys'.[3] On the other hand, Bagó's 2016 production in Vörösmarty Theatre, in a rural town, chose to avoid the problems related to Jewishness, thus deconstructing the figure of the Jew to suit the director's idea of a poeticized play and a de-politicized Stranger.

In Hungarian theatre history, *The Merchant of Venice* formerly served two major purposes: to highlight a great actor's skill as Shylock, or simply to present an enjoyable (and popular) play, an attitude which seems to haunt Bagó's 2016 production. From the early nineteenth century to the pre-Second World War period, the National Theatre used to offer one, sometimes two, productions of *Merchant* to each generation of theatre-goers, with the last one being staged in 1940.[4] These productions mostly focused on the Christian-Jew conflict, or on the tragic or romantic figure of Shylock, in the style of nineteenth-century productions such as Henry Irving's. In 1986, after a hiatus of more than four decades, the new production at the National Theatre also focused on the talent of the actor playing Shylock.[5] Since the collapse of the communist regime, *Merchant* has enjoyed a theatrical revival, and the play has regained its former popularity, though, as this chapter illustrates, directors' choices vary greatly in representing the Other, still often side-stepping potentially sensitive issues like racism and anti-Semitism.

'Jews, and we, human beings': The Mohácsi brothers' circus of hate speech (2013)

The Mohácsi brothers' heavily rewritten and idiosyncratic *Merchant* cannot be completely severed from its immediate context. It suited Alföldi's outlook for his theatre (2008–13), which was never to shy away from tackling uncomfortable questions. The National Theatre's repertoire nicely balanced classical and contemporary, Hungarian and foreign plays, and his artistic (and very Hamletian) credo, which he laid down in his job application to the National Theatre, was 'to hold up a mirror, to make us see ourselves. Or, what is even more important, to make us want to see ourselves, want to see what there really is – here, now'.[6] The three Mohácsi brothers –

director-playwright János, dramaturge-playwright István and set designer András – produced their *Merchant* at the very end of the Alföldi era. It only ran for two and a half months because of the imminent end of his mandate, though it enjoyed an audience of 9,395 spectators in the fifteen performances between 22 March and 9 June 2013.[7]

Based on those figures, it can be claimed that this take on Shakespeare's play proved more successful, influential and affective for Hungarian audiences than any other production after 1989. Critical reception, in contrast, was mixed, and rarely showed acute awareness of the complexity of this particular theatrical experience. Most reviews acknowledged its innovative character and political potential, and praised the way it reflected on the current political situation and on the context of increasing racism and xenophobia by offering 'an anatomy of hate speech' in society (Tarján 2013). At the same time, major theatre-makers and leading critics disparaged the performance, complaining about poor dramaturgical choices, the length of the playtext and the less than satisfactory acting.[8] In 2019, the Mohácsis revived their production for the National Theatre Studio in Miskolc (with a changed cast and scenic design), and although it ran for only a couple of performances – with a late premiere in the season (29 March 2019) – and in front of small audiences, it created quite a stir. Passionately positive reviews abounded, and the actor playing Shylock (László Görög) received the Critics' Award for Best Actor in the Season.

Theatre historian Zoltán Imre's *Staging the Stranger* discusses the construction of the Other on the Hungarian stage, building on the theories of Antonio Gramsci, Roland Barthes and Pierre Bourdieu. He calls attention to how hegemonic groups in power 'invent' and 'imagine' the Stranger as marginal, exotic or primitive (Imre 2018: 251–4). The Mohácsis' production employed this idea in an original way, by placing Shylock's story into a world permeated by 'casual' racism and anti-Semitism, where Jewish jokes and intolerant remarks were a source of fun for both onstage and off-stage audiences. Dramaturges István Mohácsi, Enikő Perczel, and director János Mohácsi heavily rewrote Shakespeare's play, incorporating actors' improvisations from the rehearsal process within the final prose playtext. Although they radically changed dramatic situations as well, the production remained quite close to the original play insofar as it raised uncomfortable questions in a tragicomic way. Situations from Shakespeare's play were re-modelled and 'translated' into contemporary Hungarian conditions and colloquial idiom, an approach typical of the Mohácsi brothers' workshop method which contributed to the freshness and immediacy of their *Merchant*.

Their methodology also meant that the scenic design and live stage music by Márton Kovács bore almost as much significance as text and gesture. The production was characterized by simple but effective visuals, dominated by often illuminated or colourful geometrical shapes on an otherwise empty, dark stage. Cubes, and other oblong or rectangular objects, whether on the floor or swinging above the stage, partly reproduced the theme of the three caskets (also brought in on a swing), partly created an ahistorical and simultaneously contemporary feel, which nicely balanced the dynamic between playfulness and gravity. Stairs led downwards (to the 'sea'). At the climax, in the grand *finale* of the trial scene, a flight of stairs ascended upstage, towards a cross-shaped platform, with white 'benches' swinging above. With all the actors present onstage, the three characters who had been deprived of everything (Shylock, Jessica and Antonio) stood in almost total darkness on this elevated platform, with only an illuminated paper moon swinging above them. Live string music, mixing Hungarian and klezmer styles, enhanced the emotional impact of these tragic scenes or the fun in comic moments, influencing the response of the spectators. Every detail in the performance strengthened the feeling that this Shakespearean story of Jews and Venetians was about us, the audience, here and now.

The poster showed an early modern catalogue of noses, which included a stereotypical 'Jewish nose': large, hooked and drooping. Such a nose can also refer to being downcast and sad in Hungary (the jocular expression, 'drooping nose', means being melancholy); and when Antonio seemed not to join in the general carnivalesque and abusive merriment, his friends kept asking him, 'Why is your nose drooping?' Thus, the enmity between Shylock and Antonio was re-interpreted and modified through a reference to their shared fates, more especially their loneliness, a common feature, painfully evident in the final scene after the trial, when Shylock, Jessica and Antonio stood, as if at a metaphorical parting of the ways, on the cross-shaped, elevated platform. Shylock left silently with Jessica; a little later, Antonio moved away into total darkness: a thoughtful theatrical image of a thwarted comic resolution, unrequited love and dashed hopes of mutual understanding. Only the pink chest with the three thousand ducats remained on stage, to be crushed by the falling safety curtain.

In a unique directorial take on the play, the Mohácsi brothers chose to address racism and intolerance by presenting hate speech as jokes, and infantile, often vulgar circus fun,[9] which could lead to tragedy, albeit at times unintentionally. The precise effect of this approach was ambiguous and potentially problematic. Though questions like, 'Does audience laughter mean that they sympathize with the haters, or not?' or 'Are they on the side of the victims, if they cannot refrain from laughing at them?' were inevitable, my contention is that this performance served one of its main aims well. It invited spectators to think about everyday hate speech, to which society becomes so accustomed that it cannot even recognize its presence and its possible repercussions.

At the beginning, a clownish Antonio (played by jovial-looking Gábor Hevér) was one of the chaps in an exclusive men's club in Venice. The boys were having fun at the expense of Jews, 'half-breeds' (their nickname for the Prince of Morocco), gays and clever women. In a linguistic barrage of jokes, Antonio, the Duke, Bassanio, Gratiano, Lorenzo, Salerio, even Lanzelo (Lancelet Giobbe), expressed their ingrained contempt of everyone who was 'not them', parading their superiority by degrading 'the Other' through vulgar puerile puns.

Bassanio exemplified a slightly different racist attitude – although it was not clear whether for financial reasons or in earnest belief: he wanted to make friends with the Jew, even if in a highly patronizing and therefore, humiliating manner. For the dinner he shared with Shylock, he hired a kosher cook, but then kept referring to the need to make friends with 'you Jews and we, human beings'. He never seemed to realize how his words revealed his perception of Jews as less than human. At times, he also turned anti-racist comments against Shylock: 'Does not the sun shine on you, too, Shylock? Why can't you see the beauty in beautiful things? The human in humans? What may the world become one day if we could learn to live at peace with each other? Why can't you accept us as others, Shylock? Why don't you try to assimilate?' (Mohácsi, Mohácsi and Perczel 2013: 66).

Even though Bassanio seemed less offensive in his racism when alone, the vulgarity of the Venetians was unmitigated. They called Gratiano a 'country jerk', but all lived up to this description. The lowest point of this behaviour came after the stag-party, when a drunk Antonio, helped by the equally sozzled Bassanio, Gratiano and Salerio, wanted to defecate on the doorknob of Shylock's house with the words 'Shylock, you primitive animal'. They were only stopped by the Jew's entrance and his polite greeting, 'Good morning, noble Venetian lords', uttered not in irony but in earnest (Mohácsi, Mohácsi and Perczel 2013: 65). Such clear opposition of civilized and uncivilized behaviour undoubtedly turned the audience's sympathy towards Shylock in this scene. The 'Jew' appeared as a dignified human being in opposition to Antonio and his friends' behaving as 'primitive animals'. In later scenes, however, Shylock's grandeur and moral integrity, together with the audience's concomitant empathy for the 'Jew', seemed to dissipate. His entering the wooing competition for Portia's hand, with all the Venetian men, and his unabated, brutal hatred towards Antonio in the trial scene rather created an uneasy feeling in the audience. The Mohácsi brothers' strong focus on showing everyday racism seemed to disregard at times the original Shakespearean dramaturgy or a coherent concept of character.

The main drift of the production was clear from the first scene: the performance began with Antonio's fortieth birthday party, for which the banquet table (composed of, and lit up to reveal, geometrical shapes) served as the focal point. Although Antonio's sadness was at times referred to, as in the Shakespearean text, he seemed happy to be part of this macho fun, which lasted almost twenty minutes. The men made merry, sang the traditional birthday song as they brought in the cake, ending it with a rewritten line:

> Happy birthday to you,
> Happy birthday to you,
> Happy birthday to you,
> Let them all die, all the Jews! (Mohácsi, Mohácsi and
>   Perczel 2013: 5)

Antonio responded with his own clownish mockery of the Jews' private conference with God, which was nicely replicated in Shylock's doing so in earnest later. In contrast to the jolly company, Shylock appeared as an older man, exuding seriousness yet capable, at times, to share a Jewish joke, or give a humorous answer to a racist question. His reply to Bassanio after returning from their shared (kosher) dinner was comically apt:

> *Bass.* This circumcision thing, you know, so, is it better
>   with the girls this way? I mean, is it better for you?
> *Shylock.* (*jovially*) I have had no opportunity to practise it in
>   the other way. (Mohácsi, Mohácsi and Perczel 2013: 46)

Shylock's capacity for self-irony caused laughter on- and off-stage, making him even more sympathetic – not only as a victim of Bassanio's 'polite' racism but also as the oppressed one who can fight back with humour. However, his potential for twisting words later served to subvert his moral-religious integrity, when he engaged in a battle of wits with Portia. As mentioned above, he participated in the wooing competition in an added scene. Portia rejected his suit, reasoning that it was Sabbath day. Shylock, however, found a way out instantly. He averted this trap, alluding to the (theologically correct) exception to the rule: that is, when someone's life is threatened, even a Jew can work – in this case, choose a casket on Sabbath day: 'One can work if life is in danger. If I do not open the casket, our future children's lives are in danger!' (Mohácsi, Mohácsi and Perczel 2013: 22). Such obvious and pragmatic disregard of sacred Jewish law caused laughter but diminished the audience's empathy for him: they saw an ageing man, grasping at every straw to marry a young woman. Portia could only send Shylock away finally with a trick, anticipating her hair-splitting legalizing during the trial. She asked Shylock to light a candle for her, which the Jew denied since it effected a change in the world, so Shylock left in shame. This production cleverly inverted Shakespearean situations and characters to make the audience confront their own potential for racism. Partly in a humorous way, often absurdly mixing comic and tragic, and finally, in and after the trial scene, the directors delivered a tragic, serious message: human beings can be crushed by the repercussions of casual othering.

Although the Jew–non-Jew opposition was clearly highlighted in the mayhem of anti-Semitic 'fun', the potential for tragedy appeared in four emotionally charged scenes. One presented Shylock and Jessica alone on an empty stage, returning from the harbour where they had said farewell to some of their relatives leaving the city, thus remaining the only Jews in Venice. Visually, their sad loneliness prefigured the closing scene of the play. Shylock's tragic Jewishness became significant at the end of Act 1, on discovering Jessica's elopement and baptism: in an emotionally touching *finale*, he poured out his grief at having no longer a daughter in a long monologue (one of three given to him in the production). As he spoke, he started stripping off his clothes until he bared his chest, ending with the words: 'You died, my little daughter, you died. Let the infinity of the times be easy on you. Your father loved you, your father, the last Jew in Venice' (Mohácsi, Mohácsi and Perczel 2013: 79).

Despite theatrical traditions, Antonio's near-death in the trial scene was not used to highlight oppositions such as barbarian/civilized, or Jewish/Christian. The scene shifted the focus away from the Antonio-Shylock conflict to emphasize their shared fate of loneliness. This was the point when Antonio realized that his boon companions were just as ready to help kill him, as they had been to eat, drink or joke with him. All his friends, except Bassanio, rushed to stretch him out on a grey cube, and hold him down while Shylock was whetting his knife. After he was released, Antonio's disillusionment and hurt were evident as he chose to stand apart from the others.

Shylock's fate was sealed with his onstage christening – the trial scene ended with Gratiano and Nerissa acting as godparents and the Duke as a priest. Shylock received the name 'Peter', and everyone joked about the meaning of this name. The rock-like, unyielding but dignified personality of Sándor Gáspár's Shylock was thus undermined through unpalatable comedy.

Jessica's fate contributed to the tragedy of the last Jews in Venice: her marriage to Lorenzo also ended during the trial scene. Lorenzo defied her publicly as a 'dirty Jewish slut', after he learned that Jessica had been married, but that her husband had eloped with her mother. This new take on her character could have tilted the scene towards the sentimental, but the theatrical moment of Jessica losing everything, portrayed by a talented young actress, shifted the audience's sympathy towards her as a female victim of circumstances.

Although the production took delight in characters uttering the word 'Jew', it was, rather, defined by a general mocking hatred against everyone who was different from those in the ruling 'men's club of Venice'. Apart from the Jew as the principal Other, the production panned on various other groups of Others: people of non-traditional sexual orientation, non-white people and clever women. In the casket scenes, the lesbian Great Mogul of Aragon was hooted at. When it was mentioned that she had committed suicide after her failure, no one took her tragedy seriously. Overall though, antagonism against lesbians and gay men received less weight in the production and constituted only a part of the verbal abuse; Antonio's potential homoerotic feelings were never conspicuously highlighted. On the other hand, the Prince of Morocco became a significant vehicle for talking about racism on a more general level. He first appeared on stage with the Venetian suitors in Act 1, when even Shylock distanced himself from him, holding his nose to avoid the 'stench' of the 'half-blood'. Morocco's face was painted half-brown, half-white, and his 'half-bred' appearance was already prefigured by Portia's initial comments on her father's will, not welcoming the idea of being courted by 'a Jew or a half-bred'.

In this stage world, everyone seemed unembarrassedly racist. Even the hated Others shared this intolerance. Whereas Shylock could not stand the stench of Morocco, the Prince, on his part, commented on Shylock's wooing with the following words: 'O, admirable Portia, in my beautiful country, in sunlit Morocco being a Jew disqualifies him at once, and that's enough'. In a biting satirical turn, Morocco's comments met with the Venetian lady's pretended astonishment: 'Shocking! . . . Have I just heard anti-Semitic comments? . . . What's wrong with the Jews?' In a final twist, Portia claimed that 'This prejudicial attitude cannot be tolerated within these ancient walls' (Mohácsi, Mohácsi and Perczel 2013: 25). While the utter hypocrisy of the situation was laughable, the gang-like exclusiveness and intolerance felt disgustingly real, stage racism holding up a mirror to intolerant Hungary. Morocco suffered badly: throughout his wooing, he was mocked by the Venetians, who called him a monkey, uttering monkey sounds every time he spoke. Later the audience learned that the Venetians had thrown him into the sea, taking literally the jocular Hungarian phrase 'Now the monkey jumps into the water', uttered by the Duke. This subversive use of language paralleled the references to 'drooping noses' – Jewish or melancholic – in the first scene. However, this racist 'prank' sealed the Prince's fate: he drowned, and his death led to Morocco declaring war on Venice, as we learned from the Duke in the trial scene.

In the Mohácsis' *Merchant*, Shakespeare's play was used as a starting point to focus on the 'everyday' racist and prejudicial thinking that permeates the onstage and off-stage worlds, while making the audience laugh a lot. Although this theatrical attitude may prove a double-edged weapon in a less intellectual context than the National Theatre, in its time and setting it became memorable and meaningful theatre – even if most critics considered that the production failed to meet all the expectations it had set for itself (Ascher qtd in Csáki 2013: 307).

The weightlessness of the Jew: Bertalan Bagó's *Merchant of Venice* (2016)

After the refugee crisis of 2015, amid growing intolerance and racism in Hungary, one might have expected theatres to stage Shakespeare's play about the Other, as an exploration of the 'here and now'. However, this was not the case. Two productions of *Merchant* premiered in 2016: Bagó's, in Székesfehérvár, and Péter Valló's, in the central Budapest theatre, Pesti Színház, both using the same recent translation by Ádám Nádasdy (Nádasdy [2015] 2018). The latter proved rather an artistic and financial failure, receiving little critical attention. It made light of otherness, downplaying any straightforward sign of Jewishness and only relying on the box-office attraction of the popular actor, András Kern, who, as Hungarian audiences well know, is Jewish by birth. Kern played a nondescript, bored businessman, among the young generation of Venice. Nothing differentiated him from them, either in looks or manner. Consequently, his only authentic Jewish gesture, which was to pour ashes on his head after Jessica's elopement, seemed utterly fake. Only one critic noted that the 2015 refugee crisis should have affected this performance and Bagó's production more (D. Magyari 2016). However, even he failed to pay attention to the one change made by Valló in this respect: the presence, at the beginning of each act, of a black street musician who was habitually harassed by the Venetian playboys.

Bagó's production proved relatively successful with audiences, though it did not fare too well with the critics. *Criticai Lapok* [Critical Papers], one of the two leading printed journals of theatre criticism and history, published an appreciative but rather uncritical short review by Ágnes Szűcs Katalin, while the other leading journal, *Színház* [Theatre] ignored the production entirely. István Nánay, a major critic and theatre historian, pointed out in his online review that the more dramatic moments of the *mise-en-scène* often proved too didactic, and regretted that the director's intention remained unclear, leaving 'unanswered questions'. He claimed that Bagó's staging was ambitious in its poetics, though often failing in rhythm, partly due to moving large stage props, which also attested to a directorial intent to achieve the highest theatrical effect possible (Nánay 2016). Another reviewer, Csaba B. Kiss, underlined that this production shied away from the 'real issues' of the play, adding that 'no director should stage the play without having a markedly strong concept beforehand' (2016).

This could have been otherwise: both the politically charged atmosphere and the casting, together with the poetical but modernized translation by Nádasdy, promised more. The cast featured some actors of the former National Theatre's company, which had been dispersed after the politically motivated takeover of the theatre by the new management. Antonio was played by Sándor Gáspár, the Shylock of the Mohácsi's production, while Csilla Radnay was Portia in both productions. These casting choices reflected the director's ideas on the problem of the Other, contributing to a strangely deconstructed idea of Jewishness.

The scenic design of the performance relied on geometrical shapes, as in the Mohácsis' production, without the economical and meaningful simplicity of the former. The black stage was lit up in a square pattern, with props like a piano, tables, chairs, a jacuzzi or a bed downstage. Upstage, a two-storey construction suggested doors and windows; it was sometimes hidden by a curtain, serving as a screen for the not-over-subtle use of projected images (the sea, comic video clips of Portia's suitors). Recorded electronic music counterpointed the classical music Shylock played on the piano. This design allowed for dynamic changes and good visual effects on occasion (as in the dance scene of Shylock's 'banishment/inclusion'). However, it often proved random.

Shylock was played by one of the most popular middle-aged Hungarian actors, Zsolt László, who did not fit any Jewish stereotypes. His appearance and stature rather suggested a straight-backed military man with an aristocratic flair, and a corresponding strength of character. Although he appeared in a long, dark grey overcoat, which could be conceived as a Jewish kaftan, his modern woollen cap, simple briefcase and short-trimmed beard defied any easy association with Jews. He was called, and treated, like a Jew, the Other, by the Venetians, but did not look like one.[10]

Nonetheless, the conflict between Shylock and Antonio (performed by two actors with a strong stage presence) proved powerful, even though neither of them displayed culturally identifying markers or stereotypes. Antonio first appeared in a golden-white tuxedo-like costume, playing a romantic tune on his white piano. In age, manner and musical tastes, he was conspicuously different from the Venetian playboys, who wore coloured leather jackets and looked as trendy as possible. Nor was Shylock overly hostile in any other way than the Shakespearean text absolutely demanded, so in this as well, he was opposed to the Venetian young men, for whom being anti-Semitic meant being considered fashionable. Both protagonists had an air of melancholy and quiet strength; therefore, the trial scene became the emotional peak of the performance, with Antonio stoically waiting for his end. The stage was dominated by thick red ropes outlining a square in the centre, suggestive of a boxing ring, a museum exhibit or a place for a public execution. Antonio was laid on a platform, his bared chest visibly shaking as he panted vehemently, even after Portia's sentence had set him free. For long moments, he seemed not to have noticed that he would not die, his rigid body remained frozen in a crucifix-like posture and had to be carried away by his friends. This was a theatrically compelling scene, equalled only by the added scene of Shylock's 'christening'. László's six-and-half-foot powerful Shylock was surrounded by faceless Venetians wearing white masks, who, in a dance-like choreography, arraigned him, pulled his arms apart and forced a white mask on his face, which seemed to crush his soul.

Although inclusion and exclusion played a significant part in this production, it never seemed to attribute adequate weight to the Jewishness of Shylock or to sound out the dangers of racist comments. Bagó's *Merchant* remained a praiseworthy theatrical rendition, but suffered from a siphoning away of potentially controversial issues.

In order to stage *The Merchant of Venice* effectively, theatre-makers cannot sidestep the underlying issues of otherness in the play – Shylock's, but also Morocco's – any more than they can ignore the social-political context of their production. If they fail to do so, they may prove moderately successful but fail to make a lasting contribution to the play's theatrical history. The Mohácsis' *Merchant* captivated audiences with its daring take on the play, and spectators responded positively to their bold actualization, which reflected directly on the upsurge of racism in Hungarian public life. Precisely those directorial choices, however, disappointed critics, who expected greater artistic coherence or complained about the excessively 'journalistic' approach to such delicate issues as Jewishness and anti-Semitism (Kovács 2014). The 2016 productions by Valló and Bagó, on the other hand, shied away from taking the otherness of Shylock (and Morocco) too seriously, making Shylock's character and fate somewhat weightless. What emerges from this discussion of recent Hungarian productions is that if a production of *The Merchant of Venice* shies away from darker aspects and ambiguous issues within and outside the theatre, it runs the risk of depriving itself and the audiences of everything that really matters – like Shylock in the end. The

Stranger can only be deconstructed at a cost, and needs to remain a significant and recognizable stage presence.

Notes

1 Excerpt from the poem Ádám Nádasdy wrote for Róbert Alföldi's farewell party on 30 June 2013, when he stepped down as director of the National Theatre (Csáki 2013: 321). All unacknowledged translations are mine. The theatre, which was built in 2000–2 and designed by Mária Siklós, is considered ugly by many because of its highly eclectic nature, mirroring the lack of real political and cultural compromise regarding the idea and function of the National Theatre.

2 For data on all the Hungarian *Merchant* productions between 1986 and 2016, see Imre (2018: 306–7).

3 These attacks ranged from Gábor Szigethy's invective against Alföldi's concepts of the National Theatre (22 January 2008, in the conservative weekly *Heti Válasz*) to protests in front of the theatre and parliamentary addresses by the far-right party Jobbik (Csáki 2013: 101–5, 275–89, 420).

4 *The Merchant* was one of the most popular Shakespeare plays performed in German in Pest at the end of the eighteenth century. Hungarian-language stagings began in Kassa in 1836, and the play remained a staple of nineteenth-century repertories (Imre 2018: 260–1). The National Theatre staged nine different productions of *The Merchant*, in 1840, 1865, 1877, 1886, 1889, 1907, 1923, 1927 and 1940 (Hofer et al. 1987: 369–70). For more data see Imre 2018: 260–1. For a detailed analysis of the 1940 production see Márkus (2010), Imre (2018: 254–69).

5 Tamás Major (1940) and Miklós Gábor (1986): their Shylocks had tragical grandeur and strength, mostly due to the actors' powerful stage presence. Major and Gábor were among Hungary's most talented and leading actors between the 1940s and the 1980s.

6 Alföldi as quoted in Csáki (2013: 277).

7 Csáki (2013: 390–1). The most successful performance in Alföldi's National Theatre was the Mohácsi brothers' *We*

Only Live Once . . ., with a run from 2011 to 2016, and an audience of 20,338 (Csáki 2013: 377–9), in a disturbing take on Hungarian cultural traumas from 1947 to the 1970s.

8 'It is exciting in its plan, but not accomplished in every bit and detail of the performance' (Ascher as quoted in Csáki 2013: 307).

9 See Nathalie Vienne-Guerrin's emphasis on the uneasy nature of berating in *The Merchant of Venice*. I think the Mohácsi brothers took this a step further, and their hyping up of verbal abuse proved an effective tragicomic device.

10 In contrast, the Mohácsis chose to emphasize Shylock's otherness visually. He wore a pointed Jewish black cap (a long-standing theatrical tradition), and a long, kaftan-like coat in shades of red and deep purple, which contrasted with the blueish, colder shades of Antonio and his company's clothes. The costumes looked both 'Shakespearean' and modern, colourful shirts with a belt and loose sleeves, or toga-like long coats in the trial scene, worn over modern trousers and shoes.

References

Csáki, J. (2013), *Alföldi színháza. Öt nemzeti év* [Alföldi's theatre. Five years of the National], Budapest: Libri.

Hofer, M., F. Kerényi, B. Magyar, E. Császár, Gy. Székely and L. Vámos. (1987), *A Nemzeti Színház 150 éve* [150 years of the National Theatre], Budapest: Gondolat.

Imre, Z. (2018), *Az idegen színpadra állításai. A magyar színjátszás inter- és intrakulturális kapcsolatai* [Staging the Stranger. The inter- and intracultural relations of Hungarian Theatre], 251–307, Budapest: Ráció.

Kennedy, D. (1996), 'Shakespeare Without His Language', in J. C. Bulman (ed.), *Shakespeare, Theory and Performance*, 133–48, London: Routledge.

Kiss, C. B. (2016), 'A zsidó meg a többiek. Shakespeare: *A velencei kalmár*, Vörösmarty Színház, Székesfehérvár' [The Jew and the others. Shakespeare's *The Merchant of Venice* in Vörösmarty Theatre, Székesfehérvár], review, *7óra7*, 19 February. Available online: http://7ora7.hu/2016/02/19/a_zsido_meg_a_tobbiek# (accessed 2 April 2021).

Kovács, D. (2014), 'Magyar táncok' [Hungarian Dances], *Színház*, 6 October. Available online: https://szinhaz.net/2014/10/06/kovacs-dezso-magyar-tancok/ (accessed 2 April 2021).

Magyari, I. D. (2016), 'A kölcsönös gyűlölet drámája' [The drama of mutual hatred], *Criticai Lapok Online* [Critical Papers], 2015, 7–8. https://www.criticailapok.hu/43-2016/39092-a-kolcsonos-gyulolet-dramaja (accessed 10 October 2020).

Márkus, Z. (2010), 'Two Merchants of Venice in Budapest: 1936 and 1940', in N. Pikli (ed.), *Who to Believe Expecting What: Writings for István Géher on His 70th Birthday*, 214–20, Budapest: ELTE.

Mohácsi, I., J. Mohácsi and E. Perczel (2013), *A velencei kalmár* [The Merchant of Venice], unpublished playtext, by courtesy of the authors.

Nádasdy, Á. (trans.), ([2015] 2018), *A velencei kalmár* [The Merchant of Venice], in *Shakespeare: Drámák. Nádasdy Ádám fordításai 3. Kötet*, 5–134, Budapest: Magvető.

Nánay, I. (2016), 'Bosszúra bosszú' [Revenge on revenge], *Revizor Online*, 20 March. Available online: www.revizoronline.com/hu/cikk/5986/shakespeare-a-velencei-kalmar-vorosmarty-szinhaz-szekesfehervar/ (accessed 2 April 2021).

Shevtsova, M. (2001), 'Social Practice, Interdisciplinary Perspective', *Theatre Research International*, 26 (2): 129–36.

Sokolova, B. (2018), '"Mingled yarn": *The Merchant of Venice* East of Berlin and the Legacy of "Eastern Europe"', *Shakespeare Survey*, 71: 88–102.

Stark, T. (1993), 'A magyar zsidóság a vészkorszakban és a második világháború után' [The Hungarian Jewry during the Holocaust and after the Second World War], *Regio. Kisebbség, politika, társadalom*, 4 (3): 140–50.

Tarján, T. (2013) 'Tengeren a szél' [Wind on the seas], *Revizor Online*, 1 April. Available online: https://revizoronline.com/hu/cikk/4431/mohacsi-testverek-william-shakespeare-alapjan-a-velencei-kalmar-nemzeti-szinhaz/ (accessed 2 April 2021).

Vienne-Guerrin, N. (2013), '"You have rated me": Insults in *The Merchant of Venice*', *Litteraria Pragensia. Studies in Literature and Culture*, 23 (45): 82–96.

8

Dutch negotiations with otherness in times of crisis

Othello (2006) and *The Arab of Amsterdam* (2008)

Coen Heijes

In 1964, a reviewer compared a highly successful Dutch production of *Othello* to *The Merchant of Venice*. The production was directed by Bob de Lange for the National Theatre company Haagsche Comedie, and the reviewer complimented the director for his understanding that the Moor was not to be interpreted in a racial manner, no more than Shylock should be ('Hedendaagse *Othello*' 1964). While the comment mistakenly equated race and Jewishness, its interest lies in the parallel between leading characters who are cast as outsiders. In another review, Othello was seen as a helpless but noble victim and the absence of a specific racial perspective was judged to be a positive aspect of the production, since any relation between Othello and racial tensions was considered irrelevant ('*Othello* in de Stadsschouwburg' 1964). Similar was Shylock's status on the Dutch stage during that period. Five years earlier the famous Dutch actor Paul Steenbergen had performed an acclaimed Shylock, presenting him as an honourable and dignified man, without any explicit markers of Jewishness (Doolaard 1959; Koning 1959). In the following decades, the outsider status of Othello and Shylock became more prominent, while the cautious approach to racism and anti-Semitism was a consistent element in the performance and reception of the two plays.

Forty years after the 1964 review, on 2 November 2004, Dutch society was shaken by the murder of the controversial film-maker Theo van Gogh, known for his criticism of Dutch multiculturalism. This tragedy came in the wake of two previous shocks: the 2001 terrorist attack on the Twin Towers in New York (9/11) and the murder, in 2002, of the populist Dutch politician Pim Fortuyn. These events dramatically changed the tone of the multiculturalist debate in the Netherlands and revealed a growing polarization of Dutch society. The rise of Fortuyn had begun shortly after 9/11, when he founded the political party Lijst Pim Fortuyn, which he named after himself. He was an outspoken critic of immigration, Islam, the political correctness of mainstream parties, and a multicultural welfare society. In his view, all this worked against the wishes and needs of the Netherlands' 'native', white population. Fortuyn called Islam a 'backward culture' and considered it an 'extraordinary threat, a hostile civilization', stating unequivocally that 'the Netherlands is full' (Heijden 2017). In March 2002, in local elections in Rotterdam, his party won 35 per cent of the votes, propelling him into a favourite position for the national elections. However, two months later, he was murdered in broad daylight, in the parking lot of a TV studio, by Volkert van der Graaf, a Dutch environmental and animal-rights activist who accused Fortuyn of using Muslims as scapegoats for the country's problems. This led to a rare outpour of public grief which brought about what has been referred as a 'new realism' to Dutch politics, marked by a move to the right and an increased tendency to talk tough on integration and migration (Heijes 2011; Verheul 2009).

Such was the atmosphere in which the film-maker van Gogh, a distant descendant of the artist Vincent van Gogh, was murdered as he was cycling to work. Van Gogh was known for his provocative newspaper columns, movies and public statements, in which he ridiculed Jews, Muslims and the Dutch bourgeoisie. He had been on trial for anti-Semitism and for joking about the Holocaust. His film, *Submission, Part One* (2004), criticized Islam for mistreating women. Ayaan Hirsi Ali, a political refugee from Somalia who had become a conservative member of the Dutch parliament, had helped van Gogh with the script. The film, which showed abused women with suggestive verses from the Koran around their necks, supposedly sanctioning their maltreatment, was banned in many Muslim countries. Both van Gogh and Hirsi Ali received death threats, but while Hirsi Ali was put under twenty-four-hour police protection, van Gogh refused it. Shortly afterwards, he was shot and stabbed to death by a Dutch-Moroccan member of a fundamentalist Muslim network. Following this second murder, the social debate hardened even further, particularly in relation to immigration, multiculturalism, Muslims and Moroccans in particular. Van Gogh received a posthumous award for his entire oeuvre at the annual Netherlands Film Festival. In Belgium, he received the Flemish Pallieter award for his contribution to the freedom of speech in film media. Although the assassinations of Fortuyn and van Gogh were part of a process that had started earlier, they have since been viewed as a watershed, marking the end of innocence, or the end of a delusional utopian dream of a harmonious society (Heijes 2011: 312; Heijden 2017: 18; Verheul 2009: 191). As Han Entzinger, the Nestor on Dutch multiculturalism, put it, 'This was our 9/11, the moment when the Netherlands lost its naivety. We always thought that we were the country of multicultural tolerance that could not go wrong' (Entzinger 2004; Prins and Saharso 2008; Verheul 2009).

One might think that such radical developments would inevitably leave their mark on the representation and reception of the Other in literature. In this chapter, I look at how these events affected the first two major productions of Shakespeare's Venetian plays that were staged after 2004: *Othello*, by Nationale Toneel, in 2006, and *Arab of Amsterdam*, in 2007, an adaptation of *The Merchant of Venice* by De Nieuwe Amsterdam. At first sight, these productions seemed to veer away from the traditional construction of the Other in the Dutch history of the plays' performance. As suggested by interviews with actors, directors and critics, they aimed at a more nuanced and topical view of outsiders. However, a closer analysis reveals a complex and ambivalent picture. In both cases, the underlying narrative remained much closer to the traditional Dutch approach to the plays, suggesting a tendency to gloss over uncomfortable truths regarding identity and tolerance.

Othello, directed by Johan Doesburg (2006)

In the Netherlands, *Othello* has long been one of the most-performed Shakespeare plays and, since 1945, one of the ten most popular canonical plays. Johan Doesburg's production for Nationale Toneel was undoubtedly affected by the aforementioned events. The connection between Thijs Römer, the actor playing Othello, and van Gogh, was explicit. Römer was a relatively young actor who had recently captured the spotlight, thanks largely to van Gogh with whom he had worked extensively. He had starred in *Cool!* (2004), a film about Moroccan criminal youngsters, in *06/05* (2004), a film about Fortuyn's murder, and in *Medea* (2005), a posthumously broadcast TV adaptation, which won the special prize at the Netherlands Film Festival. The events of 2004 had a deep impact on Römer and affected his thinking about Othello:

> I have become aware that it is not self-evident to have an open and honest approach to life. You can also see that in

Othello. . . . It is really frightening. . . . it is so simple to destroy a person. After what happened to Theo, it would be very easy to become cynical and lose one's innocence. This did not happen to me, but it could. Still, I would like to hold on to this innocent approach. (Römer qtd in Schaap 2006)[1]

Following van Gogh's murder, the debate in the Netherlands focused on Muslims and migrants from Morocco, and this found its way into this production.

Moroccans and citizens of other countries around the Mediterranean had started arriving in the Netherlands in the 1960s in response to the shortage of national applicants for low-skilled jobs on the Dutch labour market. Prior to van Gogh's murder, the Moroccan community had already received negative media attention, because of a group of Moroccan youngsters engaged in criminal activities (Heijes 2001; Schuhmacher 1987; Tinnemans 1994). After 2004, the negative coverage increased dramatically, and this *Othello* cut directly into this debate. Although Römer avoided taking sides, he saw parallels between Othello's situation and that of van Gogh's murderer, between the radicalization of the Dutch-Moroccan who killed the director and what was happening to Othello:

Othello is in the position of an outsider, he needs to be whiter than white. But when he gets into problems, and the white world rejects him, he has nothing to fall back on. You see the same happening to . . . Theo van Gogh's murderer. He did everything to become a part of the white world. And when that did not work out . . . at a certain moment he snapped. The fact that Othello has nothing to fall back on explains the speed of his radicalization. (Römer qtd in Takken 2006)

Although Römer mentions skin colour in his comments, the production was less concerned with race than with religious and ethnic difference, and the vulnerability of the outsider.

Neither the director nor Römer nor Anniek Pfeifer, who played Desdemona, considered skin colour important. Instead, they emphasized Othello's isolation, vulnerability and loss of cultural traditions ('Actuele' 2006; Doesburg 2020; Jager 2006; Schaap 2006). Nevertheless, the production started with a direct reference to skin colour, through a close-up of Othello in blackface, slowly removing the make-up with paper tissues to reveal his white skin, although his eye sockets remained black. The process was recorded by Iago with a handheld video camera, then magnified through a projection onto the set, which was dominated by a wall of forty dark freight containers.

This memorable opening clearly suggested Othello's attempts to integrate in a white society; however, the black make-up around his eyes indicated that no matter how hard he might try, he would always be an outsider. Originally, the production used brown make-up to highlight Othello's 'Arab nature', but during the rehearsals, the decision was taken to switch to 'jet black', since it worked better to differentiate Othello (Doesburg 2020; Takken 2006). Although the removal of blackface had been employed in neighbouring Germany to probe sensitivities about its use in racial discourse, this was not the case with Doesburg's production, and critics paid no specific attention to it (Dercksen 2006; Freriks 2006; Veraart 2006).[2]

As with previous Dutch productions which employed blackface and brownface, colour was used to indicate the complex vulnerabilities of the outsider: not only the Other's vulnerability in a multicultural society, which might lead to radicalization, but also vulnerabilities of a more general kind. These could be intimately personal, like being in love and being overcome by jealousy and suspicion. Römer (qtd in Takken 2006) argued the importance of this aspect:

> Just before the production starts, something drastic has happened to Othello: he has discovered love. Love has made him uncertain and vulnerable . . . I hope that after this

Othello, people in the audience will look at each other and say: 'God forbid anything like that should come between us.' I'm mainly thinking of couples.

Undoubtedly, the production wanted both to address the political and social repercussions of recent events and to remain a tragedy of love, jealousy and misdirection. This also transpired in the reception, which mostly saw the production as a tragedy of love and loss everyone could relate to:

Othello is the odd one out, an outsider, insecure and because of this, susceptible to influence – it is not only him, all the other characters are affected in this way, and that's what's important in this staging, much more than the potential political connotations. Everyone is an outsider yearning for affection, and when it does not come, something snaps. (Veraart 2006)

Iago (Michel Sluysmans), too, fitted the pattern of the vulnerable outsider: a smooth guy from an unsavoury neighbourhood, constantly slicking back his hair with a pocket comb, he was a prototypical populist voter. In an interview, Sluysmans argued that Iago was a vulnerable, pained figure, and this was a new take on a character who is traditionally represented on the Dutch stage as a Richard III-like humorous villain (Sluysmans 2006a).

Iago's isolation and vulnerability in this production had two different sources, a political and a personal one. On the political level, he was presented as a disgruntled, xenophobic character, who feels he has been left behind, and resents the social success of the Other. On a personal level, Iago's isolation and pain came from his relationship with Othello. Both actors were in their late twenties, both wore the same type of youthful, slightly tattered/frayed clothes; they were bonded by a long-established friendship. It was the loss of this friendship that pained Iago, who felt rejected by Othello. The assistant director, Costiaan Mesu, spoke of Iago's fury 'as the close bond with Othello, his mirror image, was broken' (Mesu 2006: 10). Referring specifically to this problem, Römer (qtd in Takken 2006) suggested that

> Iago was Othello's best childhood friend. They have done everything together for years and years on end and when they turn sixteen, Othello suddenly gets a girl-friend . . . takes her home. Iago becomes the jealous friend who's left behind.

The feeling of isolation was central to the production. Sluysmans has spoken about how this is experienced by all the characters, each of whom longs 'for something they cannot get: Iago for Othello, Roderigo for Desdemona, Cassio for Desdemona, Desdemona for Othello, Emilia for Iago, Bianca for Cassio, Brabantio for Desdemona. In the end, they are all alone' (Sluysmans 2006b: 5). Although the female characters were set apart by the red colour of their costumes, they were subject to the same general sense of longing. Emilia could not help loving Iago in spite of his manipulations, and Desdemona remained loyal to the end. The production did not focus on any specifically gender-based otherness, in line with the general trend among Dutch *Othellos*. This was confirmed by the reviews which paid no specific attention to the female characters, apart from applauding or criticizing the quality of acting.

Tom Schenk's set strengthened the sense of loss and isolation. Crushed by the massive wall of freight containers, the actors looked diminutive and lost; the cold, anonymous world completely overwhelmed them. Adding to the general sense of isolation, some of the containers opened at times to reveal individual characters physically boxed in and separated. This design underpinned the director's vision, which looked beyond the politics of otherness and stressed mankind's helplessness in an uncaring universe: 'man is small', Doesburg reflected on the use of the set (qtd in Takken 2006). A video camera was used throughout to magnify the characters' emotions and bring them closer to the audience. It zoomed in on Othello's despair, Iago's pain, Emilia's helplessness, through haunting video-stills of isolated individuals. This heightened the focus on personal emotions, rather than on political content.

Although interviews with members of the cast and the director suggested that their intentions were partly political, the production sidestepped this in favour of a more general sense of vulnerability – ultimately, everyone was an outsider. While it might be argued that this reflected the collective sense of loss felt after 2004, the link was tenuous. The reception firmly saw the play slip back into the realm of love, passion, jealousy and existential loneliness. Review headlines like 'Downfall by violent love affair' (Schaap 2006), 'A young Othello with an old message' (Jager 2006), 'Romantic Othello does not buzz' (Dercksen 2006) and 'Above all a soldier in love' (Takken 2006), indicated a conformity with the tradition which has dominated the play over the past decades on the Dutch stage. Likewise, audience reactions mainly focused on the tragic love story and the quality of the acting (Moose 2006). In that sense, the reception did not differ from Ivo van Hove's much publicized 2003 and 2012 *Othellos*. Nor did it mark a specific change in its view of the Other. It chose not to explore sensitive topics such as racism, the use of a white actor for Othello, blackface traditions onstage or offstage, broad popular dissatisfaction with immigration or the challenges of an imploding Dutch multicultural society. To a large extent, it was business as usual on the Dutch stage.

The Arab of Amsterdam, directed by Aram Adriaanse (2008)

The Merchant of Venice is popular in the Netherlands and enjoyed four professional productions between 2002 and 2008. The first, after van Gogh's murder and its ensuing impact on the migration and integration debate, was not Shakespeare's play but an adaptation by Justus van Oel (2007) for De Nieuwe Amsterdam, directed by Aram Adriaanse. The theatre company, known for its focus on diversity, staged a production which marked a departure from previous Dutch *Merchants* by adapting the play in a way which seemed to allow a critical interrogation of multiculturalism and the position of the Other in these circumstances. Like the 2006 *Othello*, this production was closely connected with van Gogh. Van Oel was the script writer for *Najib and Julia* (2003), a TV series directed by van Gogh about the clash between two different cultural and social circles. Based on *Romeo and Juliet*, it told the story of a love affair between a Dutch hockey-playing girl from a well-to-do family and a spirited pizza delivery boy from a traditional Moroccan family. The series won the prize for best television drama at the Netherlands Film Festival, although van Gogh's harsh criticism of multiculturalism elicited a strong reaction from Moroccan respondents who argued that he was exploiting the negative stereotype of Moroccans created by the media (Olie 2004).

It looked as if Adriaanse's production would be the perfect vehicle to address topical issues. Shakespeare's title was changed to *The Arab of Amsterdam*. Antonio (Hein van der Heijden) was a Dutch merchant, who traded illegally in marijuana and was awaiting three new shipments. The Shylock character was named Rafi (Sabri Saad El Hamus). In a prologue, he introduced himself as a 'Jewish Arab, an Arab Jew' (Oel 2007: 2) who ran a chain of shawarma snack bars in Amsterdam. Having migrated to the Netherlands from Iraq as a political refugee, Rafi recalled an incident in which his Iraqi professor of English had found out that he was an Arab Jew. Consequently, he was forced to write his thesis on Shylock:

> If I was to graduate, then it had to be with maximum pain: by prostrating myself, apologizing on behalf of an invented Jew, by spitting on myself and my people, to satisfy a group of sniggering students. (Oel 2007: 2)

Rafi was furious with Shakespeare for wilfully creating a Jewish scapegoat, while also making Shylock a fool: Shylock, he reasoned, could have taken less than a pound of flesh, as no Venetian would ever resist a discount. Taking his cue from Karen Blixen's *Out of Africa*, Rafi further argued that the use of a red-hot knife would have prevented the loss of blood, as it 'makes clean wounds, / and in cutting immediately sears all veins, / so that no blood would flow' (Oel 2007: 2).[3] In fleeing from Baghdad to Amsterdam, however, the outsider status of the Jewish Arab Rafi had not changed – from a Jew in an Arab country, he had become an Arab in the Netherlands. Either way, he remained an outsider, an Other, whether Jew or Arab, to be discriminated against.

In a further intertwining of the two Others embodied by Rafi/Shylock, Bassanio (Raymi Sambo) was given paraphrased lines from *Der Müll, die Stadt und der Tod* [*Garbage, the City and Death*], Rainer Werner Fassbinder's (1975) controversial play, which was banned on grounds of anti-Semitism. In the new context, his words became a violent attack on Arabs: 'Fleas! All of them little black fleas! The city is suffering from these fleas. It groans and shudders. The fleas are becoming a plague' (Oel 2007: 17). This was a direct comment on the explosion of xenophobia. As the director stated in an interview, the framework of *Merchant* was used 'to address the problems surrounding the migration of North Africans and [more specifically] Moroccans to the Netherlands' (Adriaanse 2020). This was made explicit by the insertion of Shylock's lines about the humanity of the Jew (3.1.53–64), which, subtly adapted, Rafi used twice as his identities shifted. First, he spoke them when he was taunted as a Jew, on his arrival in the Netherlands:

You are not a Jew, you are a man amongst men, you are not a Jew, Jews don't exist, you just suffer from hallucinations, from paranoia . . . Nobody wants to hurt you, boy, people only want to be kind to you, we live in a peaceful country, Hitler is dead, how can you remember him, you were not even born at the time, Saddam is dead, you survived the bastard, it is safe here, everything is fine, what more can a man want? (Oel 2007: 51)

Later, at the trial, Rafi responded with 'I am a Jew. Hath not a Jew eyes?' to which Portia retorted, brutally: 'Us against them, the Jews with their dead against the eternal anti-Semite, do me a favour and think of something else!' At this point, Rafi repeated the lines, substituting 'Arab' for 'Jew': 'I am an Arab. Hath not an Arab eyes?' In this way, the final lines of Shylock's speech (*MV* 3.1.63–4) gained an additional, ominous dimension in the Dutch context: 'If a Christian wrong an Arab, what should his sufferance be by Christian example? Why, revenge!' (Oel 2007: 52).

El Hamus spoke about how the Netherlands had changed, becoming less tolerant. Reflecting both on the rise of populist parties and on the events of 9/11, he noted:

the Arabs of now are the Jews of then. [The situations] may not be so extreme, but you can draw a comparison, unfortunately. No gas chambers, no concentration camps, but ways in which today's Arabs will be isolated, kept apart. . . . Time has taught us how victims can turn into perpetrators. . . . and how Arabs will take revenge. They fly an airplane into the Twin Towers. Does that make them happy? No. Why do they do it? That is something we have to face. (El Hamus 2007)

In his adaptation, van Oel made several changes to communicate these ideas. While they might seem profound from an Anglophone perspective, to van Oel they were minor touches (Oel 2020). Act 5 was cut, as was the plot involving Portia's suitors, which, van Oel argued, would have been a distraction, 'because [he] wanted to focus on the unjust treatment of the immigrant' (Oel 2020). With the removal of Belmont, Morocco and Arragon, 'the conflict between . . . [Rafi] and his environment [became] central' and the production conveyed 'the pain of the newcomer', the isolation of 'the Arab who was misunderstood' (Adriaanse 2020). The set supported this stark vision: a couple of chairs and tables, with a scaffolding in the background, created a sinister atmosphere. The use of a dark scrim enabled the audience to see characters eavesdropping on each other and conveyed a pervasive atmosphere of suspicion between the different groups. The actors were dressed in black, some of them wearing long, leather trench coats, which added to the general sense of gloom.

The production closed with the heavily adapted trial scene where Shakespeare appeared as a character on trial. Dressed in a way which clearly identified him as the author, bearing close resemblance to the Cobbe portrait, with his lace ruff, moustache and trimmed beard, he came across as a slightly comic figure, out of his depth, unable to deal with a virulent and persistent hatred, for which he was supposedly partly to blame. In a moment of rare unanimity, the actors sat down on the chairs, turned to the audience and, breaking the fourth wall, launched into a devastating attack on Shakespeare for creating a Jew who was such an easy vehicle for anti-Semitic propaganda:

> The anti-Semitic start-up capital from which you draw interest! A Shylock such as this would sell like hot cakes, William, and you knew it. No, probably you never spoke to a Jew. They had been driven out of England for centuries, no, you didn't do it out of malice, if only you did, then you'd have revealed yourself honestly, like I do. No, you trampled me thoughtlessly, the power of habit, your 'art' stems from a cesspool. (Oel 2007: 57)

Another addition to the final scene was based on observations of the award-winning British journalist, Robert Fisk, a veteran Middle East correspondent, with whom van Oel had discussed the region's ethnic and religious divisions. In the production, this was translated to the Dutch multicultural context and the way Amsterdam is divided into Muslim and non-Muslim enclaves. By interconnecting Rafi's Jewish and Arab identities, the production made three major points. First, in line with the general performance history of *The Merchant of Venice* in the Netherlands after the Second World War, it offered a critique of anti-Semitism. It then employed Shakespeare and the Dutch sense of revulsion against anti-Semitism to address discrimination against Muslim immigrants, by drawing a parallel between what had happened to Jews and what was happening to Muslims. In doing so, *The Arab of Amsterdam* presented a fierce defence of tolerance, particularly regarding Muslim immigrants, in the troubled context of the early 2000s. The result was a sledgehammer adaptation, rather than a nuanced one, which was echoed in El Hamus's comment on the production:

> We chose a frontal confrontation, just as it is happening today in the Netherlands. We pulled out all the stops to confront others with hatred. Bluntness seems to be the order of the day. Our production needed to make a brutal statement. (El Hamus 2007)

The production was very well received by critics and audiences alike. It was seen as a timely and relevant 'denunciation of the increasingly vehement political and social climate in the Netherlands' (Jong 2007) and as a 'masterly orchestrated commentary on racism' (Zonneveld 2007). Although Dutch reception of the *Merchant* is generally critical, using terms such as 'Shakespeare's blackest comedy' (Embrechts 2007) or the 'anti-Semitic culmination of Western play-writing' (Heuven 2007), this adaptation was seen as resolving these problems and expanding the play's potential for critiquing anti-Semitism to embrace other forms of othering. The changes made to the text, the introduction of Rafi and Shakespeare, the topicality of this production, were generally praised. This Dutch adaptation of *The Merchant of Venice* was a powerful plea for tolerance within a multicultural context through its use of the Rafi/Shylock transposition to critique anti-Semitism, xenophobia and anti-Muslim sentiment. In this it contrasted with the two previous *Merchants* staged in the Netherlands, by the Amsterdam Theatre Company in 2002 and Delfts Toneelgezelschap in 2004, which had presented Shylock as a sympathetic outsider (Janssen 2002; Kleef 2004). Rather than address topical events in the manner of this production, they had emphasized the comedic elements of the play. Nevertheless, even though *The Arab of Amsterdam* deconstructed Shylock to construct Rafi, it conformed with the traditional Dutch apologetic approach to Shylocks, by making Rafi a dignified and sympathetic character, worthy of respect and understanding, rather than a more ambiguous figure.

At the end of the production, after Rafi had countered Portia's arguments against cutting the pound of flesh, he used a welder to heat the blade, in order to avoid the drop of blood. However, he did not use it, not because he was forced to stop, but out of his own choice. Although his final words were about mercy, they also demonstrated the difficulty of reconciliation and the perpetuation of a deep chasm: 'Look at me, Antonio . . . Rafi is your friend now, you have to be grateful. I am not the Shylock Shakespeare made, Rafi is my name. I show you my meekness, and you will hate me for it' (Oel 2007: 62). The closing lines were spoken by Jessica and Rafi, who cited Shakespeare's Sonnet 1 ('From fairest creatures we desire increase'), thus ending on a quiet, tentative note of hope while still leaving the audience aware of the negative climate around the theatre.

Epilogue

The two productions discussed here were influenced by tragic events which changed and polarized Dutch society. Both stood in defence of tolerance and multiculturalism, denounced xenophobia and populism, and presented the Other in a sympathetic and understanding light. However, the change of approach was less profound than might have been expected. In

Othello, although the Other was linked to radicalized Muslims, the connection was tenuous and the production focused more on a generalized outsider and a sense of isolation which embraced all the characters in the play. It hovered uneasily between the personal and political, while its reception focused mostly on the former, on the universal emotional appeal of love, jealousy and betrayal. *The Arab of Amsterdam* was more focused and direct in relating the Other to the specific Dutch context of discriminated Muslims. Although both productions were responses to the murder of van Gogh, with whom some of their members had had close personal and professional connections, they did so in ways that may not have pleased him. In conversation, van Oel agreed that van Gogh might have derided all this as 'subsidized immigrant theatre' (Oel 2020). The productions played 'safe' in criticizing Dutch populism and xenophobia, and in choosing the moral high ground of the tolerant 'us' versus the critics of multiculturalism. This approach inevitably left little room for self-scrutiny, the absence of which dogs the Dutch performance history of *Othello* and *Merchant*, by largely avoiding the exploration of sensitive issues. The Dutch have yet to come to terms with their colonial history, their complicity in the deportation of Jews, the tensions between Jews and Muslims in the Netherlands, and with pervasive institutional racism. But then again, perhaps that would have been too much in this tumultuous timeframe. After all, a society can only endure so much, or can it? And perhaps there are limits to what Shakespeare can possibly deliver.

Notes

1 Unless otherwise specified, all translations are mine.

2 On *Othello* in Germany, see Chapter 10 in this volume (Bettina Boecker).

3 Van Oel considered that Rafi, as a student of English, would have known *Out of Africa*. John Gross also refers to this story (1992:

231–2) in his discussion of the cultural differences that underlie responses to fiction.

References

06/05 (2004), [Film] Dir. Theo van Gogh, Netherlands: Column Productions.
'Actuele *Othello* van Thijs Römer' [Topical *Othello* by Thijs Römer] (2006), *De Telegraaf*, 17 October.
Adriaanse, A. (2020), personal interview, 27 February.
Cool! (2004), [Film] Dir. Theo van Gogh, Netherlands: Column Productions.
Dercksen, L. (2006), 'Romantische *Othello* zindert niet' [Romantic *Othello* does not buzz], *8Weekly*, 4 November.
Doesburg, J. (2020), personal interview, 28 February.
Doolaard, C. B. (1959), '*De Koopman van Venetië*: Onderhoudende opvoering rond gave Shylock van Steenbergen' [*The Merchant of Venice*: Entertaining production around flawless Shylock by Steenbergen], *De Tijd*, 8 January.
El Hamus, S. S. (2007), qtd in N. de Boer, 'Sabri Saad El Hamus. Hier kan ik zijn wie ik wilde zijn' [Sabri Saad El Hamus. Here I can be who I want to be], *Nico De Boer Teksten*, October.
Embrechts, A. (2007), 'Shakespeare in een Falaffelimperium' [Shakespeare in a shawarma empire], *Volkskrant*, 23 October.
Entzinger, H. (2004), in A. Evans-Pritchard, 'Exodus as Dutch Middle Class Seek New Life', *The Daily Telegraph*, 11 December 2004.
Fassbinder, R. W. ([1975] 1998), *Der Müll, die Stadt und der Tod* [Garbage, the city and death], Frankfurt am Main: Verlag der Autoren.
Freriks, K. (2006), 'Zaal medeplichtig aan Othello's moord' [Audience complicit in Othello's murder], *NRC Handelsblad*, 30 October.
Gross, J. (1992), *Shylock: Four Hundred Years in the Life of a Legend*, London: Chatto and Windus.
'Hedendaagse *Othello* in smetteloze voorstelling. Voortreffelijke regie van Bob de Lange' [Contemporary *Othello* in spotless production. Excellent work by Bob de Lange] (1964), *Algemeen Handelsblad*, 2 March.

Heijden, C. van der (2017), 'Vijftien jaar na de moord op Pim Fortuyn. Dat zeg je niet!' [Fifteen years after the murder of Pim Fortuyn. You don't speak of these things!], *De Groene Amsterdammer*, 3 May: 18.

Heijes, C. (2001), *Met Andere Ogen. Wonen en Werken in Multicultureel Nederland* [Through Other Eyes. Living and Working in the Multicultural Netherlands], The Hague: Sdu Uitgevers.

Heijes, C. (2011), 'Diversity Management in the Public Sector: Moving from Hobbyism toward Integration', *Public Personnel Management*, 40 (4): 309–26.

Heuven, R. van (2007), '*De Arabier van Amsterdam*' [*The Arab of Amsterdam*], *Dagblad De Pers*, 22 October.

Jager, G. (2006), 'Een jonge Othello met oude boodschap' [A young Othello with an old message], *Leeuwarder Courant*, 8 November.

Janssen, H. (2002), 'Mafaalani, een diamant met scherpe kantjes' [Mafaalani, a diamond with sharp edges], *Volkskrant*, 26 March.

Jong, S. de (2007), '*Arabier van Amsterdam* geeft te denken' [*Arab of Amsterdam* is food for thought], *De Gelderlander*, 20 October.

Kleef, A. van (2004), 'Verrukkelijke *Koopman van Venetië* van DTG' [Delightful *Merchant of Venice* by DTG], *Delftsche Courant*, 25 March.

Koning, D. (1959), 'De Haagsche Comedie: *De Koopman van Venetië*' [The Haagsche Comedie: *The Merchant of Venice*], *Haarlems Dagblad*, 8 January.

Medea (2005), [TV series] Dir. Theo van Gogh, Netherlands: AVRO.

Mesu, C. (2006), 'Spiegels en scherven' [Mirrors and broken parts], in *Program Notes Othello*, 8–10, The Hague: Nationale Theater.

Moose minirecensies (2006), *Othello Het Nationale Toneel*. Available online: www.moose.nl/minirecensies/othello-het-nationale-toneel-stichting-annette-speelt/index.html (accessed 2 April 2021).

Najib en Julia (2003), [TV series] Dir. Theo van Gogh, Netherlands: AVRO.

Oel, J. van (2007), *De Arabier van Amsterdam* [*The Arab of Amsterdam*], Amsterdam: DNA.

Oel, J. van (2020), Personal interview, 26 February.

Olie, D. (2004), *Onderzoek naar Betekenisgeving aan de Multiculturele Televisieserie Najib en Julia* [Research into the

meaning of the multicultural television series *Najib and Julia*], Amsterdam: University of Amsterdam.
'*Othello* in de Stadsschouwburg' [*Othello* in the Municipal Theatre] (1964), *Algemeen Handelsblad*, 11 March.
Prins, B. and S. Saharso (2008), 'In the Spotlight: A Blessing and a Curse for Immigrant Women in the Netherlands', *Ethnicities*, 8 (3): 365–84.
Schaap, W. (2006), 'Ondergang door stormachtige liefde' [Downfall by violent love affair], *De Stentor/Gelders Dagblad*, 15 September.
Schuhmacher, P. (1987), *De Minderheden. 700,000 Migranten Minder Gelijk* [The minorities. 700,000 migrants less equal], Amsterdam: Uitgeverij van Gennep.
Sluysmans, M. (2006a), in M. Landeweer, 'Met frisse blik Shakespeare tegemoet' [Facing Shakespeare through fresh eyes], *Algemeen Dagblad/Haagse Courant*, 27 October.
Sluysmans, M. (2006b), 'Hunkeren' [Yearning], in *Program Notes Othello*, 5, The Hague: Nationale Theater.
Submission, Part One (2004), [Film] Dir. Theo van Gogh, Netherlands: Column Productions.
Takken, W. (2006), 'Bovenal een verliefde soldaat. Acteur Thijs Römer over zijn vertolking van Othello' [Above all a soldier in love. Actor Thijs Römer on his interpretation of Othello], *NRC Handelsblad*, 27 October.
Tinnemans, W. (1994), *Een Gouden Armband. Een Geschiedenis van Mediterrane Immigranten in Nederland 1954–1994* [A golden bracelet: A history of Mediterranean immigrants in the Netherlands 1954–1994], Utrecht: Nederlands Centrum Buitenlanders.
Veraart, K. (2006), 'Innemende *Othello* van Doesburg' [Engaging *Othello* by Doesburg], *Volkskrant*, 30 October.
Verheul, J. (2009), '"How could this have happened in Holland?" American Perceptions of Dutch Multiculturalism after 9/11', in D. Rubin and J. Verheul (eds), *American Multiculturalism after 9/11: Transatlantic Perspectives*, 191–206, Amsterdam: Amsterdam University Press.
Zonneveld, L. (2007), 'Een Pond Vlees. *De Arabier van Amsterdam*' [A pound of flesh. *The Arab of Amsterdam*], *De Groene Amsterdammer*, 26 October.

9

'Were I the Moor, I would not be Iago'

Radical empathy in two Portuguese performances of *Othello*

Francesca Rayner

Empathetic engagements

In his chapter on the improvisation of power in *Renaissance Self-Fashioning*, Stephen Greenblatt takes issue with sociologist Daniel Lerner's claim that the global spread of empathy is accelerating. For Greenblatt, such universalizing assertions hide the workings of power that determine the conditions in which empathy occurs. In a challenge to such decontextualized understandings of empathy, Greenblatt devotes the rest of the chapter to an analysis of *Othello* which illustrates that 'what

Professor Lerner calls "empathy", Shakespeare calls "Iago"' (1980: 225).

Greenblatt's reminder of the more sinister implications of putting oneself in the place of the Other is an important one and opens up a distinction between empathy and sympathy. As Martha Nussbaum has argued, 'a malevolent person who imagines the situation of another and takes pleasure in her distress may be empathetic, but will surely not be judged as sympathetic. Sympathy, like compassion, includes a judgement that the other person's distress is bad' (2003: 302). Yet even this distinction constructs both empathy and sympathy as essentially individual attributes and sidesteps Greenblatt's insight that empathy operates within particular regimes of power.

Greenblatt notes that '[t]here are periods and cultures in which the ability to insert oneself into the consciousness of another is of relatively slight importance, the object of limited concern; others in which it is a major preoccupation, the object of cultivation and fear' (1980: 227). In the last few years, authoritarian leaders such as Donald Trump and Jair Bolsonaro, and populists like Nigel Farage, Marine le Pen and Matteo Salvini have constructed forms of empathy with their supporters based on supposedly anti-elitist politics which, Iago-like, obscure the accumulation of wealth and power by global financial elites. They have adopted strategies that recall Iago, such as the mobilization of calculated stereotypes of immigrants and immigration that deflect feelings of discontent and anxiety onto others in times of crisis and promote nationalist sentiment. At the same time, such strategies actively discourage empathy with immigrants, the poor, ecological activists, Mexicans, Muslims, women and LGBTQI activists, who are denigrated as 'losers' or non-citizens. Some European countries, such as Portugal, have continued to criticize the use of such stereotypes and to reaffirm the need for a humanitarian European response to refugees and immigrants, while the Covid-19 pandemic, in 2020, seems to have instituted a temporary lull in the direct use of such strategies within

Europe. Yet, the measures adopted during the pandemic have shown that those who are already in precarious economic and social positions continue to suffer disproportionately, whether the elderly and the poor in several European countries or the African American community in the USA. Moreover, the economic crisis that has come in the wake of the pandemic may well intensify once more these opportunistic discourses of directed hate. In such a context, outlining the basis for a more radical form of empathy based on collective struggles for social and political justice, rather than forms of individual empathy or sympathy constructed within the parameters of the status quo or a return to normality, constitutes a necessary act of political solidarity with those considered undeserving of either empathy or sympathy.

Cultural theorist Carolyn Pedwell's *Affective Relations: The Transnational Politics of Empathy* is an excellent attempt to think through the limitations and radical possibilities of empathy. Deliberately reading empathy against the grain, Pedwell argues that this 'might allow us to move away from visions of empathetic politics animated by neoliberal and neoimperial logics towards empathetic engagements which actively promote a collective commitment to social and political justice' (2014: xiv). She acknowledges that 'there is no necessary or straightforward link between the generation of empathy and the achievement of transnational social justice'. She also suggests that 'empathetic engagement can distance as much as it connects, exclude as much as it humanizes, fix as much as it transforms and oppress as much as it frees'; she does, however, envisage a more radical form of empathy created around 'the possibility of embodied *relationality and connection* that it [empathy] offers' (2014: 190).

This chapter explores the possibilities of radical empathy in two Portuguese performances of *Othello* from the twenty-first century. The first took place in 2007, one year before the international financial crisis that led to several years of austerity measures in Portugal and elsewhere in Europe. It was directed by Nuno M. Cardoso and performed at Porto's Teatro Nacional São João (TNSJ), Portugal's second national theatre. It followed a series of international performances of the play at this theatre, including a 2001 performance by the Lithuanian company Meno Fortas, directed by Eimuntas Nekrošius, a 2004 visit by Cheek by Jowl, directed by Declan Donnellan, and a 2006 performance by the Brazilian company Folias d'Arte, directed by Marco António Rodrigues. The second performance, directed by Nuno Carinhas at the same theatre in 2018, took place at a quite different European moment marked by the closing of national borders, an increase in populist nationalism and the mobilization of anti-immigrant and anti-refugee sentiments for political gain. It was the only performance of the play at the theatre during this period and the choice of the play was clearly influenced by the increase in anti-refugee sentiment in Europe.

Both productions had strong Iagos, performed by Nuno Cardoso (2007) and Dinarte Branco (2018) respectively.[1] Iago's textual dominance complicates empathetic engagement with the play's other characters. As Michael Goldman has observed, *Othello* is a difficult play to perform successfully because of the 'jeopardizing of our [the audience's] regard for the tragic and our temptation to affiliate ourselves emotionally and philosophically with the villain' (1985: 46). Iago is given the opportunity to address the audience directly through his soliloquies and the audience tends therefore to see events from his perspective. Such processes of identification make it harder to disengage from the racist, sexist views espoused by Iago. This chapter explores whether it might be possible to construct forms of radical empathy in performance that work against such an affiliation with Iago and his normative gender and racial politics, or whether the current political environment tends to reinforce such politics in performance. Radical empathy is understood here as a process of disidentification with gender and racial stereotypes, underpinned by a sense that such stereotypes demand artistic and political transformation.

The winter of our discontent: Nuno M. Cardoso's 2007 *Othello*

Both *Othello* productions discussed here suggest that the performance that took place in the theatre was shadowed by a potentially more radical one, which it hinted at, but which did not materialize. The reasons for this were varied, but instrumental in limiting the potential for radical empathy.

Cardoso's 2007 production was one of the highlights of the theatre's season, but it attracted few reviews. In the *Diário de Notícias* newspaper, Miguel-Pedro Quadrio was critical of the production. He argued that the problem was 'an insurmountable mismatch between a text which breathes and signifies only in the changes made to it, and the well-intentioned performance which it suffocates' (Quadrio 2007: 38).[2] The director used a nineteenth-century translation by the Portuguese king, D. Luís de Bragança, D. Luís I (1861–89),[3] which was substantially cut and reshaped. Its archaic feel contrasted with the contemporaneity of the setting, the costumes and the lighting, to create the mismatch Quadrio correctly identified. He also suggested that the director sought to interrogate the melodramatic elements of the play in the light of the contemporary desire for frank communication. Indeed, the director's comments in publicity material stressed that rather than being about jealousy, this was 'a tragedy of communication', of 'its failure, absence and distortion', ranging 'from the manipulation of information to lying, omission and deliberate misleading' (2007). *Othello* as a tragedy of failed communication was an innovative attempt to move understanding of the play away from individual characters and towards social networks of information and communication.

Eschewing readings of the play which concentrate on the heat of passion, Paulo Capelo Cardoso's scenography and Nuno Meira's lighting were characterized by coldness. A large ice cube at the back of the stage melted throughout the course of the play, emphasizing the passing of time and the impossibility of turning back the unfolding tragedy. A small white platform was positioned in the centre of the stage in front of an abstract, inverted 'forest' made up of thin pieces of wood hanging from the ceiling, which resembled icicles when lit by bright, white light. For the director, this was ice that could burn, a stage metaphor for Iago's cold rationality and its effect on those around him. By stressing the calculating side of Iago's character, Nuno M. Cardoso suggested that 'passion and jealousy . . . usually associated with heat . . . [are] created in the mind' (qtd in Rosado 2007: 29), thus disengaging *Othello* from a Portuguese tradition of melodramatic performance stretching back to the nineteenth century. By locating the tragedy in an environment that emphasized the rational calculation of the white manipulator rather than the exaggerated passion of the Moor Othello as the catalyst for the tragedy, the production created a world which challenged Iago's racist construction of Othello as responsible for his own tragedy.

Born in Equatorial Guinea to parents from S. Tomé and Principe, then educated in Cuba before enrolling in the Chapitó circus school in Lisbon, Ângelo Torres (Othello) had a parallel career as a professional storyteller, an interesting biographical detail considering Othello's tendency to narrate his life history as a form of self-defence. Torres's background in an oral tradition helped him create an Othello based on the rhetorical power of the spoken word. For some in the audience, his distinctive speech patterns might have been read negatively, as 'non-Portuguese' or 'non-Shakespeare'. Others would have responded to the rhetorical qualities of Torres's verse speaking as a positive mark of difference. As Marianne Novy notes, 'the importance of empathy and its related quality sympathy in literary and dramatic response differs for different people, and this makes for different experiences' (2013: 118). In this context, different views of Portugal's colonial past and post-colonial present would have influenced audience responses to the differences within spoken Portuguese that Torres's performance highlighted. While some in the audience may have constructed forms of radical empathy based on positive valuations of linguistic and cultural difference, others may have empathized or even sympathized with Othello's predicament while judging his performative difference in less positive terms.

The actress Rita Loureiro (Desdemona) compared her part to a musical score constructed around the spoken word. Conceptualizing individual roles in terms of musical scores potentially enabled each character to construct a more egalitarian position for themselves within the ensemble and the world of the play. Desdemona, for instance, was represented as a modern woman. The costume designer, Carlota Lagido, dressed her in trousers and boots, while the director wanted her murder performed not in her bed but at the front of the stage.[4] Nevertheless, despite this expressed desire to create a woman who did not conform to conventional gender stereotypes, this radical potential was undercut by both the gender ideology of the text and the performance itself. Novy has pointed out that 'at some point every woman in this play will be called a whore by the man closest to her' (2013: 104); in addition, in the performance, the actress was consistently marginalized physically by the actors playing Iago and Othello. In an interview, Loureiro explained that she had consulted a doctor during rehearsals after feeling physically ill (Loureiro 2019). She connected this with playing Desdemona and, in particular, with the difficulties of her last scene where, alone at the front of the stage, she spoke her final words while Othello approached from behind to murder her. This extraordinary report of a link between the real-life, physical experiences of an actor and the condition of the character she performs is an important reminder of the verbal/physical violence and isolation that characterize Desdemona's experience after leaving for Cyprus. Her condition is so painful that it can take its toll on contemporary actresses for whom ideologies of gender submission and obedience or gender violence are repugnant.

The production's emphasis on the spoken word meant that there was less attention to stage movement or relationships. This created a rather static performance and reinforced Iago's dominance. Nuno Cardoso was taller than the other performers and more often centre stage, which gave him two immediate advantages. He was the best-known performer and the one who attracted the most laughs from the audience, who were invited to enjoy his manipulation of other characters. After the scene with the drunk Cassio, when he exclaimed 'And what's he then that says I play the villain?' (*Oth* 2.3.331), there were predictable laughs.[5] However, when he suggested to Othello the justice of strangling Desdemona in her bed rather than poisoning her (4.1.204–5), some members of the audience also laughed. Similarly, when Desdemona appealed to Othello to kill her the next day, rather than that night (5.2.79), this, bizarrely, also produced laughter. Much of this laughter resulted from Cardoso's obvious playing-up of the performativity of the role. It could also have been prompted by Iago's accessible language and the audience's relief at understanding these parts of Shakespeare. Stereotypical villains are a staple of Portuguese and Brazilian television soaps or *telenovelas*, a more contemporary form of melodrama, and thus recognizable because rooted in local culture. However, the consistent empathy for Iago's sexist remarks, and attendant lack of empathy for Desdemona's predicament as a woman in danger of losing her life, warrant some consideration.

The director claimed explicitly that he wanted to avoid political readings. He told Ana Sofia Rosado of the *Primeiro de Janeiro* newspaper that he 'swapped all the political charge of the first act for a detailed study of a Venetian character like Roderigo and centred the second act on Cassio' (2007: 29). This concentration on Roderigo, to the exclusion of the racial and sexual politics of Act 1, which was cut completely, and on Cassio, rather than Desdemona or Othello, seemed wilfully perverse. Perhaps Cardoso felt that the racial politics of Act 1, in particular Iago and Brabantio's racial slurs, would be unacceptable to contemporary audiences and should therefore be cut. It is debatable, however, whether simply removing the parts of the play that might cause offence would encourage an anti-racist perspective. On the contrary, it tended to make Othello's vulnerability to Iago almost incomprehensible.

Moreover, although Cardoso wished to make Emilia (Sara Barbosa) the conscience of the play, there was little sign of this apart from her final textual denunciation of Othello and Iago. Most of the time, she simply followed Desdemona around the stage like a mournful shadow. She was constantly bullied by Iago and seemed almost pleased when Desdemona began to lose favour with Othello. Her bitter comment that men vomited out women when they no longer needed them was followed by her world-weary monologue about inequality (4.3.83–102), which did manage to raise some laughs from the audience in an uncomfortable moment of empathy. However, Cardoso's deliberately non-political reading meant that the gender and racial politics were left unexamined, despite his attempts to create a context and a vision of Othello and Desdemona that might encourage a more radical empathy from twenty-first-century audiences.

A performance elsewhere: Nuno Carinhas's 2018 *Othello*

Miguel Ramalhete Gomes's article 'A Day in Aleppo', in the programme of Nuno Carinhas's 2018 production of *Othello*, concentrated on parallels between Othello's precarious position in Venice and that of the many refugees from war-torn or pauperized countries who have travelled to Europe over the past decade. Ramalhete Gomes notes in relation to Othello that '[i]t is typical of Shakespeare to force us to contemplate tragic figures for whom there might be less empathy rather than the easy image of the refugee with the baby on their back' (2018: 64). His presentist essay mentions empathy three times, suggesting the political saliency of the term in the current period and for contemporary discussions of *Othello*.

Unlike Cardoso's *Othello* and all major post-revolutionary performances of the play in Portugal, the actor playing the role in this production (João Cardoso) was white. Crucially, he resembled the white actor playing Iago (Dinarte Branco), as both were bald and stocky. The only visual sign of their difference was Iago's moustache, a somewhat ironic statement on difference. In comments made to Queirós for the *Público* newspaper, Carinhas said that 'the physical resemblance between the two actors' made 'irrefutable' a reading of the two as doubles (2018: 29). Such casting, which emphasized the similarities rather than the differences between Iago and Othello, rendered the racist comments of Iago, Brabantio and the Duke frankly unreliable, although somewhat confusing, as they were directed at an obviously white actor.

In a conversation included in the production programme, Carinhas explained this casting decision, which the translator Daniel Jonas believed would be controversial:[6]

> There is no way I would want to see a black man kill a white woman onstage at this moment . . . I accept the view of Othello as the other, the one who's different, homeless, who comes from another place to a white continent. *Politically, what really interests me is to interrogate this white continent . . . These questions interest me more than skin colour.* (2018: 52, my emphasis)

Carinhas's comment conflates sensitivity about portraying refugees and immigrants as killers of white European women with theatrical arguments around the greater representation of black performers on a national theatre stage. The 'white continent', that appears to be Europe, has long since ceased to exist after successive waves of immigration and second- and third-generation children born in the countries of Europe. Portugal itself has seen several waves of migration from its former African colonies of Mozambique, Angola, São Tomé e Principe and Cape Verde since 1975, as well as, more recently, from Brazil under Bolsonaro. Moreover, the idea that performance would 'interrogate' this 'white' continent was not borne out. The all-white cast functioned instead to naturalize whiteness as the racial marker that needs no explanation or justification. As Lisa Young suggests, '[p]art of the success of "Whiteness" is that most of the time it does not appear to exist at all' (qtd in Hall 1995: 171).

This is not to suggest that a white Othello cannot examine critically questions of race. In his analysis of Portuguese writings on Africa from the medieval to the early modern period, the historian Josiah Blackmore proposes a view of whiteness and blackness as a continuum rather than a binary opposition. He argues that:

> Whiteness or lightness appears in Portuguese writings on Africa, but it is important to note that it is not only a European trait but an African one as well. Whiteness, like blackness, is a relative, rather than absolute characteristic.... And, it is important to note that Iberian whiteness is not necessarily English or French whiteness. The sexual unions and marriages between Portuguese and Africans during the centuries of colonization produced varied forms of whiteness (as did the unions between Iberians and Moors since the eighth century), and to invoke a white/black binary distinction is often an idealizing gesture. (2009: 24)[7]

Blackmore adds that '[b]lackness . . . proved a "slippery concept" for dark-skinned Portuguese' in their attempts to impose absolute distinctions between black and white. As such, rather than naturalizing whiteness, the production might have emphasized instead this uneasy separation between black and white and the ways in which Iago manipulates distinctions within whiteness itself in explicitly racist terms.[8]

While the notion that the production would interrogate the construction of whiteness seemed notably absent, an interesting faultline emerged around the question of gender roles and domestic violence. Domestic violence is a huge problem in Portugal and several controversial legal judgements have hit the headlines in recent years. In one, a judge considered the woman's adultery to be a mitigating factor in her murder and quoted the Bible to back up his judgement. In another, a woman with an independent income was considered too 'modern' to be a victim of domestic violence. In 2019, the same judge who had quoted the Bible refused to impose house arrest on a man who had shattered his partner's eardrum. He threatened to sue all who had publicly condemned his decisions, claiming for himself a vulnerability and sensitivity that he had refused to show to the women before him in court.[9]

Maria João Pinho, the actress playing Desdemona in Carinhas's production, was keen to raise the question of domestic violence. Carinhas acknowledged this concern in the programme, noting that '[t]here are going to be actresses who are not able to deal with Othello's violence out of conviction, just as there might be . . . feminist men who don't want to be Othello' (Jonas et al. 2018: 50). The assistant director, Sara Barros Leitão, remarked that '[j]ust because the play carries the name of Shakespeare' did not mean she could forgive Othello. For her, 'he's a man who assaults women, a murderer. [The play] is about domestic violence, it's about women's liberation, not about jealousy' (2018: 51).[10] The extensive conversations around domestic violence in the publicity suggest the production took seriously the need to challenge normative construction of gender in the play.

However, such expectations were not met in performance and the concern with domestic violence remained on the margins – a shadow production ghosting the events on stage. Elements already present in the text, such as each of the women being called whores by their partners, Othello slapping Desdemona in public (*Oth* 4.1) and Emilia's speech about female equality (4.3.83–102) remained. Physical prominence was given to Emilia when she denounced Othello and Iago at the end of the play. She was placed centre stage with her back to the audience, which suggested that her denunciation of Desdemona's murder represented also the perspective of the audience. However, the potential for a feminist statement was negated by Bianca's appearance as a stereotypical prostitute and by cutting Emilia's important speech about why she stole Desdemona's handkerchief (3.3.294–303). As Novy points out, this is the only monologue by a woman in the play, so cutting it paradoxically rendered the women even more silent (2013: 28).

Turning back to the discourse around the play, I'd like to explore this absence further by focusing on a moment of the round table discussion between members of the creative team and critic Ramalhete Gomes. At one point, the translator, Daniel Jonas, remarked:

> Desdemona constantly reaches new lows for tolerance in love. At a certain point, as we stretch the limits of tolerance, we reach a point of madness, in which respect for the other and for ourselves becomes almost a test of vanity. (2018: 48)

Jonas then likened Desdemona to a nun, or to a woman involved in good works because of this supposed 'vanity', and asked why she did not respect herself. In response to the discussion that followed along very similar lines (i.e. how low can Desdemona go in her love), Ramalhete Gomes intervened. Drawing a parallel with the ways in which judges blame women victims of rape rather than their rapists, he argued that there was a need to examine the patriarchal structures of the play rather than make Desdemona's submission an individual fault of character. He pointed out that:

> We are questioning her motives and forgetting that these motives are shaped by the walls that are erected around her and that she seems unable to think beyond them. . . . Asking why she does not run away after Othello assaults her, is not to take into account the social element, her context. (2018: 50)

After this, the other participants in the discussion moved quickly away from this uncomfortable point, via Carinhas's mutterings about political correctness destroying the classics. This somewhat tense exchange illustrated the underlying unease of the production with a social and political rather than individual approach to gender violence. Indeed, the translator's comment suggested, rather disturbingly, that Desdemona is somehow responsible for her own death.[11]

Differences among the creative team also led to a largely incoherent production. The steps linking the stage and the audience space were used by the characters in the first scene to involve the audience in the play yet not in the rest of the production. The dance in Cyprus celebrating the defeat of the Turks brought onstage around ten record players for no creative reason beyond visual display. When artistic choices did work, this owed more to accident than design. The financial necessity that led to one actor playing both Brabantio and Graziano, for instance, meant that when the latter stood over Desdemona's dead body, the ghost of her now-dead father was inevitably present. While all the performances sold out and the press obediently reprinted the theatre's own press release showcasing a production that dealt with racism and domestic violence, the possibility of constructing forms of radical empathy that drew a connection between the gendered or racist premises of the play and Desdemona and Othello's deaths was notably absent.

Or was it? There was one moment that seemed to point to the possibility of just such a radical, transformative empathy. As Othello entered the bedroom to murder his wife, he lay down on the floor in a position that closely mirrored the sleeping Desdemona. In *Engaging Audiences*, Bruce McConachie outlines a cognitive approach to empathy. He considers the role of mirror neurons and describes 'the tendency to automatically mimic and synchronize facial expressions, vocalizations, postures, and movements with those of another person and, consequently, to converge emotionally' (2008: 65). This stage image, with Desdemona and Othello as mirror images of each other, raised the tantalizing possibility of Othello rejecting notions of Desdemona as the gendered Other and deciding not to murder her in a liminal moment where he feels 'pity' for the 'dangers' *she* has passed.[12] In its emphasis on physical mirroring, such a moment also resonated with Pedwell's understanding of a radical empathy in the 'possibility of embodied *relationality and connection* that it offers' (2014: 190). Additionally, taking into account the longstanding history of audience intervention in these final moments to prevent Desdemona's murder, if the audience empathize with Othello's decision not to kill Desdemona, the murder and Othello's suicide are interrupted in a way that does not position questions of gender *against* questions of race. In this case, the brief moment of radical empathy gave way to the murders and suicide that constitute the play's tragic conclusion; but it did temporarily challenge the gendered and racial inevitability of Desdemona's and Othello's deaths.

Concluding remarks

In an article for the first post-revolutionary performance of *Othello* in Portugal in 1993, Maria Helena Serôdio concluded that 'there is no place for the "Other" who is successively demonized, made fragile and repressed so that the only characters who remain onstage at the end are all men, all of them white' (1993: 45). Her intersectional approach to questions of gender and race in *Othello* seems to have fragmented in the performances of the new millennium, where gender and race have become separated or even pitted against each other. Although both productions discussed here were aware of the ways in which gender and racial stereotypes make the play problematic for contemporary audiences, they seemed unwilling to challenge such norms and to unsettle expectations about performing Shakespeare at national theatres. This led to a sense that they were shadowed by more radical performances they disavowed, but which might have made a case for the continuing relevance of Shakespeare more effectively.

One of the reasons why these performances were not successful in constructing forms of radical empathy was that neither questioned the binary that defines (by omission) white, heterosexual, Christian males as subjects and those outside this formulation as Others. Indeed, it could be argued that the artistic and critical insistence on Othello as Other and on gender and sexual 'difference' in the play no longer acts progressively in the twenty-first century, but shores up instead the very binary distinctions that ensure Iago's continued dominance in performance. And what of Iago himself, the man who thinks wives have too much power, that white women should not marry black men, the man who thinks his own merit has been passed over for an intellectual who is not even local? Is he not the type of figure who believes that Trump will make him great again? That Bolsonaro will understand his actions as a military man? That Brexit will send back the foreigners who give him orders? In these circumstances, despite the good intentions of both productions, the political balance of forces seemed to be more in favour of Iago and the kind of cynical empathy Greenblatt associates with him. In such a context, constructing forms of radical empathy in performance that acknowledge not only that the distress of Desdemona, Othello and Iago is bad, but that it also serves particular political regimes and that the tragedies that result from such distress are by no means inevitable, is both an urgent and transformative task.

Notes

1 Nuno Cardoso is no relation to Nuno M. Cardoso and the similarity of the names explains why they are known respectively as Nuno Cardoso and Nuno M. Cardoso.
2 All translations from Portuguese are my own.
3 Various twentieth-century translations of the play existed which could have been used in 2007. Yvette Centeno's translation, for instance, had been used for the Companhia de Teatro de Almada performances of the play (1993 and 2005) and might perhaps have been a better choice in this regard, although the type of substantial alterations the director made to the text might have been controversial for the translator.
4 It might also be argued that, as in performances during the dictatorship, this decision showed a preoccupation with

questions of sexual decorum in a national theatre setting rather than a desire to challenge gender norms.

5 William Shakespeare, *Othello*. All references from the play are to Shakespeare 2016.

6 To my knowledge, no review of the production even discussed this casting decision, let alone dealt with it critically.

7 Historically, Moors were often involved in the Portuguese slave trade of sub-Saharan African slaves and such complex intersections between whiteness and blackness reinforce Blackmore's argument.

8 Such a perspective is borne out by contemporary materials in other national contexts. The excellent North American *Whiteness Project* (http://whitenessproject.org), for instance, interviews young millennials in Dallas, Texas, about what it means to be white. The complexity at the heart of contemporary understandings of whiteness it reveals suggests that unpacking whiteness in *Othello* could have functioned as a way of politicizing notions of race and constructing forms of radical empathy that challenged the construction of whiteness as the unmarked, naturalized opposite of blackness.

9 The judge, Neto de Moura, was later transferred to deal with cases that did not involve domestic violence by socialist politicians concerned about the bad publicity he had generated. There were some interesting overlaps between *Othello* and media discussions of domestic violence during this time. The newspaper *Correio de Manhã* is notorious for its sensationalist reporting of so-called crimes of passion. One headline from the newspaper ran 'Man murders wife he suspects of betrayal'. However, this was not a crime story but a review of the 2018 *Othello* production. A more progressive journalistic approach to domestic violence in *Othello* appeared in an opinion column by the left-leaning Bloco de Esquerda Member of Parliament, Mariana Mortágua. Under the title 'Is *Othello* a domestic tragedy?', Mortágua dismisses the notion of the play as a domestic tragedy and positions it clearly as a political tragedy (Mortágua 2018). At the bottom of Mortágua's opinion article, there is a link to an article on domestic violence by the investigative journalist Fernanda Câncio with the title 'Othello and Desdemona in the Portuguese courts', which outlines the ways in which crimes of passion are still

considered less serious than premeditated murder under the law and are therefore punished less severely (Câncio 2018).

10 There was a somewhat moralistic discourse around whether it might be possible to 'forgive' Othello or not from both the Assistant Director Sara Barros Leitão and Maria Sequeira Mendes in her workshop on the play.

11 The fact that Carinhas had known João Cardoso for many years but was working with Maria João Pinho for the first time also inflected the onstage relationship between the two performers. According to Sara Barros Leitão, differences during the rehearsal process over personal space between Pinho and João Cardoso led to a lack of stage chemistry on stage.

12 The notion of Othello feeling 'pity' for the 'dangers' Desdemona has passed reverses the gender politics of their first encounters where it is Desdemona who feels 'pity' for the 'dangers' Othello has been exposed to as a soldier: 'She loved me for the dangers I had passed / And I loved her that she did pity them' (*Oth* 1.3.168–9).

References

Blackmore, J. (2009), *Moorings: Portuguese Expansion and the Writing of Africa*, Minneapolis: University of Minnesota Press.

Câncio, F. (2018), 'Otelo e Desdemona nos tribunais portugueses' [Othello and Desdemona in the Portuguese courts], *Diário de Notícias*, 18 April. Available online: https://www.dn.pt/portugal/otelo-e-desdemona-nos-tribunais-portugueses-9275937.html (accessed 2 April 2021).

Goldman, M. (1985), *Acting and Action in Shakespeare's Tragedies*, Princeton: Princeton University Press.

Greenblatt, S. (1980), *Renaissance Self-Fashioning: From More to Shakespeare*, Chicago: University of Chicago Press.

Hall, K. F. (1995), *Things of Darkness: Economies of Race and Gender in Early Modern England*, New York: Cornell University Press.

'Homem mata mulher por suspeita de traição' (2018), [Man murders wife he suspects of betrayal], *Correio da Manhã*, 8 October [unattributed]. Available online at: www.pt.cision.com/s/?l=1fd04331 (accessed 2 April 2021).

Jonas, D. et al. (2018), 'A Valsa Dissonante: Conversa com Daniel Jonas, Miguel Ramalhete Gomes, Nuno Carinhas, Sara Barros Leitão e Fátima Castro Silva' [The Dissonant Waltz: A conversation between Daniel Jonas, Miguel Ramalhete Gomes, Nuno Carinhas, Sara Barros Leitão and Fátima Castro Silva], in *Manual de Leitura: Otelo*, 37–52, Porto: Teatro Nacional São João.

Loureiro, R. (2019), interview with the author, 1 July.

McConachie, B. (2008), *Engaging Audiences: A Cognitive Approach to Spectating in the Theatre*, Basingstoke: Palgrave MacMillan.

Mortágua, M. (2018), 'Otelo é uma tragédia doméstica?' [Is *Othello* a domestic tragedy?], *Jornal de Notícias*, 2 October: 2.

Novy, M. (2013), *Shakespeare and Outsiders*, Oxford: Oxford University Press.

Nussbaum, M. (2003), *Upheavals of Thought: The Intelligence of Emotions*, Cambridge: Cambridge University Press.

Pedwell, C. (2014), *Affective Relations: The Transnational Politics of Empathy*, Basingstoke: Palgrave MacMillan.

Quadrio, M. P. (2007), 'Interrogar a frio os silêncios de Otelo' [Interrogate coldly the silences of Othello], *Diario de Notícias*, 21 January: 38.

Queirós, L. M. (2018), 'Otelo: quando a palavra é um veneno que devora a alma' [Othello: when the word is a poison that destroys the soul], *Público*, 3 October: 29.

Ramalhete Gomes, M. (2018), 'Um Dia em Alepo' [A day in Aleppo], in *Manual de Leitura: Otelo*, 59–66, Porto: Teatro Nacional São João.

Rosado, A. S. (2007), 'Dizer positivamente a verdade' [Speak the truth honestly], *Primeiro de Janeiro*, 9 January: 29.

Serôdio, M. H. (1993), 'A Demonização d'*o o outro* em *Othello* de Shakespeare' [The demonization of the *other* in Shakespeare's *Othello*], in *Othello* production programme: 37–46.

Shakespeare, W. (2016), *Othello*, ed. E. A. J. Honigmann, rev. edn, intr. A. Thompson, The Arden Shakespeare, third series, London: Bloomsbury.

The Whiteness Project (n.d.). Available online: http://whitenessproject.org (accessed 2 April 2021).

10

A tragedy? *Othello* and *The Merchant of Venice* in Germany during the 2015–16 refugee crisis

Bettina Boecker

The refugee crisis of 2015–16 with its largely unmonitored influx of migrants into Germany and Chancellor Angela Merkel's by now notorious 'We can handle this' ('Wir schaffen das!') caused heated and polarized public debate in Germany. In this controversy, theatres have almost unanimously sided with the government position. Many of them have made a sustained effort to contribute to the *Willkommenskultur* (culture of welcome) established in reaction to the arrival of hundreds of thousands of 'wretched strangers' (*STM* 6.85) in need of food, clothes, housing and some sort of pathway into the German host culture. The theatres' range of activities has been wide and varied, including not only professional productions of plays considered relevant to the issues raised by the sudden increase in immigration, but also forms of community theatre featuring amateur (or sometimes professional) refugee actors or social projects utilizing the theatre as a public space. This has not been uncontroversial. Latvian director Alvis Hermanis, for example, cancelled a production planned at Thalia Theater Hamburg because he felt that a commitment to the culture of welcome directly or indirectly fostered terrorism on European soil. Press reactions to this decision, in turn, are an object lesson in how Germans (or, more precisely, those writing for the arts sections of major German newspapers) think of their theatres. The German daily *Der Tagesspiegel* spoke for many when it claimed that 'Hermanis betrays the consensus that theatre is pluralistic, a place of freedom and a safe space' (Schaper 2015).[1] That this consensus is not an illusion is testified by the many refugee-focused projects and initiatives launched by major houses, like Thalia Theater in Hamburg, Deutsches Theater Berlin and Kammerspiele München. This is further confirmed by numerous publications since 2015 which suggest that theatres should be aware:

> that they are *theatre* in everything they do – that their actions should always have something of the symbolic or paradigmatic about them. Whether they do it through projects, performances, guest productions or support initiatives involving refugees, they should offer society an example of welcome that is . . . disappearing from parts of the population. If theatres thus succeed in creating a lived or staged counter-model to the ideal society propounded by [far-right movements such as] *Pegida* and the *Alternative for Germany*, then that indeed does them credit. (Brandenburg 2016)

In the 2015–16 season, it was hard to avoid the impression that theatres were profiting from, perhaps even capitalizing on, the migration crisis, which put them in a position to reclaim a public relevance that had declined since German reunification in 1989–90. Theatre in the German Democratic Republic (GDR), as in many other East European countries, often worked in opposition to the communist government and is sometimes seen as instrumental in the fall of the Berlin Wall.[2] However, in spite of the influence of East German directors like Frank Castorf on the all-German theatre scene, the theatrical institution has been unable to establish a broad public relevance after 1989. At the same time, the standards and principles of West German practitioners like Peter Zadek and Peter Stein had been questioned without being replaced by a new agenda. While the anti-bourgeois impetus of West German directors like Zadek and Stein had become mainstream by the early 1990s, East German directors like Castorf seemed unable to establish an identifiable political position vis-à-vis Western capitalism. The latter seemed to have 'won' over communism, the political system they had spent large parts of their career opposing. In a sense, this put them on the same side as those now in power; a position hard to reconcile with the subversive habits cultivated during the GDR years. All this left German theatre in crisis, as diagnosed by David Ashley (Ashley 2007). That this crisis revolved also around a perceived lack of political purpose might explain why many theatres embraced the culture of welcome with such gusto and organized a plethora of paratheatrical activities aimed at helping refugees find their place in German society.

This essay investigates two Shakespeare productions from the 2015–16 season, which were planned and rehearsed before the actual refugee crisis: *Othello*, directed by Christian Weise for the Maxim Gorki Theater in Berlin, and the Munich Kammerspiele *Merchant of Venice*, directed by Nicolas Stemann. Theoretically at least, both productions spoke directly to the issues facing Germany from the summer of 2015 onwards. Staged at theatres with a particularly active role in the culture of welcome, the two productions spotlighted the tensions between how the theatres understood their role in the political process, their preferred aesthetic agenda, and the public's expectations of what theatre, and Shakespeare, should do and look like.

Othello, Maxim Gorki Theatre, Berlin, 2016

The Maxim Gorki Theatre has had a reputation for politically engaged theatre at least since the 2013–14 season, when Shermin Langhoff and Jens Hillje took over joint directorship and employed an unusually heterogeneous troupe of actors which mirrored the ethnic diversity of contemporary Germany (Kolesch 2016: 90). They went on to stage productions, many of them world premieres, in which issues of diversity, identity and inclusion were central. All this led some theatre critics to describe the company and its productions as *postmigrantisch*, 'post-migrant', a label that Langhoff refutes. However, their first production of *Othello* in February 2016 engaged with the post-migrant context through what one might call a post-colonial adaptation of Shakespeare's play by Soeren Voima.[3] This text is not, and does not aim to be, anything like a translation of Shakespeare's original play. It follows the plot only loosely, makes major alterations to the dialogue, and in some respects positions itself as a response to the work of Gayatri Spivak (Spivak 1988) – or so it would seem from the programme, which, setting the tone for the evening, asked in large letters (larger than either the title of the play or the name of its author): 'Can the subaltern speak?' Voima addresses Spivak's concern about representing the Other by modifying the character of Othello to suit twenty-first-century sensibilities about race – of which more in due course – and by adding an additional character, a chorus of Cypriots repeatedly venting their frustration with the succession of colonizers who have landed on their island. The chorus complains:

> They wage war only so that they can rebuild everything later on, they create chaos so that they can establish a new order. They hunt, they imprison, they exploit us! ... If they had not found refuge in some bay or another, their ships would have been lost, and we would have been spared both armadas,

the one from Turkey *and* the one from Venice; spared the
World Bank, free trade and economic assistance.... Give a
salute, subaltern people of Cyprus! Brighten up your brute
faces, you disorganized chorus of island existences, to greet
the Italian privateers. Free traders, I mean, free traders, not
privateers. (Voima 2016: 20ff.)

Explicit though it is, the chorus's protest is far from coherent.
It is liberally interspersed with humorous metatheatrical
gestures – the principal speaker is not satisfied with the relative
importance of his part – and with sexual and scatological
jokes. As a result, its rote-like enumeration of (post-)colonial
grievances sounded almost ironic.

By contrast, there is not the slightest hint of irony about
Othello in Voima's text. Played by Taner Sahintürk, a German
of Turkish descent, this 'Moor' (a Tunisian in Voima's
adaptation) is capable of naming and reflecting on the racism
to which he eventually falls victim, delivering long monologues
where he ruminates on race and his position as an outsider in
Venice:

Sin is dark, virtue is light, I am guilty. Yes. I don't know
why, but I know I am a vile, dismal, ridiculous creature. An
outcast. An animal.... I am connected to my alien ancestors,
my alien tribe, my alien clan. I am connected to an entire
alien continent, connected to the heart of darkness. I'm in
really deep shit. (Voima 2016: 49ff.)

Alongside Othello's self-awareness – or self-deprecation – the
text suggests a higher degree of self-control compared to that of
Shakespeare's Moor. In Voima's text, Othello does believe Iago,
and he does harbour a desire to kill Desdemona, but when Iago
charges him to actually do the deed, Othello demurs. Visually,
the production set Othello apart from the other characters in a
way that appeared to invite identification. All the other actors
were dressed in costumes in the style of *commedia dell'arte*
and heavily made up with white face paint, to appear almost

like puppets. Sahintürk, by contrast, wore almost no make-up.[4] Thus the Gorki production turned the tables on the consistent dehumanization of Othello by Shakespeare's Venetians in that only Othello appeared as fully human. As the play progressed and the 'Moor' exchanged his faux-Renaissance leather doublet for jeans, an Adidas jacket and trainers, the contrast between him and the other characters, who continued to sport their flamboyant attire, became even starker. Yet, as the production neared its end, the chorus, rather than Othello, became the focus of attention. From his final speech onwards, they moved in an increasingly synchronized, puppet-like manner: these were not individuals, this was a mob whose treatment of Othello was just as pre-scripted as the part that the Moor himself was expected to play. Heaping racist insults on him ('Barbary ape'), loudly hoping that 'at least two or three of them [blacks] will get themselves killed tonight' (Voima 2016: 71), the chorus made no effort whatsoever to conceal their racism. In the last few lines of the play, they urged him to get on with killing Desdemona because this was necessary to prove their racist prejudice 'true'. Seconds later, however, they reflected on the callousness with which they had been treating him:

> Have pity? Us? No pity for that blockhead! A human being, who, because he suffered, took a lot of things seriously: Equality. Justice. Love. Who didn't understand that he was being played games with precisely for those reasons. A human being like us, broken and mutilated. Accustomed to any form of death. And incapable of living. What do we care? What's that to us? No pity for the general of Venice. (Voima 2016: 75)

Pity was a sentiment the production had indeed worked hard to nip in the bud up to that moment – even though the chorus's admitted lack of pity might have made the audience feel for the protagonist, albeit very late in the play. Sahintürk's Othello may invite identification, but by turning Shakespeare's tragedy into farce – thus taking up a tendency some critics (Bristol

1996: 181) have attributed to the play itself – Voima's playtext largely prohibits any overly emotional response to the plight of the Moor. Anti-illusionistic features, like the clownish costumes or the cymbal and drums being sounded every time a character tumbled through the curtain onto the raked stage, appeared designed to counteract anything like empathy on the part of the audience. Most importantly, perhaps, Voima's script clearly rejects many features of Aristotelian tragedy, above all the high style traditionally associated with the genre, as is obvious from the chorus's crude joking, deliberate incoherence and short, often incomplete sentences which leave room for improvisation. Conventional ideas of tragic determination are countered by foregrounding the pre-constructed nature of ethnic prejudice which brings about (or, in this production, did not quite bring about) Othello's downfall.

In one of the most poignant moments of the production, right after Iago attempted to persuade the Moor to kill Desdemona, the 'honest' ensign painted Othello's face gold. This is how the critic Wolfgang Behrens, writing for the popular reviewing platform *Nachtkritik.de*, describes this moment:

> Iago approaches Othello with brush and paint-pot – and there is no doubt: He's going to paint him! This Othello is not black, so the Venetians need to make him black. Already the spectator's mind is reeling: Is blackfacing tolerable under these circumstances? Is it okay for the German Wodianka [the actor playing Iago] to paint the German Sahintürk [Othello] black in order to demonstrate that race is a mere construct? Hmm, difficult . . . But then, disembarrassment, salvation: It's gold. Golden paint. Gold-facing. Praise the Lord! One knew it all along: they have the right consciousness at the Gorki. (Behrens 2016)

As in earlier German Othellos,[5] which flaunted the artificiality of blackface, foregrounding the set of clichés, stereotypes and notions of racial superiority in which the convention is grounded, the scene also contributed to the ongoing debate about performing race in German theatre. In 2012, *Bühnenwatch* ('stage watch'), an initiative against racism on the German stage, intervened against a production using black make-up on (white) actors playing African migrants.[6] The debate about blackfacing has been led with renewed vigour ever since.[7] Weise's production of *Othello* for the Gorki was very much aware of this controversy, and visually presented a kind of photo-negative blackfacing by means of the white make-up everyone but Othello wore in the first half of the show. In that everyone *but* Othello was stereotyped as comical, repulsive or a mixture of both, the production also effectively reversed the codes that informed white blackface minstrelsy in the United States from the nineteenth century onwards.

The use of regional dialect was another important means of code reversal. Emilia joked in *Kölsch*, the dialect of the Cologne area, which would have comical connotations for the audience because of the region's strong carnival tradition. Roderigo spoke the Saxon dialect and turned out to be a member of Pegida, the right-wing movement that started in Dresden, the capital of Saxony. Instead of dehumanizing the Other – traditionally, Othello – the production dehumanized the Venetians, or at the very least held them up for ridicule. Reviewers Jonas Kellermann and Lukas Lammers describe Roderigo as 'a moron [whose] private parts smell, [whose] dialect, . . . constant whining and . . . thoroughly ridiculous anger are a source of constant amusement for the audience. . . . In the context of the production . . . this figure . . . is marked as exotic and alien' (Kellermann and Lammers 2017: 202). While the production was explicit in its denunciation of othering, it seemed unable to do without it: everyone but Othello seemed parodic and cheap.

Like many recent German productions of *Othello*, Weise's ended in *aporia*. We never learn whether Othello actually murdered Desdemona, and at the end, the actors addressed the audience to request an alternative playtext they might use (though one wonders what the alternative to an already alternative playtext might look like). This classically Brechtian move was a fit ending for a production that did not so much stage Shakespeare as upstage him, dismissing notions of his 'timeless relevance' in order to point towards a perceived failure to make 'the stranger's case' in a manner that spoke to today's German liberal, progressive sensitivities.

The Merchant of Venice, Kammerspiele Munich, 2015

While the Berlin *Othello* effectively disposed of the original Shakespeare text, the Munich *Merchant* turned it into an exhibit, something almost resembling a character in its own right. Director Nicolas Stemann had it projected onto large screens for the entire duration of the production, with actors often reading directly from the monitors and giving their opinions on the absurdities and injustices of Shakespeare's Venice. The audience were offered a rehearsal-in-progress, watching the actors' efforts to come to terms with the play. Less obviously, the screens could also be interpreted as a tongue-in-cheek comment on *Werktreue*, 'fidelity to the text', an idea that had played an important role on the German stage after the Second World War. 'Fidelity to the text' was supposed to counter the Nazi appropriation of canonical literary texts, *Merchant* being prominent among them. By the same token, the abolition of *Werktreue* was a decisive move in the revolt of the 1968 generation against established theatre practices, opening the way for what has since become known as German 'director's theatre'. In the context of the 2015–16 season at Kammerspiele, the screened text could also be interpreted as a nod to the particular situation that the theatre found itself in at this point. Directorship of the house had just been taken up by Matthias Lilienthal, known for his roots in the Berlin fringe scene as well as his preference for post-dramatic theatre practices over what he had once called

'Kunstkacke' (art shit). This sobriquet referred to traditional, text-centred productions that sought to create the illusion of closed fictional worlds. Lilienthal's appointment was met with considerable apprehension, both by the ensemble and the Kammerspiele audience. This theatre, some would say, had a reputation for quality character acting and a perceptive approach to classic drama. Against this backdrop, the fact that Lilienthal included a Shakespeare play in his first season could be read as a conciliatory gesture. Though ironical, the screened presence of the text was a nod to the presumed expectations of an aesthetically conservative audience.

The other defining features of the production, however, were unambiguously post-dramatic, to the extent that one reviewer described the evening as 'a private lesson for performance illiterates' (Leucht 2015). The twenty-odd roles were shared by six actors, with the partial exception of doyen Walter Hess (Shylock), and the female lead, Julia Riedler (Portia). Regarding the other parts, there was hardly any mapping of one role onto one actor. Pop songs, dances and stage fights were interspersed throughout the performance; at times actors vociferously complained about the opacity of the text, or refused outright to speak certain passages. Hassan Akkouch, an actor born in Lebanon, spoke some lines in Arabic while Shylock and Antonio were arguing during the trial scene: his were the only interventions for which neither English nor German subtitles were provided, thus doubly alienating Akkouch from Shakespeare's original text. Critics noted that Stemann's work on *Merchant* drew on techniques used in his productions of Elfriede Jelinek's post-dramatic playtexts. They thought that the success was rather mixed. If the dispersal of roles among the cast was a textbook example of how post-dramatic theatre becomes political (Lehmann 2006: 175), then his version of the trial scene took this beyond the realm of the 'merely' aesthetic into that of the explicitly stated. In one of the most notable deviations from Shakespeare's play, Shylock's 'Hath not a Jew eyes?' (*MV* 3.1.53ff.) was turned into a general complaint of the disenfranchised, though with individual variations. While the Shylock 'voice' spoke the lines in translation, other actors voiced similar grievances concerning their marginalization as Muslim, Roma or female. The scene ended with the equivalent of a WASP complaint about all that complaining: 'I am a white man, and I am fed up with all this shit'.

Not a single reviewer failed to notice the central 'message' of the production. Writing for *Nachtkritik.de*, Tim Slagman remarked: 'It is easy to understand why the characters dissolve into one another, why an essential core is being removed from them – after all, a belief in the latter is the basis for any kind of resentment and prejudice' (Slagman 2015). The overall success of the method, however, was questioned by many. The influential German weekly *Die Zeit* commented: 'This is a play about marginalization, though without an inner space from which people (who don't exist in any case) could be excluded in the first place. Shylock's famous ["Hath not a Jew eyes?"] was addressed to an empty centre by a chorus of minorities' (Kümmel 2015).

Such de-centring resonates with the reverse stereotyping in Weise's *Othello*. While Weise's way of un-othering the Stranger entails the othering of almost everyone else and promoting the Moor from the periphery to the centre, Stemann also others everyone, but altogether does away with the idea of a centre: there is no 'Us' to give substance to the Other. Ironically, both productions create situations that might come straight out of the textbook of right-wing dystopias: a host culture displaced and marginalized by the Stranger, as in the case of the Gorki production, and a host culture devoid of any defining features, at the Kammerspiele. Both are object lessons in how post-dramatic theatre approaches the political, and in particular, the issue of alterity as 'destabilizations of the authentic used to unfix stable and possibly oppressive perceptions of strangers and the unfamiliar' (Garde and Mumford 2013: 149). In the case of *Merchant* in particular, it is easy to discern how the political impetus is primarily the result of specific techniques of representation.

Fluid identities, empathy and the refugee crisis

The German refugee crisis of 2015–16 endowed both *Othello* and *The Merchant of Venice* with an unexpected topicality. Although both productions made a point regarding the fluidity and/or constructed nature of identity, and largely disenabled anything seeming like empathy with the protagonists, the wider policies of both houses spoke of a perceived need to supplement representation-as-politics with something more tangible.

Around sixty theatres participated in the culture of welcome throughout 2015 and 2016, and the Gorki as well as the Kammerspiele were certainly among the most active. The Gorki organized several festivals, funded a separate *Exil Ensemble* made up exclusively of actors who had fled from the Middle East, and offered various theatrical ventures, specifically for newcomers to Berlin. In addition, it hosted a number of migrant-led initiatives like a 'refugee café', and provided help ranging from support for obtaining visas and finding lodgings to making its workshops, tools and materials available for the construction of temporary housing. The Kammerspiele ran the Open Border Kongress in October 2015, which included talks on the refugee crisis and on how to foster a culture of welcome, led theatre projects with migrants, and organized performances by resident actors with a focus on the migration crisis. The theatre temporarily renamed itself the Munich Welcome Theatre, much to the chagrin of Bavaria's ruling conservative party. Like the Gorki, the Kammerspiele created an additional ensemble made up entirely of refugees, the Open Border Ensemble, to perform its own repertoire. The Munich Welcome Café on the theatre's premises on glittery Maximilianstraße attracted up to 500 people at one go, and offered regular 'cookery evenings' for refugees and non-refugees alike.

All these projects were very much directed at actual individuals – no fluid identities here – defined as Strangers in their current environment, and they arguably appealed very much to the fellow-feeling of those doing the welcoming, that is, they worked from completely different premises than the productions discussed earlier. In an interview with Germany's *Islamische Zeitung*, Björn Bicker, one of the main organizers of the Open Border Kongress and other similar projects in Munich, said: 'That's what we need: compassion. And that is what theatres are able to do – produce art. . . . These are human beings, like you and me. And these human beings are refugees. Therefore, I need to take care of them' (qtd in *Islamische Zeitung* 2015).

That the theatres felt compelled to cultivate such virtues in their fellow Germans was somewhat of a novelty in the autumn of 2015. Obviously, however, it was part and parcel of a long German tradition of moralizing, didactic theatre going back at least to Gotthold Ephraim Lessing's championing of empathy as the main effect drama should aim for (Lessing [1769] 2019), as well as Friedrich Schiller's treatise, 'The stage as a moral institution' (Schiller [1784] 2015). And 'institution' is indeed a key term here, as testified by the energy invested during that season by both Kammerspiele and Gorki in projects that were not 'theatre'. Asked in what sense, if any, the Refugees Welcome Café had anything to do with theatre, director Matthias Lilienthal stated:

> I couldn't care less whether it's only a social project. I would always prefer a good social project over a bad theatre project. That includes this café, about which one can indeed say, what has that to do with theatre. The moment something takes place in the theatre space, it turns into an intellectual metaphor and has its effect. Theatre, to me, is a laboratory to try out urban lifestyles, and the Kammerspiele – like many others in Munich – try to anticipate a future society in which refugees and *Münchner* [locals] live together. (Krone 2016)

Unsurprisingly, this caused outrage in some quarters; in some respects the statement is hard to beat for its presumptuous arrogance. Lilienthal and the Kammerspiele receive subsidies that are extremely generous, and he is paid to make theatre, not to engage in social work. One may also wonder whether theatre is indeed a laboratory for 'urban lifestyles', especially given that a majority of taxpayers live in rural areas, and ask to what extent the theatre has the right to teach the population how to live together in the future. What Lilienthal describes entails a massive expansion of the tasks and functions of theatres. It is easy to wax enthusiastic about the renewed social and political relevance of theatrical work, but given the extreme polarization of the political debate and the rise of the right-wing Alternative for Germany that followed the refugee crisis, it is not unproblematic for a largely state-funded institution to propound what at the time were highly controversial government policies with such gusto. More importantly perhaps, any re-claimed political relevance was arguably achieved by non-theatrical means. Wiesbaden director Michael Thalheimer offers a concise summary of why this could seem problematic:

> It has become fashionable [for theatres] to take on tasks that fall under the responsibility of other institutions. When new [theatre] directors present their programme, I frequently feel as if Amnesty International, Help for the Homeless and the United Nations Refugee Agency have together created a space in which to rehearse the future. What gets completely forgotten though is that we are talking about theatre. . . . On the one hand, these colleagues curry favour with the *Zeitgeist;* on the other, they ignore the actual tasks of the theatre. Behind all of this is a big lie. Nobody is being helped – everyone is only pretending. And then the theatres fall in love with these social projects, which are nothing but vain posturing. . . . This is the way for theatre to abolish itself. . . . Theatre must remember its archetypical task. It must remember text, ensemble, the art of acting. (Thalheimer 2015)

Thalheimer's rejection of 'social projects' at the theatre goes hand in hand with an aesthetic agenda perhaps not incorrectly described as post-post-dramatic. Another option would be simply to call it conservative, but in a theatrical landscape in which post-dramatic theatre has become 'established' (Birkner, Geier and Helduser 2014: 11), this does not necessarily do justice to a stance which from some points of view can seem distinctly avant-garde. One could argue, as Lilienthal seems to do, that even supposedly non-performative social projects are, in some way, theatre, simply because they take place in locations primarily dedicated to that purpose. That, however, would only strengthen Thalheimer's argument about the 'posing' inherent in such ventures.

Overall, the response of German theatres to the refugee crisis testifies to the decidedly political self-image of the institution as such. However, the two productions discussed in this essay highlight a profound ambivalence, even anxiety, as to what constitutes a political intervention – and whether representational means alone are enough to effect one. With regard to the two Shakespearean Strangers under discussion, I have argued that one reason for this inconclusiveness is that both theatres stage their Shakespeare in ways that largely preclude audience identification and empathy. '[T]here is something degrading in suffering and something elevating and productive of superiority in pitying', Nietzsche states in *Daybreak* (Nietzsche 2012: 139), and the two productions clearly seem to concur. At the same time, the 'culture of welcome' as practised both at the Kammerspiele and at the Gorki is unthinkable without genuine fellow-feeling, pity, empathy, compassion, whatever you call it. A certain discrepancy between the way the productions approach the Stranger on stage and the way the institutional policies of the two theatres approach the Stranger in real life is hard to overlook.

It goes without saying that both *Merchant* and *Othello* offer unique challenges when produced on the contemporary stage, especially in Germany, and it cannot come as a surprise that both productions revealed a complex, if not outright difficult relation with the source text. The Berlin production effectively rewrites *Othello*, aiming to expose the supposedly unabashed racism of Shakespeare's play. The Munich *Merchant* similarly turns the source text into an exhibit, to be dissected and ultimately condemned and discarded. Both productions highlight the intersection of the still mostly iconoclastic tendencies of much German Shakespeare, a post-dramatic production style with an anti-illusionistic, anti-identificatory bent, and institutional policies that depend on empathy and perhaps even something like identification, in their dedication to a 'culture of welcome'. It remains to be seen whether those policies, insofar as they are still extant at the time of writing (early 2020), will eventually lead to a reconsideration of currently dominant representational paradigms.

Notes

1 Unless otherwise specified, all translations are mine.
2 For a debunking of the myth – circulated especially by (West) German television – that Heiner Müller's 1990 production of *Hamlet/Maschine* was instrumental in bringing down the Berlin Wall, see Oliver (2015).
3 This is a pseudonym used by theatre practitioners Robert Schuster, Tom Kühnel and Christian Tschirner, who often work as a collective.
4 Marvin Carlson points out that given the almost-clown-like make-up of everyone else on stage, Sahintürk's lack of facial make-up makes his 'the only visage on stage which can be read as conventionally "white"' (Carlson 2016).
5 Blackfacing was a central feature in Peter Zadek's notorious 1976 *Othello* at Schauspielhaus Hamburg. Ulrich Wildgruber presented Shakespeare's Moor as an almost ape-like savage, with the black paint on his face rubbing off on a white-clad or mostly naked Desdemona (Eva Matthes) over the course of the production. By flaunting the artificiality of blackface, the production also foregrounded precisely the set of clichés, stereotypes and notions of racial superiority in which the convention is grounded.

Thomas Ostermeier's 2010 *Othello* for the Epidauros Festival, later transferred to Berlin's Schaubühne, seems to have used the convention in some versions of the production – for example, the one brought to France (Sceaux) in 2011. Unlike Zadek, however, Ostermeier focused less on the victim (Othello) than on Iago as the perpetrator. In a move that provides an interesting contrast to the golden face paint used at the Gorki, Ostermeier's Othello has the Moor blackfaced by Iago and Desdemona at the very beginning of the show (Darge 2011).

6 Michael Thalheimer's production of Dea Loher's *Unschuld* [Innocence] at Deutsches Theater Berlin.

7 Notably, the Gorki's dramaturge for the 2015 *Othello*, Joy Kristin Kalu, has been a high-profile contributor to this debate.

References

Ashley, D. (2007), 'Notes on the German Theatre Crisis', *The Drama Review*, 51: 133–55.

Behrens, W. (2016), 'Sieh da, ein Mensch!' [Look, a human being!], *Nachtkritik.de*. Available online: http://www.nachtkritik.de/index.php?option=com_content&view=article&id=12161 (accessed 2 April 2021).

Birkner, N., A. Geier and U. Helduser (2014), 'Geschlecht und Alterität im postdramatischen Theater: Zur Einführung' [Gender and alterity in postdramatic theatre: an introduction], in N. Birkner, A. Geier and U. Helduser (eds), *Spielräume des Anderen. Geschlecht und Alterität im postdramatischen Theater*, 9–20, Bielefeld: transcript.

Brandenburg, D. (2016), 'Symbolisch handeln!' [Act symbolically!], *Die deutsche Bühne*, 5: 3. Available online: http://www.die-deutsche-buehne.de/sites/default/files/archiv/files/03_DDB_2016_005-Editorial.pdf (accessed 2 April 2021).

Bristol, M. (1996), *Big-time Shakespeare*, London: Routledge.

Carlson, M. (2016), 'Some Quadricentennial Shakespeare in Germany', *European Stages*, 7. Available online: http://europeanstages.org/2016/10/19/some-quadricentennial-shakespeare-in-germany (accessed 2 April 2021).

Darge, F. (2011), 'L'*Othello* sauvage de Thomas Ostermeier' [Thomas Ostermeier's wild *Othello*], *Le Monde*, 21 March. Available online: https://www.lemonde.fr/culture/article/2011/03/21/l-othello-sauvage-de-thomas-ostermeier_1496312_3246.html (accessed 2 April 2021).

Garde, U. and M. Mumford (2013), 'Postdramatic Reality Theatre and Productive Insecurity: Destabilising Encounters with the Unfamiliar in Theatre from Sydney and Berlin', in K. Jürs-Munby, J. Carroll and S. Giles (eds), *Postdramatic Theatre and the Political*, 147–64, London: Bloomsbury.

Islamische Zeitung (2015), 'Interview mit Björn Bicker über den ersten OPEN BORDER KONGRESS auf den Bühnen der Münchner Kammerspiele' [Interview with Björn Bicker on the first OPEN BORDER CONGRESS at the Munich Kammerspiele], 28 October. Available online: http://www.islamische-zeitung.de/interview-mit-bjoern-bicker-ueber-den-ersten-open-border-kongress-auf-den-buehnen-der-muenchner-kammerspiele (accessed 2 April 2021).

Kellermann, J. and L. Lammers (2017), '"I am not what I am": Versuche der (postmigrantischen) Dekonstruktion in Berlin' [Attempts at (post-migrant) deconstruction in Berlin], *Shakespeare Jahrbuch*, 153: 196–206.

Kolesch, D. (2016), 'Wie Othello spielen?' [How to play Othello?], *Shakespeare Jahrbuch*, 152: 87–103.

Krone, T. (2016), 'Refugee-Welcome-Theatre an den Münchner Kammerspielen: Große Bühne für Flüchtlinge' [Refugee-Welcome-Theatre at Munich Kammerspiele: A Grand Stage for Refugees], *Deutschlandfunk Kultur*, 16 July. Available online: http://www.deutschlandfunkkultur.de/refugee-welcome-theatre-an-den-muenchner-kammerspielen.2159.de.html?dram:article_id=360317 (accessed 2 April 2021).

Kümmel, P. (2015), 'Nein, Sie bluten nicht' [No, they don't bleed], *Die Zeit*, 15 October: n.p.

Lehmann, H.-T. (2006), *Postdramatic Theatre*, London and New York: Routledge.

Lessing, G. E. ([1769] 2019), *The Hamburg Dramaturgy by G. E. Lessing: A New and Complete Annotated English Translation*, ed. N. Baldyga, London: Routledge.

Leucht, S. (2015), 'Livecams und Tigerauge. Nachhilfe für Performance-Analphabeten und irritierende Empathie: Matthias Lilienthals Marathon-Auftakt beginnt eher mau' [Live cameras and 'The Eye of the Tiger'. Lessons for performance illiterates and irritating empathy: Matthias Lilienthal's marathon kick-off underwhelms audiences], *Taz*, 13 October. Available online: https://taz.de/Intendanz-der-Muenchner-Kammerspiele/!5237725/ (accessed 2 April 2021).

Munday, A. et al (2011), *Sir Thomas More*, ed. J. Jowett, The Arden Shakespeare, third series, London: Bloomsbury.

Nietzsche, F. (2012), *Daybreak: Thoughts on the Prejudices of Morality*, ed. M. Clark and B. Leiter, trans. R. J. Hollingdale, 2nd edn, Cambridge: Cambridge University Press.

Oliver, E. (2015), 'Shakespeare und die Wende: Heiner Müllers Hamlet/Maschine', in C. Jansohn (ed.), *Shakespeare unter den Deutschen*, 283–93, Stuttgart: Franz Steiner Verlag.

Schaper, R. (2015), 'Auf der Flucht vor Flüchtlingen' [Fleeing refugees], *Der Tagesspiegel*, 9 December. Available online: http://www.tagesspiegel.de/themen/reportage/alvis-hermanis-auf-der-flucht-vor-fluechtlingen/12696680.html (accessed 2 April 2021).

Schiller, F. ([1784] 2015), 'The Stage as a Moral Institution', in *Aesthetical and Philosophical Essays*, 487–96, Redditch: Read Books.

Shakespeare, W. (2010), *The Merchant of Venice*, ed. J. Drakakis, The Arden Shakespeare, third series, London: Bloomsbury.

Slagman, T. (2015), 'Tanz der Vampire' [Dance of the vampires], *Nachtkritik.de*, 9 October. Available online: http://www.nachtkritik.de/index.php?option=com_content&view=article&id=11616:der-kaufmann-von-venedig-nicolas-stemann-steuert-zum-intendanzauftakt-von-matthias-Lilienthal-an-den-muenchner-kammerspielen-einen-karnevalesken-politischen-shakespeare-bei&catid=99&Itemid=100089 (accessed 2 April 2021).

Spivak, G. C. (1988), 'Can the Subaltern Speak?', in C. Nelson and L. Grossberg (eds), *Marxism and the Interpretation of Culture*, 271–313, Basingstoke: Macmillan.

Thalheimer, M. (2015), 'Michael Thalheimer über Anbiederung, Posen und Gegenwartsdramatik' [Michael Thalheimer on currying favour with the public, posing and today's theatre], interview by Martin Eich, *Wiesbadener Kurier*, 28 November: np.

Voima, S. (2016), *Othello: Nach William Shakespeare*, Berlin: Henschel Schauspiel Theaterverlag Berlin GmbH.

PART THREE

Performative propositions

Induction 3

Lawrence Guntner

In this final section (Part Three: Performative propositions), three directors reflect on their experience of directing *The Merchant of Venice* and *Othello*. The task of a director, according to Plamen Markov, is to mediate between past significance and present meaning through the medium of the Shakespearean text. However, it is the director's respect for the text (in translation), or lack thereof, plus a national tradition and personal style, which finally define his choices.

For Karin Coonrod, the Stranger 'inspires political provocations and more mysterious openings for hospitality'. Among the 'provocations' she included in her open-air production of *The Merchant in Venice* – at the Venetian Ghetto Nuovo, for its 500th anniversary in 2016 – was the 'estrangement' of Shakespeare's text through strategies of multilingualism and doubling. Different languages – English, Venetian Italian, Ladino (the Spanish dialect spoken by Sephardic Jews), Yiddish, Judeo-Venetian and Hebrew – suggested the multiplicity of diaspora and that anti-Semitism comes in a multitude of tongues. The character of Shylock, performed by five different actors, offered another composite portrait – merchant, father, mother, widower, and (potential) killer. At the end, the word 'Mercy', in English, Italian and Hebrew, was projected on the walls of the houses surrounding the square. Yet, there was no mercy in Shakespeare's Venice, nor in Coonrod's production.

The origins of Arnaud Churin's production of *Othello* (France, 2018–19) went back to his experiments with *A*

Midsummer Night's Dream in New Caledonia with a Kanak team. *Othello*, for Churin, cannot be narrowed down to racism. It is rather a complex play about diversity, hatred of the Other, and the mechanisms of patriarchy, all driven by language, rather than action. Othello's storied world of magic, fantasy and adventure is vulnerable to the insinuations of Iago that stem from a pragmatic world. Set in a Samurai-like elsewhere, the all-black cast, with a white Othello, performed in a choreography of gestures and body rhythms inspired by the martial arts. Despite much shortening of Shakespeare's text, the roles of Emilia and Bianca were left uncut, and Bianca's role and significance was enhanced. In the closing scene, she stood centre stage as the only woman still alive.

For his production of *Othello* (2020), Markov also sidestepped the topics that have recently defined otherness in *Othello* – race, sexism and age – to focus instead on the anxieties of migration, the tensions arising within a migrant community and the emotional fallout of severing traditional loyalties and familial bonds. The performance included some dialogues in Nigerian Ibo for the Moors and Turkish for the Cypriots, including Bianca. Large puppets, used to illustrate parts of the action, de-familiarized the narrative and infused it with comedy. In the European tradition, enriched by earlier Marxist readings of the play, a minor character like the Clown was upgraded to an agent and mediator between the stage and spectators.

While all these productions preserve the coherence of story-telling, they reshape and re-assemble Shakespeare's plays by opening them up to audiences that share different ideas of the limits of strangeness and tolerance. In their sensitivity to the alien they address the painful moral quandaries surrounding the Other.

11

The Merchant in Venice in the Venetian Ghetto (2016)

Director Karin Coonrod in conversation with Boika Sokolova and Kirilka Stavreva

Karin Coonrod is an Italian-American theatre director and pedagogue who works across theatrical genres. Her theatrical adaptations of poetry, fiction and non-fiction have given canonical and lesser known texts a modern licence to life. Her theatre is characterized by extensive use of music and movement, and by a particular interest in on-location experience. In 2004, Coonrod formed Compagnia de' Colombari, whose ambition was to open up the twenty-first-century stage for the medieval mystery plays. Since then, they have done much more, performed across the US and Europe, seeking resonances and dissonances among languages, cultural traditions and genres, engaged in civic projects and gained numerous accolades.

In 2016, Coonrod and the company put on a production of *The Merchant of Venice* in the Venetian Ghetto Nuovo, under the title of *The Merchant in Venice*. This was dedicated to a double anniversary: 500 years since the foundation of the Ghetto and the 400th anniversary of Shakespeare's death. *The Merchant in Venice* was performed at other locations in Italy and the USA, notably at the high-security prison for men in Padua.

BS&KS *How important is the character of the Stranger in your theatre work? What has drawn you to it?*

KC I am writing these thoughts in April 2020 during the time of the coronavirus here in New York City. No respecter of persons, the coronavirus is a kind of Stranger that strikes where it will. We are stopped in our tracks and catalyzed into a new consciousness.

The Stranger creates a conflict to which I am repeatedly drawn in my theatre work, that is true. It inspires political provocations and more mysterious openings for hospitality. I see the Stranger through both ends of the telescope: from the far end as Stranger to the community and close-up as Stranger to oneself. In *The Merchant of Venice*, Shylock, the quintessential Stranger (the Jew, the immigrant, the outsider, the Other) is the object of cruel mockery by the community – those in the mainstream of the culture. Shylock calls out his mockers, and they escalate the cruelty until in the end he is jettisoned from the court (and the play) in complete humiliation. My adaptation changed the ending by bringing Shylock back onstage as an interlocutor directly addressing the audience and reprising the hallucinatory speech he had spoken with seeming impunity to the Duke and the court:

You'll ask me why I rather choose to have
A weight of carrion flesh than to receive

Three thousand ducats. . . .

. . .

. . . I [can] give no reason, nor I will not,
More than a lodged hate and certain loathing
I bear Antonio, that I follow thus
A losing suit against him! Are you answered?
(*MV* 4.1.39–41, 58–61)

The mirror is held up to the audience in a direct encounter, a wake-up call.

Shylock the Stranger is the most memorable character in the play, for the vitality of his language that expresses his flawed humanity. Not a comic villain nor a tragic hero, but rather a fully human character. The mainstream culture scorns and despises him for his religion, his money, his otherness. In the end, the Venetian citizens self-righteously hold the word 'mercy' over him – yet their treatment of him exposes their hypocrisy. Here the Stranger is a catalyst to his fellow characters inside the play and to the audience directly.

In a play like *The Tempest*, that telescope is flipped. Prospero is a Stranger, yes, but to his parading self. The moment of self-strangeness crystallizes when Ariel, not himself a human, but speaking on behalf of everything non-human, summons Prospero to realize in himself what it is to be human. In my production of *The Tempest* (2014), this is the turning point. At this moment, everyone in the company, actors and musicians, stand with Ariel in a force field of attention – fixed on Prospero. In this distended, visceral silence, Prospero recognizes and feels this call to his lost humanity, now a Stranger. In a way Ariel, too, has become a Stranger to himself, by gathering within him/her/their-self everything that is not human, to provoke the human into action of human conscience.

BS&KS *A striking quality of your* Merchant *was the estrangement of the English language. Several of the actors were non-native speakers; Shakespeare's English was peppered* *with other languages; the musical contour included a range of traditions.*

KC Minting the production of the *Merchant* in the Venice Ghetto informed many choices. When I was invited to create the production, the first consideration was which language to use. It made sense to perform in the writer's own English language, as we were going to play in front of an international audience and commemorate the 400th anniversary of *his* death. Yet, we were also playing *in Italy*, the land of *commedia dell'arte* which had clearly influenced Shakespeare. I made *commedia* part of the performance, in a number of scenes; *commedia* is so expressive in costume and gesture that the playfulness and broad, risqué humour would translate, no matter the language. It also made great sense to incorporate Venetian-Italian in the *commedia* scenes with Lancillotto and Gobbo.

My adaptation also used Ladino, Yiddish, Judeo-Venetian and Hebrew: I wanted Shylock to call upon his tribal mother tongue to express heightened moments of feeling when English failed him. For example, in the second Shylock scene we included a phrase of Ladino when Shylock speaks closely to his daughter: 'Jessica, m'ija, / Mira a mi casa' ('Jessica, my girl, look to my house'). Later, when Shylock is deeply lamenting the departure of his daughter he says 'me fia', Judeo-Venetian for 'my daughter', more intimate than the Italian 'mia figlia'.

When the Venetians hurl insults at Shylock, they erupt in a multitude of languages, a way to put Shylock on the world stage through an onslaught of anti-Semitism.

When thinking about the music I didn't go in the direction of period music. Instead, I went to Frank London, the founder of the Klezmatics Band in New York, and found a collaborator, game to set text to music in the most intuitive way. He and I talked about how scholars had discussed Shylock's dislike of music. Sure, Shylock is a strict *single* parent who doesn't want his adolescent daughter to be seduced by the carnival music – and anything attached to secular culture. Is that so strange? It does not indicate he is a music hater. Informed by the rich repository of Judaic music, Frank composed theme music for Shylock's ritual costume change; from a high rooftop, he also played a haunting trumpet lament at the moment of Jessica's flight from her father's house.

Two other musical moments come to mind. The entire company launched the play in a carnivalesque song in Italian, to signal the spirit of Italy to the audience. (Frank was loosely inspired by Nino Rota in the composition of the passage of Ruzante we used for the prologue.)[1] The intention was to collide the exuberant musical opening with Antonio's singular moody gloom: 'In sooth I know not why I am so sad' (*MV* 1.1.1).

Another moment, later in the play, was when Lorenzo's mates have duly kept the appointed time for meeting him, but not seeing their 'lovestruck' friend, they mock his tardiness. Their text is, 'O ten times faster Venus' pigeons fly / To seal love's bonds new made than they are wont / To keep obliged faith unforfeited' (2.6.6–8). Sure, this could be spoken with great aplomb, about how new love eclipses old love. Yet, I wanted some razzmatazz variety and it occurred to me that the antiquated imagery of Venus's doves would be hilarious if sung by Graziano and Salanio in competition – in the operatic Italian of two tenors – while killing time. Frank obliged with a fiery duet and it was a riot every single night.

BS&KS The Merchant in Venice *was a site-specific production, born and formed by its location in the Ghetto Nuovo. How did this particular location affect the production? How did it shape the portrayal of otherness?*

KC The stones of the Ghetto embedded with centuries of history informed the entire production. They are infused with memories from Shakespeare's day, and all the lives and tragedies since. I didn't have to do anything but let the stones speak. My designer, Peter Ksander, understood that immediately and chose the exact location where the audience should be seated: we built stadium seating and positioned it directly in front of the oldest and most beautiful architecture – complete with its two synagogues – in the Campo Nuovo of the Ghetto. The stage was the thing itself. There the audience could gaze at a palimpsest of history serving as a backdrop to the action. The stones provided a most resonant platform for our international stage.

In my adaptation, Shylock let out his wail of grief at the departure of Jessica. It was as if the unheard voices, captive underneath the stones, found a channel through the actor's body to be released finally into the air, a moment in which play and history collapsed into each other.

BS&KS *One of your signature approaches is to split a main character into several parts – something you did in the production of* King Lear *(2000), in* texts&beheadings/Elizabeth R *(2015), and in* The Merchant in Venice *(2016). What did the multiple figurations contribute to the character of Shylock?*

KC I would call my approach a composite, not a split. When I look at a Rothko painting – that might first appear as a stack of stripes – I see it as a whole thing, not broken up, colour by colour, and I enter its compelling drama. So, too, with the mosaic of character. We are so many things at different times and, sometimes, all at once. I respond to the play, the history of the character and the context of its performance.

In my *texts&beheadings/Elizabeth R*, I wanted to dig down into the infinite variety of Queen Elizabeth I's mind and persona in a way that would engage the audience in puzzling her out. In a way, I was playing these contradictions against the familiar biopics of her life.

With Shylock, I was intrigued to open up his character to what is Jewish and what is universal, by having each of the five scenes played by a different actor. Each scene emphasized a particular aspect of his character: the merchant, the father, the mother, the widower and the killer. Each actor playing Shylock also played another character, often in opposition with Shylock, thus inviting the audience into the theatricality of an actor's single body containing this dilemma.

Each Shylock actor donned an elegant golden-yellow silk sash, yellow having been historically the colour of the Jew in Venice. With this design, my costume designer Stefano Nicolao and I sought a mark of the Stranger that would signal the otherness, the stigma of a non-citizen, but also the dignity and self-respect Shylock held in himself. I wanted a large gesture that would be witnessed by the audience: each actor stepping into the role of Shylock was to be changed ceremoniously by the crew. In this way, we could all share the emotional burden of playing the Stranger.

BS&KS *In your approach to Shylock you alternate between character layering (for which you use different actors) and their grouping into a composite entity. Can you say a bit more about this dynamic in representing the Stranger?*

KC There are two intense moments in the play's trajectory when the five actors who play Shylock appear together, almost as a collective person. The first is when Shylock becomes distraught at the flight of his daughter Jessica, his only child. Seduced by Lorenzo, she turns her back on Judaism. For Shylock, this is personal, political and metaphysical. His grief and loss are overbearing; it turns every part of his being toward hatred and revenge. The only worthy theatrical response is for the five Shylocks to be called into presence with each other, to merge in their shared understanding: 'for sufferance is the badge of all our tribe' (*MV* 1.3.106). It is a spiritual impasse, a moment when Shylock's grief twists into revenge.

So, in the theatre we did this: the moment Jessica takes the torch as the torchbearer for Lorenzo and his mates, a plaintive trumpet begins to sound from high over the rooftops of the Ghetto. The music operates as a poetic call to the five Shylocks, who very slowly enter into a huge circle occupying much of the Ghetto stage space. It's a poetic, theatrical moment, not literal. It's as if the parent knows in his heart that something's up, a kind of musical premonition that calls him into an appointment with himself. The five actors playing Shylock walk into a massive circle where crew members ceremoniously change them from their previous character's clothes into the Shylock desert cloaks and golden sashes. As the character emerges in five incarnations, the company begin to mutter insults at Shylock and the Jews. The five actors hear the taunts, but say nothing. The invectives grow and become poisonous (all passages from Salanio and Salarino's parts) while the five Shylocks slowly walk towards each other until they come close together, only stopping when one of them – Shylock #3 – lets out an unearthly howl that stops every sound and action on the stage and in the Ghetto itself. A stunning silence attends the distended howl containing the grief of all parents, fathers, mothers, disenfranchised parents, the grieving voice of the voiceless.

In one of our early rehearsals, I realized we had recreated an image of Rodin's Burghers of Calais as Shylock #3 spoke and the others remained in still silence, in solidarity. Shylock's rage was born in this howl of grief, which grew unchecked in a universe of greed and loneliness. Shylock had been the recipient of 'Christian' revenge; and he warned Salanio and Salarino, 'The villainy you teach me I will execute, and it shall go hard but I will better the instruction' (3.1.64–6).

By multiplying the presence of Shylock on the stage, the sense of the Stranger looms larger and the community pales in comparison in moral authority.

BS&KS *The female voice and body are crucial in the affective power of the scenes with the composite Shylocks. In addition to the keening of 'mother Shylock', Jessica in the final scene also embodies the lived experience of otherness. To what extent was gender important in portraying the Other?*

KC I suppose it would be easy to say that as a female director I would place women in key roles in a Shakespeare drama, something we see often today, which I applaud. But to me, it was the opening of the extraordinary role of Shylock to its full dimension that engaged my attention. I would not want to create a prism and block out half its colours. The choice to have Jenni Lea-Jones play Shylock #3 in the naked moment of grief, after the famous speech 'Hath not a Jew eyes?' (*MV* 3.1.53), made visceral and poetic sense. There is a reason I refer to Shylock the mother as one of the five aspects of Shylock. He was a single parent, whose wife, Leah, had probably died some years before (we imagined perhaps six or seven years before and the loss had been deeply mourned between the father and daughter). Now Shylock had taken on the whole burden in his daughter's turbulent adolescent years. Though Jenni played the role as a man, her own apparently powerful female presence shone through this moment.

Regarding the final scene of the play, what came to mind was Jessica's response to the cumulative understanding of the hollowness of the world she had entered. Interestingly, she is silent after her 'In such a night' (5.1) scene with Lorenzo, which I chose to interpret not romantically, but rather as a further sign of their moving apart spiritually. The build-up of information about Venetian culture has brought her to a point of a primal scream against the citizens' greed and cruelty, against her father. That, along with Lorenzo's incessant chastisements, brings her to a place of watching without speaking. I had staged Jessica to witness the courtroom scene so that she could see how the Duke and all the Venetians (including members of the audience wearing red stoles like the Duke) stand together in solidarity against Shylock, forced him to be a Christian convert and therefore never really belong to any community. Jessica's silent scream at the end of the play is hurled at the culture that allows these injustices to thrive.

It is important to me to play with the fluidity of gender on stage, to keep a light touch in the 'play' of the play. So, when the actors first confront the audience, some men play women and women men. But when Antonio and his boys take over the first scene, it is clear that they are men and only men. The play is about them, until Portia is introduced into it by Bassanio and then Shylock is approached for a loan.

The scamp, Lancillotto, was played by Francesca Sarah Toich, because she was the best for the role. With her extraordinary voice and androgynous manner, she brings us right into the mischief of the character. Shakespeare makes the point – inside the plot – that women must play men in order to be heard, hence Portia's only way to 'win' is to enter the court disguised as a male lawyer, as well as her two assistants, Nerissa and Balzarina. In our production I changed the gender of Balthazar to Balzarina, thus creating a kind of island of women in Belmont – women, I imagined, who cherish each other's presence and don't want to be subservient to men. This occurred to me in the second scene of the play when Portia and Nerissa engage in hilarious and cruel mockery – quite xenophobic – against the suitors who have arrived to win Portia's hand.

BS&KS *In the Ghetto, your* Merchant *culminated with projections of the word 'mercy' in English, Italian and Hebrew. Did 'the quality of mercy' acquire different significances in the different venues the play was performed? Why did you choose to end in this way?*

KC There is no mercy in this play. The first time the word appears is when – more than halfway through – Shylock says to Antonio, 'Tell me not of mercy!' (*MV* 3.3.1). Venice has never demonstrated mercy, yet now that Antonio, one of their own, is endangered, mercy is being required of the Jew. Through the trial with Portia, this is being driven home to him, with a vengeance. The word stands out like a photographic negative. For this reason, it had to stain the Ghetto walls, an imprint of what was not, and a question of what is.

I end the play not with the return of the rings, but rather with a return of Shylock's speech when he first appears at trial before the Duke: 'You'll ask me why I rather choose to have / A pound of carrion flesh than to receive / Three thousand ducats. I'll not answer that / But say it is my humour . . . Are you answered?' (4.1.39–42; 61). As the play concludes, each of the five Shylocks speak the line 'Are you answered?' to the audience, followed by the shofar's blast and Jessica's silent scream, while MERCY in English, MISERICORDIA in Italian and RAKHAMIM in Hebrew are writ large on the Ghetto walls. What was missing in the play – mercy – is the handwriting on the walls of the Ghetto, which look down on the stage and at the entire audience.

It has been an interesting thing to listen to the audience at the end of the play, whether in the Ghetto or in North America. I wanted to leave them with the sense of the inanimate walls saying what no human could say, like a prophetic handwritten imperative.

BS&KS *After the Venetian Ghetto, your* Merchant *travelled to the high-security prison for men in Padua, Italy. How did this site affect the production? Did you find that you had to modify some of the components?*

KC For a production for the inmates in the high-security prison, we created a shorter version, since we were limited to only seventy minutes in the afternoon. We decided to excise the Portia scenes with the exception of the courtroom. We kept all the scenes with Lancillotto and Gobbo because they were in Italian and thus easily understood by the inmates. The audience of men vociferously enjoyed that we were fearlessly bawdy. (Francesca Sarah Toich – playing Lancillotto – is a striking young woman who in her male role boldly donned a codpiece and spoke out in a fierce deep voice; Andrea Brugnera, playing Gobbo, was not afraid to make his salacious quip about women.) The inmates had been prepared for our performance by reading and studying the play and watching the Al Pacino film. We involved the Prison's Drama Group to participate as members of the audience, standing in solidarity with the Venetians, donning red stoles, against Shylock #5 (played by Ned Eisenberg) in the trial scene. It is a very poignant moment. We used all the music, except for whatever marked the Belmont scenes.

BS&KS *What resonances emerged between* The Merchant *and the histories of the 'Others' incarcerated in the prison? How did this audience respond to the production?*

KC The inmates seemed to appreciate the piece. I greatly regretted that we did not have time to have a talkback, but we were able to greet all personally with handshakes and hugs.

One of our actors, Michele Guidi, who played Bassanio, was initially frozen backstage, weeping. I went to find him to talk. He told me he could play in front of thousands, if necessary, but before this group of prisoner men, many of them for life, he couldn't. His eyes were red with grief at their plight. We had all been terrified by the thickness of walls and the number of gates that clanged shut behind us, stripped of all our ID papers, phones, money, keys. It was intense. It was real. It was playing for keeps. All I could quote to Michele was something from Beckett: 'I can't go on. I'll go on' (*Waiting for Godot*). As Beckett is one of our high priests in the theatre, Michele listened. He knew they needed us as we needed them. He went on and played with his heart in his eyes.

As we were allowed to bring all our costumes and props inside the walls – including the knife that Shylock held to Antonio's heart – we captured every eye at that sustained moment, with attention at a peak. It heightened viscerally the exchanges between Portia (Linda Powell) and Shylock #5 (Ned Eisenberg). For all of us, inmates and actors, the stakes were unforgettably high in that moment when experiences collided.

For many of us, this was our first experience performing in prison. Since then, we've played in numerous American prisons and jails, under many different projects. It's been a growing and deepening level of engagement.

Note

1 Angelo Beolco, known as Il Ruzante, was a sixteenth-century actor and playwright known for his plays and monologues. Largely composed in the Venetian language, they offer a keen satiric outlook of the local country-life of the era.

12

Inverting *Othello* in France (2019)

Director Arnaud Churin in conversation with Janice Valls-Russell

This interview took place in singular circumstances. When Arnaud Churin and I first spoke over the telephone in early March 2020, his production of *Othello* was on tour. After premiering in Alençon in March 2019, the reprise in Paris in October that same year attracted critical attention. A few days after that first telephone call, theatres closed in France and actors, like the rest of the population, were in lockdown, in the context of the Covid-19 global pandemic. We carried out the interview by Skype.

Arnaud Churin is an actor and a director, born of parents who belonged to the 1968 generation and endorsed the ideals of the May uprising. They brought up their children in accordance with their principles, in a rural area three hours' drive from Paris. It was through popular culture, and stand-up comedians he heard on the radio, such as Coluche and Raymond Devos, through language, therefore, that Churin discovered the world of entertainment, as well as through his father's whimsical creativity. The family was not wealthy and seized upon all forms of free culture. One favourite, perpetually fascinating destination was the Centre Beaubourg, with its exhibitions and its forecourt, where all kinds of live arts performances (theatre, music, mime) took place. Summer camps also stimulated Churin's taste and talent for telling stories, playing music and organizing festive events.

At the age of twelve, he was invited to take part – as a fairy – in an amateur production of *A Midsummer Night's Dream*. At the age of fourteen, he played Figaro – a form of consecration that conditioned what followed. He went on to study at the drama academy of Rennes (which became the academy of the Théâtre National de Bretagne), and from there moved on to the Paris Conservatoire national supérieur d'art dramatique (CNSAD). He appears in plays, films and telefilms, as well as directs his own productions.

JVR *Was this your first engagement with Shakespeare? Why Othello?*[1]

AC This *Othello* originated in the southern hemisphere. In 2006 nine Kanak actors – men and women – were invited from New Caledonia to the Caen National Drama Centre (CDN) for a production of Seneca's *Oedipus*, which I had been invited to direct.[2] Offering presents is very important in Kanak culture, so I went to buy a few books, including Jean-Michel Déprats's translation of *A Midsummer Night's Dream*. One of the actors, who is also a poet, a wonderful old man, told me: 'Isn't it funny that someone like you, who is so knowledgeable, should think that Shakespeare is English. In fact, he's Kanak! We know them, those spirits he talks about, the one who's a cobweb, the one who drops dew into the flowers.' Sometime later, another member of the same company came to Paris to train with a drama school. He floated the idea of exploring

Shakespeare as a Kanak; we talked about *Dream*, and the way the whole of nature is affected when a man and a woman quarrel. We had the play translated into Nengone and, in 2011, I went to New Caledonia for a theatre residence on the island of Maré. We asked the old actor-poet and others to tell us the story of the lizard and the sea urchin (that is to say Oberon and Titania): One night, at the full moon, the lizard (a metaphor for man) saw the sea urchin (a metaphor for woman). He had never seen one before. He approached, parted the needles and pricked himself. All of his substance drained away, until only his skin was left. Then the sea urchin said to him: 'If you accept to be what you are, I'm willing to marry you'.

We wished to explore intersections between the island myths and the world of Shakespeare in a production of *Dream*, which would incorporate (as a play-within-the-play) the story of the lizard and the sea urchin. I was the only white person on the island, I lived like my Kanak friends. Unfortunately, the project was never completed: there was an uprising, with tensions that crystallized around the hatred of Others, and people were wounded and even killed.

Later, back in France, a staging I wanted to make of Kateb Yacine's *Le Cadavre encerclé* [The encircled corpse] was turned down on the grounds that I had not chosen a North-African actor. In my view, the universal power of this text is such that its casting need not be racially or ethnically conditioned. It seemed to me that there was something hypocritical in this: as if non-European texts should necessarily be performed by non-European actors, who, regrettably, are underrepresented in productions of the mainstream French – or more widely, European – repertoire.

That is how, irritated by this kind of presupposition, but also drawing on my own experience in New Caledonia, I decided to stage an *Othello* in which all the characters except the lead role would be black. At that stage, I still considered that the play spoke about racism, questioned the Other, his/her ability to find a place in a given society. During the rehearsals, it appeared to us that racism was not the heart of the tragedy. Iago is bent on essentializing Othello, and his manoeuvring succeeds all the better in that Othello lacks self-confidence, has few friends, is isolated. Yet, every time, Shakespeare is careful to contradict Iago. Besides Iago's role, therefore, the overall vision of the play cannot be reduced to racism – even if, as an academic pointed out to me, Othello's speech on the anthropophagi, based on travel accounts, can have suggested representations of Africans as 'savages' and carried the seeds of future racial theories.

In my view, Othello invites us to explore the mechanisms of patriarchy. Such mechanisms function through language, and that is what emerged during rehearsals: language, in *Othello*, is the driving force behind the tragedy. The Turks everyone fears so much do not come. It is not action, but what is said, that drives the play.

JVR *How did you choose the actors?*

AC I did not audition them, I did not choose them. It would have been dreadful to tell them, 'I'm choosing you because you are black' – downright abjection, in the meaning Jacques Rivette gives that word.[3] I approached actors I had met over the years, and co-opted others through people I knew. This project was grounded on mutual trust. I told each one of them: 'I'm going to build the part with you'. Our cast reflects a wide range of journeys and backgrounds: some of the actors grew up and studied in France, others come from elsewhere. Two are from the Republic of the Congo, one is from the Democratic Republic of the Congo.

JVR *Othello kills his (white) wife, which is why some non-white actors refuse the part. Others see in Othello a victim of white racism, even as he seems to belong in Venice (he's a Christian, a general), and consider that this is a role for non-white actors. What do you think? Couldn't your inversion of racial signifiers suggest that the white Othello is a victim of black racism?*

AC Unless I'm mistaken, Othello's skin colour is mentioned nineteen times in the play. Importantly, Desdemona never essentializes Othello, except as a fighter, a warrior. In order to read anti-black racism in the play, it would need to represent Othello as stupid, 'inferior', or bloodthirsty; once again, the text is not inherently racist. Of course, there have been blackface productions, where Othello is mocked, and stripped of his tragic stature.

I'm a little wary of the word 'racism', which covers so many notions that it sometimes ends up not really meaning anything anymore. There's what one might call systemic racism, the difficulty to find a job depending on the community, or neighbourhood, you come from. But all too often, there's a confusion between racism and hatred of the Other: in Italy or France, for instance, you'll have the inhabitants of neighbouring villages feuding even though they are all related. And one finds that in Iago: he hates Cassio because he's a Florentine.

I find the notion of inversion problematic. I'm not sure I'm inverting, or reversing, Shakespeare's text, I'm changing usages. When a white actor plays Othello in a white cast, no one talks about inversion – and anyway, when Othello was first performed there were only men in the cast, usages have changed. And performances change as those usages evolve. If today we have difficulties with blackface, it's because of the way this convention was used in America in cabarets to mock black people. Actors should be able to play any part, because all human beings are entitled to occupy any place in society. If some, because of their skin colour, are excluded from some sectors of society, then their presence on stage conveys significances that may elude us.

In 2015, there was a controversy here in France, when Luc Bondy wanted Philippe Torreton, a white actor, to play Othello. At the time, I was already thinking about my own project. Perhaps my own casting choices will be critiqued someday, perhaps in a staging where all the parts are played by non-white actors?

As for 'anti-white' racism, I never imagined for a second that anyone might see my production from that angle! First of all, because I don't see that anti-white (systemic) racism exists ... In our society, white people do not find themselves excluded from certain areas of social life (jobs, discos, housing and so forth) because of their skin colour. One or two critics attempted to go in that direction, but they are a tiny minority.

JVR *What did you seek to achieve by setting the racial dichotomy which operates in the play in a third cultural space? Why did you turn to Asia?*

AC Once I had decided to play around with the casting, I had to rethink the cultural starting-point of the play, that is to say Venice. It seemed to me that if I kept a Venetian setting with that cast, I would be imposing on my audience a representation of the city which did not correspond to their personal idea of Venice. I like to aim at an internal coherence, some form of plausibility. The solution therefore was to find a third space, to let go of my own, familiar representations of Venice, to imagine a place that was definitely elsewhere, a universe of tales and legends, where hierarchical ranks are clearly signalled, where you know who's the ensign and who's the general, a world where the issue of warriors gathered to fight an enemy is made visible – even though the enemy is internal.

I entered the world of theatre through art, I like to work in period. Just before staging *Othello*, I had adapted *L'Enfant de demain* [Tomorrow's child], the story of a child soldier in the Congo wars (Amisi 2011).[4] I asked the author of this autobiographical account, Serge Amisi: 'When you are a stolen child, who has grown up without family values, what is your cultural base?' He replied: 'Karate films.'

Karate is universal, like Shakespeare – whose precolonial humanism has nothing to do with the abstract universalism against which Maurice Merleau-Ponty cautioned.[5] Karate is familiar to children all over the world, regardless of their social background. When I knew that our play was going ahead, and that for many teenagers in the audience this would be their first encounter with Shakespeare, a popular author who wrote for his contemporaries, I wanted to tell them: this show is for you. That is how the idea of a universe suggestive of the world of the Samurai took shape. Through the designs, created by Virginie Mira: black scrims suspended from sophisticated machinery that made them turn and fly, almost, suggesting sails, partitions of Japanese palaces, a camp. Through the magnificent Samurai costumes designed by Sonia de Sousa, with long jackets over hakama, in different hues, decorated with graphic codes. And through the actors' gestural codes and body rhythmics, which we borrowed from karate. What I also like about karate is the way it contributes to creating a world that clarifies choices. While the overall design may have seemed too deliberate and even artificial to some spectators, it worked with younger audiences: it enabled them to get into the play, to respond to the rhythm of the choreography and the characters' movements.

JVR *Why a black handkerchief?*

AC Almost everyone imagines a white handkerchief, as an attribute of purity, and virginity. Ian Smith has argued that it's a black, embroidered handkerchief, 'dyed in mummy' (*Oth* 3.4.76) (Smith 2013). The text gives us two sets of information about the handkerchief: what Othello tells Desdemona (3.4.57–77) and what he says after killing her (5.2.210–15). In his first version, he seems to lay it on, insisting on the magic. I was struck by the importance of magic in the play. It's extraordinary how white people don't acknowledge that their own cultural roots are steeped in legends and magic, they often tend to relegate magic to the world of black people. Brabantio considers that the magic Othello supposedly used to seduce Desdemona is a crime, he has 'enchanted her' (1.2.62–79, 63), and used 'witchcraft' (1.3.60–5, 65).

In fact, to perform *Othello* is to question the place allowed magic. All of Iago's arguments are materialistic, while Desdemona's cannot be verified. And Othello, who has played on magic – the magic of words, of a fantastical elsewhere – and woven his stories of magic, to win and keep Desdemona's love, ends up making his the non-magical vision of the world relentlessly fashioned by Iago, to such an extent that he ends up demanding proof of Desdemona's supposed faithlessness. When I was in New Caledonia, I witnessed the extent to which local cultures and myths were crushed by a narrowly rationalistic, European outlook. Through Iago, the audience is invited to be wary of such a vision of the world, of its destructive power, of the aggression of the Other it entails, driving one to question what produces beauty, what is not verifiable.

JVR *There are several recent translations of* Othello. *Why commission a new one?*

AC Initially, we chose an existing translation. We applied for permission, presenting our project: we wanted to shorten the text, have female senators, and replace Moor/Black by Caucasian/White. We were granted the right to use the translation, and the actors started learning their text. But then we were told we couldn't use it with the changes we wanted to make. So we commissioned a new version, working closely with the translator. In this refusal, one of many setbacks we had to face, I see a form of dominant thinking: adaptations seem to be legitimate only in one direction, when a white actor plays Othello alongside other white actors, and I really see this as a problem.

JVR *What did you cut? Did you cut anything from the women's speeches, or on the contrary, did you play up the presence of the women through other cuts? Would you say this is a post-#MeToo production?*

AC As I said, everything turns on the language, rather than the action. Our show lasts about two hours and forty minutes. We cut Act 2 substantially, and part of Act 5. We did away with the Clown, but gave Roderigo and his manipulation by Iago a comic dimension, which went down very well with the public: the two actors formed an excellent duo.

The cuts enhanced the presence of the women. We did not cut Emilia's part, and we left Desdemona's virtually untouched. And we heightened Bianca's role: the same actress also doubled as the Duke's advisor (conflating Senators 1 and 2, as well as the Messenger in 1.2 and 1.3). In the final scene, Bianca replaces Gratiano, which enables her to share a final exchange with Emilia and to comment on her death. The two women understand that they've been tricked. The decision to have Bianca return at the end of the play reflects the company's collective approach to adaptation, and was taken in response to Nelson-Rafaell Madel's uneasiness with the misogyny of his character, Cassio. Shakespeare plunges us into a gendered vision of the world. Audiences may laugh when they hear Cassio's misogynistic mockery, but moments later they wish they hadn't laughed when Othello strikes Desdemona. The play probes male-female relationships, and we chose to hold out the possibility that Cassio might end up loving Bianca. She never says she is a whore. Not so long ago, women living in rural communities, who had no children and perhaps several partners, were easily described as prostitutes. In the last scene, Emilia is centre stage, and all the others gravitate around her. Then Bianca moves centre stage. Without saying a word, she becomes the Duke's councillor, approaching Othello as if to take him (gently) to prison. Bianca is the only woman still alive at the end of the play. After Othello's suicide she stands front stage looking at the audience: she is both Bianca and the councillor – a woman. The suspended décor rises and one steps out of the world of fiction.

When I started thinking about the play, no one was talking about #MeToo yet. That movement has helped to liberate language and given the play an additional resonance. Spectators, mostly men, told me they had initially thought of the play as being about violence against a black character, and they had 'discovered' the double femicide, which they had forgotten about. This is another way in which the play invites us to think about diversity, about our interactions with the Other. Our production may contribute to giving a disquieting familiarity,[6] to borrow Freud's concept, to a play audiences think they know.

JVR *Desdemona is taller than Othello. At one moment, she carries him in her arms, reversing the traditional bride-bridegroom conventions. Does this aim to deconstruct 'black male virility' representations of Othello?*

AC I didn't choose Julie Héga because her Desdemona would be taller than Othello, I chose her because I had followed her career. I immediately thought of her for Desdemona, even before I knew who would be playing Othello (Mathieu Genet). The way I see things, Brabantio has brought Desdemona up like a boy, she is strong-willed, she's grown up too fast, and her father hasn't realized this.

Our karate coach is a woman, Laurence Fischer, a world champion. She's active in sports and social programmes for women victims of violence in France and abroad: all this was very important in defining the role of Desdemona, and Julie's way of embodying it. Laurence's personal experience, and her work with our team gave physical coherence to our casting reversal, as you call it, redistributing the usual active/male passive/female assignations. Julie seized all the options and her inversion of gendered stereotypes when she took Othello in her arms was a joke intended for the audience watching a production which wanted to shift things. Everything is very labile in Shakespeare's plays, and our perspectives too need to shift, on minorities – whoever, wherever they may be – and on our vision of society.

Othello is a peaceful man and initially he intends to call Cassio back very quickly. Yet, although he may belong to a minority, he's also a general. As such he belongs to that patriarchal community of men, that male collective who, through Iago, enjoin him to kill Desdemona. Iago's reasoning, which he borrows from Brabantio's last words to Othello, is implacable: she betrayed her father, she may betray you, you must chastise her, punish her. What we have there is the infantilization of a daughter and a wife.

JVR *Would you say that your approach invites audiences to think about what the sociologist Edgar Morin calls a 'communauté de destins' rather than (merely) in terms of minorities (racial, gender, ethnic, etc.)?*

AC I'm no intellectual. I follow current debates, and I'm fascinated by everything that relates to post-colonial thinking. The universalism I believe in, which I explore in theatre, is connected with the reality that our planet is not well: given the number of us there are living on this planet, we are going to have to allow the Other into our lives. That's what the philosopher Souleymane Bachir Diagne, whose outlook has been a strong presence throughout my work on *Othello*, tells us. Everywhere, one hears authoritarian, divisive responses to the question of the Other. It is important that gay, Jewish, feminist, black communities should all make themselves heard in France and elsewhere. When women talk among themselves, they discuss issues they can only share with other women. In his last words, Othello says: I've fought my original religion, I've killed a co-religionary, in killing myself like that Stranger I become a Stranger, a Stranger to myself. As if the social narrative was made flesh.

There is a lot of violence in the narratives of people of North-African or African background, who have no other affiliation than the (French) national community in which they have grown up, into which most of them were born, and who nonetheless feel that they are denied access to this community. The same thing has been happening during this Covid-19 pandemic, with members of the Asian minority who have been hassled or insulted, because the pandemic started in China! Once again we have a recurring pattern of rejection of a minority figure within a given community.

The play is about all that too: when one believes in the idea of a social contract, and yet everyday life sends back a contrasted reality, the ultimate response, for some people, is violence, violence against unkept promises. I feel close to that form of universalism Edgar Morin writes about, a left-leaning, secular, universal outlook, but in my view this outlook is not sufficiently alert to the gap between its ethos and the everyday reality of experience. Through *Othello*, I wanted to address otherness, which is a very complex issue.

JVR *Can you tell us something about the reception of this production (by theatre/festival directors, critics, audiences)?*

AC We performed for very different audiences, which responded eagerly, regardless of their sociology. Spectators told us: we didn't miss a single line, you enabled us to hear the text. In the end, the few tepid responses we met came from some producers and theatre directors. They were not used to seeing a cast like ours perform that play, it didn't match their idea of the play. As a few of them told us, 'It's great, but we would rather have a "more classical" *Othello*'.

Notes

1 The interview took place in French. The translation is by Janice Valls-Russell.

2 The impulse for this project came from the actor Jean Boissery, who is from New Caledonia.

3 Arnaud Churin is alluding to an article by Jacques Rivette, 'De l'abjection' [On abjection], in which he reviews *Kapo* (1960), a film by Gillo Pontecorvo set in a Nazi concentration camp. Rivette analyses Pontecorvo's use of a tracking shot that shows the suicide of a woman, and considers the ethical standpoint

of the film director and, more widely, 'the standpoint of a man, the author, a necessary evil, and that man's attitude to what he is filming and, therefore, to the world and to all things' (Rivette 1962: 54).

4 For a discussion of the book and of Churin's stage adaptation, see 'Serge Amisi' (2015).

5 Merleau-Ponty advocated 'no longer the overarching universalism of a strictly objective method, but some form of lateral universalism that we would acquire through ethnological experience, a continuous testing of oneself through the Other and of the Other through oneself' (Merleau-Ponty 2008: 52).

6 Churin used the phrase 'inquiétante familiarité', the most accepted French coinage of Sigmund Freud's 'Das Unheimliche', which is usually translated into English as 'the uncanny'.

References

Amisi, S. (2011), *Souvenez-vous de moi, l'enfant de demain* [Remember me, tomorrow's child], La Roque d'Anthéron: Vents d'ailleurs.

Merleau-Ponty, M. (2008), 'Rapport de Maurice Merleau-Ponty pour la création d'une chaire d'anthropologie sociale' [Report by Maurice Merleau-Ponty on the creation of a chair in social anthropology], *Claude Lévi-Strauss, centième anniversaire*, special issue of *La Lettre du Collège de France*, 2: 49–53.

Rivette, J. (1962), 'De l'abjection' [On abjection], *Cahiers du cinéma*, 120 (June): 54–5.

'Serge Amisi ou la resilience perpétuelle d'un enfant soldat' (2015), *Osi Bouake*, 15 February. Available online: http://osibouake.org/?Serge-Amisi-ou-la-resilience (accessed 2 April 2021).

Smith, I. (2013), 'Othello's Black Handkerchief', *Shakespeare Quarterly*, 64 (1): 1–25.

13

Migrant *Othello* (2020) in Bulgaria

Director Plamen Markov in conversation with Boika Sokolova and Kirilka Stavreva

Plamen Markov is an eminent Bulgarian theatre director and pedagogue. Through his prolific career, he has directed over ninety plays, nationally and internationally, and received a number of prestigious prizes. As professor at the National Academy for Theatre and Film Art in Sofia, he has nurtured a generation of distinguished actors. Since 2012, in addition to his pedagogical and directorial work, he has also served as Artistic Director of the Varna Drama Theatre 'Stoyan Bachvarov'. His production of *Othello* opened on the Varna stage in January 2020, launching a year-long programme to celebrate the centennial anniversary of the theatre.

BS&KS *Could you tell us about your experience of directing Shakespeare and what prompted your interest in staging* Othello *at the Varna Theatre?*

PM In my career, I have worked with Shakespeare several times, both nationally and internationally. However, I reached for his plays (and Chekhov's) after I reached a certain age. They are both generous authors. My productions and adaptations of Shakespeare include *Macbeth* at the National Theatre in Sofia (2003), *Love's Labour's Lost, A Midsummer Night's Dream* (2004), *As You Like It* (2005) and *Julius Caesar* (2009). The Varna Theatre has a long Shakespearean tradition. After directing *Richard III* (2011) and *Shakespeare in Love* (2017) there, I felt that the troupe was energized for an unconventional *Othello*. So I decided to put it on.

Shakespeare is a 'classic' and in the theatre, 'classic' is what always sounds contemporary. It is for theatre practitioners to find the intersection between history and the present without forcing it, so that those who – unlike the theatre buffs – have never seen a classic play, would think that this is how it *was* written. World drama offers a wealth of 'evergreens', plays any director would like to put on. However, it is not easy to say why it is you who should put your name to them, or what revelation you will bring to the audience. We all work for a hypothetical, ideal, virtual, if you wish, imaginary audience, which, when it becomes real, intervenes in its own unpredictable ways and puts things into their proper places.

BS&KS *You have a long-standing interest in adapting the classics. How did you imagine* Othello *for this moment in history? Your interpretation involves the theme of migration, doesn't it?*

PM I started with the idea that the Moor Othello is made Commander-in-Chief at a critical moment for Venice, a recognition that the city lacks able leaders for its maritime wars. There is no authoritative, experienced and talented local person, and they know it. The situation is not unlike the brain drain occurring in our own time when talent moves from the poorer to the richer countries. Because of the military situation, Venice is ready to accept the fact that Othello has seduced the daughter of a senator and married her without her father's permission. The Duke's and the Senate's moral relativism indicates their tenuous position vis-a-vis the Turkish danger. They legalize Desdemona's abduction by Othello in order to use his exceptional military abilities to save their skins. As soon as the Turkish danger blows over, they demote him and put their own boy, Cassio, in his place. These are acts of sheer expediency, overriding racial, class or moral considerations. For the Venetians, the appointment of a non-Venetian, whether a Moor or another, is a price worth paying to protect the Serenissima. There is no drama here, because this interest-driven compromise is above the board.

For our production, I worked on the hypothesis that Iago is also a Moor. Neither of the two is black; we are not interested in racial dichotomies. Both he and Othello are noble Africans from one of the Western African empires, which are multiracial and multi-tribal. In my interpretation, the conflict is most intense among the Moors who have followed Othello to Venice. Once there, he refuses to promote Iago who is second in noble rank in their group, as well as his friend; instead, he chooses for his lieutenant a local, Cassio, who does not display great abilities.

To complicate the conflict of allegiances, Othello intends to abduct Desdemona, in accordance with his tribal tradition, something Cassio is prepared to help with. Iago and Othello are life-long friends who have shared adversity, also as pirates, after their banishment from their West-African kingdom. Besides, Iago is married to Emilia, a Venetian and friend of Desdemona's (not her servant). His circumstances and ambitions are not unlike Othello's. The intertwining of personal and political considerations however, leads Othello to denying Iago what he deserves.

Once Othello reveals that he is actually of high birth, and 'fetch[es] his life and being / From men of royal siege' (*Oth* 1.2.21–2) – something that the Senate did not suspect of the pirate they chose to lead the naval war against the Ottomans – he becomes aware of danger bells ringing among the senators, fears that one day he himself might have a claim to power. He can hear people saying things like, 'if such actions may have passage free / Bond-slaves and pagans shall our statesmen be' (1.2.98–9). Thus he realizes that it would be politically short-sighted to employ Iago and stack the cards against himself. Surely, in Othello's calculation, Iago, intelligent as he is, must have reached the same conclusion and would not take things amiss. For people who have been through so much together, this seems to go without saying.

BS&KS *So this set-up allows you to crack the mystery of Iago's destructive hatred of Othello?*

PM Right. This is the moment when Iago, who is until then considered by all 'honest', 'just', 'good', etc., dramatically changes. He becomes what he tells Roderigo: 'I'm not what I am' (*Oth* 1.1.64). In our production, this is the hidden, underestimated conflict which unfolds to a destructive effect. An honest person, who is simply taken for granted, and never rewarded, can at some point snap: a question of a professional promotion can become an existential one. Here is the big transformation, culminating in 'I am not what I am'! Besides, Iago's disappointment is like a highly contagious virus without an antidote, a forest fire that burns all to ashes.

By creating this new set of circumstances, I gave a push to the events. From the middle of the play on, Othello begins to speak publicly about his so far well-hidden uncertainty regarding his newly achieved status, or the devoted love of his young, beautiful wife. He turns into a conduit for Iago's intrigues and brings them to their tragic end. Because of his trust, he is infected with Iago's virus, and spreads it around. Such are the additional energies I instilled in our production.

The principal actors, Simeon Lyutakov (Othello) and Penko Gospodinov (Iago), used them well, as they grappled with the reformulated conflict and developed the ideas in their acting.

BS&KS *Iago and Othello are not the only immigrants in your Venetian world. Can you tell us about the others?*

PM Yes, there are others. In my version, such is the Clown, a man of the theatre who has followed Othello in exile. He comes from the West-African, Yoruba, theatre tradition, which uses marionettes and a single musical instrument. Like any artist separated from his natural audience, he is barely surviving in Venice. Still, he and his actors continue to make their traditional puppets, which look like the people around them, some African, some Venetian. But African stories now have no audience, so they need a new story to enliven with their art.

At that moment, Iago steps in, allegedly to help the Clown with ideas, and shares his revenge plans as hypothetical plots for a show. Together with the Clown, they elaborate the intrigues by enacting them with the marionettes. When the Clown begins to realize how Iago intends to use their ideas, and play with people instead, he tries to distance himself from Iago by attempting to return the story to its role of a plot for a marionette play, while Iago's intrigues get out of control and bring about a tragedy.

BS&KS *Your Clown seems to represent yet another, let's call it, compliant minority of people, adrift in an unfamiliar new world, easily mislead, deceived, even betrayed. Indeed, the concept of 'betrayal' is central to the production. Could you say a little about how it applies to such different characters as the Clown, Iago, Othello and Desdemona?*

PM Yes, it is a complex world. The Clown finds himself adrift, he doesn't know the new language well and is incapable of devising stories for his European audience. With Othello and

Iago, he prefers to speak Ibo; from time to time, he tries to speak 'Venetian' (the words Shakespeare wrote for the part). However, his accent is so heavy, his speech so clumsy, his grammar non-existent, that he sounds comical. When Iago begins to explain his ideas by playing with the marionettes, the Clown originally goes along with him, because he feels that Iago is right about his grievances. However, he does not understand all; he does not comprehend Iago's briskly spoken 'Venetian'. It takes him a while to realize the full implication of Iago's ideas, and the connection between play and reality, between a theatrical plot and the monstrosity involving real people. So, in a sense, he is betrayed. He then tries – and fails – to stop an avalanche of events in which human characters, not marionettes, would be irreversibly damaged in the plotting.

'Betrayal', indeed, is something of a fulcrum for us. (By the way, a few seasons ago, I put on Pinter's eponymous play, also here in Varna.) 'Betrayal' has many shapes and forms. Some actions are unforgivable, like betraying one's community, or family. So, if the immigrant Mauritanian community helped Othello, the exiled prince, if they risked their lives and livelihoods to transform him from a pirate into a respected leader in a country different from their own, and if then that same Othello started to ration his own people's chances for upward mobility in that society, well, then . . . Simply put, the question which Iago is asking is: 'Who are you to control my life's chances with your political shenanigans when I gave up everything to follow you?'

Desdemona also in some way betrays her community. The audience inevitably empathizes with her, becaus she is a romantic and sympathetic character. In our production, too, we empathize with Desdemona (Paulina Nedkova), but we also underline the trauma to her family by suggesting a connection between her elopement and her father's death. In the production, Brabantio's death is announced by his twin brother, Gratiano, who arrives with the Venetian delegation to bring the order about making Cassio governor. The same actor, Stoyan Radev, performs both Brabantio and Gratiano.

Thus, the impact of the news was compounded by the physical similarity. Desdemona is distraught by the news, brought by a man in her father's image (though of course, we dressed the characters in different colours). She is smitten by guilt, which leads to her passive acceptance of her own demise, to her lack of resistance in the final scene.

BS&KS *In the history of Bulgarian Othellos, the eponymous character has always been played by white actors. Bulgaria has no colonial history, and the acting profession is racially, though not ethnically, homogeneous. For the first time, in your production, a young Nigerian-Bulgarian actor, Bistra Okereke, makes an appearance. She has an added part, along with another black actor. How did you weave these characters into the fabric of the production?*

PM Because of the absence of black actors, Othello has always been a somewhat exotic play in Bulgaria. When you offer actors to play it, the first thing they ask is, 'Are we doing blackface?' Both my principals asked that, because they were both going to play Mauritanians. In fact, in the Western African empires there were black people, Arabs, Tuaregs, light-skinned Berbers. In this case, we had two black women actors (Bistra Okereke and Regina Elaui-Stoicheva). They appear as actors and dancers from the Clown's troupe, who had come along with him to Venice. Bistra Okereke was also our language and dance consultant, and translator for sections of the text into Ibo.

BS&KS *Since Othello, Iago, the Clown and his dancers form a racially diverse group, how did you mark their belonging to the same immigrant community in Venice?*

PM Language is the country that immigrants inhabit. It is what turns them into a tribe. It binds them together much more than skin colour. When on the streets of New York people speak Bulgarian, usually loudly because nobody can understand them, they *are* in Bulgaria. The critic Toncho Zhechev used to say about Aleko Konstantinov's character, Bay Ganyo,[1] that for all his travels across Europe, he has never been abroad; he only speaks Bulgarian, his habits remain unchanged and wherever he goes, he brings his Bulgaria along. The tongue, which the Mauritanians in Venice speak, is their community, their common biography. To convey this, Bistra Okereke translated some of the dialogues into Ibo, one of the languages of Nigeria. We used it for some conversations between Iago, the Clown, Othello and the two women, both of whom speak good Ibo. These dialogues are partly translations of various bits of Shakespeare's text, partly devised for the occasion; the audience can't follow what the actors say, but the stage context suggests the meaning.

BS&KS *Are the Mauritanians the only Others in your production?*

PM No, you can also hear Turkish, the language of the Muslim community in Cyprus. We imagined Montano and Bianca as Turkish-speaking locals, who are Venetian-ized, and have taken Italian names. Not unlike modern Asians adopting Western names instead of their own. Bianca is flattered that a Venetian gentleman appears to be interested in her and leaves her lover, Montano, the Venetian protégé from among the locals.

The Cypriots are further characterized by Oriental touches to their costumes, though they are perfectly fluent in the language of the Venetians. The Mauritanians who live in Venice also wear a combination of West-African and Venetian clothes, not unlike modern diplomats who don traditional garb for official functions and wear mainstream clothes the rest of the time.

BS&KS *Two of the three female characters in* Othello *are murdered by their husbands; the third is a socially marginalized prostitute. Was violence against women something you actively engaged with?*

PM Just as we do not focus specifically on race and racism, we do not foreground the obvious sexism. Nor do we make much of the age difference between Desdemona and Othello, though we have preserved Iago's argument that in such cases love is problematic. Bianca is not a prostitute in our production, either. There are plenty of productions about the racial nature of the conflict, about their unequal marriage, about the plight of women, about the perfect villains with their webs of intrigue; these have become rather standard. All these elements are present, because they are in the play, but they are not central to us. Nor is our handkerchief white and embroidered; it is a piece of red voile, light enough to fly in the air, not something to wipe your nose with. To hell with the stupid, philistine handkerchief, the great symbol of marital infidelity, jealousy, magic, maternal legacy, or what you will!

We are much more interested in how people, whose honesty, nobility, truthfulness and selflessness the world is ready to vouch for, at some point can become capable of the most atrocious things. We kept asking ourselves, 'What does "I am not what I am" mean'?

BS&KS *Yet, humour is generously used in your production. Modern audiences appreciate this approach, but it can also be a slippery slope. How did you avoid skidding, or did you?*

PM I like inter-genre spaces in drama and believe that when theatre does not make people laugh, it is laughed at. That is why I kept the Clown from the original play, though he is often cut in performance, and gave him a troupe with quite a bit of stage action.

The theatricalized presentation of the play's intrigues with the marionettes creates a sense of fun and lightness. Then, Iago tries the same intrigues on real people and what was comical becomes tragic.

Keeping the balance was, of course, difficult, but in *Othello* Shakespeare also alternates scenes with different genre characteristics, as Chekhov does. People who do not understand this produce school-book performances; the audience then respectfully sits to the end; it already knows the story. Luckily, in the theatre there is no remote control to change the channel. To avoid audiences feeling the need for it, we must make intense, dynamic theatre, where points of view and genre expectations shift all the time. I am not saying it is easy, but it is worth the effort. As in the previous productions of the Varna Theatre, *Richard III*, *Uncle Vanya*, *The Government Inspector* and *Shakespeare in Love*, we worked with the same wonderful group of actors. I believe we offered our audiences intense, moving, surprising and varied productions.

BS&KS *Your production does not end exactly as Shakespeare's play does. What did you change?*

PM The change has to do with Iago's demise. We had the Clown stab him, instead of Othello. Though at the beginning he is something of an accomplice, during the play he tries several times to stop Iago, and at the end, uses the weapon himself. Destiny itself intervenes in Iago's death. He ends up, in a way, like a marionette, which cannot die, rising again and again, and repeating, 'I bleed, sir, but not killed' (*Oth* 5.2.285).

BS&KS *What about love, in the tense field between the individual and the tribe? Will daughters always carry the burden of guilt for marrying an Other? Where does our modern world stand in this respect?*

PM We had no ambition to deal with patriarchal mores. We are simply examining a particular case. Nor are we philosophers, or educators. What we do is offer different points of view. Our motto is, 'We are not the answer to a problem, we are the raw pain'.

All in all, throughout the whole process of working on *Othello*, we had the wind in our sails. Except that on the day of our guest performance at the National Theatre 'Ivan Vazov' in Sofia, our bus had to turn back midway and return to Varna, because of the announcement of the coronavirus quarantine. We are in a lockdown now and hoping for better times ahead.

Note

1 Aleko Konstantinov's satirical short stories about Bay Ganyo, published as newspaper feuilletons and collected in 1895 under the title, *Bay Ganyo: Improbable Short Stories about a Contemporary Bulgarian*, offer an uncompromising portarait of the boorishness and self-importance of the nascent bourgeoisie in the newly restored Bulgarian state (1878).

Coda

Staging Shakespeare's Others and their biblical archetype

Péter Dávidházi

Words hardly ever shed their former meanings entirely, as J. L. Austin acutely observed; their etymology often preserves a model of action that keeps governing even their most sophisticated later applications (Austin 1979: 201–3). If so, we cannot ignore the archaic idea still hidden in the word *crisis*, the hallmark term of the twenty-first century. When the authors of this volume survey some of the recent crises of their respective countries – gruesome terrorist attacks, waves of mass-migration, the (re)emergence of hard-line politics, domestic violence – they invariably use the same word and its latent paradigm, which also apply to the ongoing crises of the Covid-19 pandemic and global warming. The Greek verb *krino* means to decide, or make a judgement, the noun *krites* refers to an arbiter, so *krisis* is like the crucial moment of a trial just before the sentence is revealed. Indeed, our current crises entail that our condition has been worsening, reaching a *critical* point when we still do not know whether the outcome is life or death. The supposed agency of the implied verdict, human or divine, is not defined, but there is still a chance to appeal and avert the worst.

Waiting for the verdict, and also hoping to influence it, this volume's European scholars (who are also *critics*, trained to judge dramatic works and performances) explore the possibilities of theatre helping us to survive. This is not a time to stay aloof: the authors of this volume may profess different views, but their strong commitment is always evident. Focusing on recent productions of *Othello* and *The Merchant of Venice*, they analyse the two plays by foregrounding the aliens, whether alienated because of origin, gender, race or religion. They also testify to the creative effort the best productions make in order to remind us of our acute problems, by letting the Other speak through Shakespeare.

However, their analyses also reveal the ghost of an old acquaintance from the Bible, haunting these new European performances. Paradoxically, the only time when the Bible is mentioned in this volume is when we learn from Francesca Rayner (Chapter 9) about a Portuguese judge who quoted it to justify his judgement that a woman's adultery can be a mitigating factor in her murder. The frames of reference used in this volume are resolutely secular, even if occasionally somebody (most emphatically Arnaud Churin, Chapter 12) may criticize the narrowly rationalist matrix of secularism, its lack of a mythical sensibility, and the wide gap between its ethical norms and the startling world of our everyday experience. Yet, as Janice Valls-Russell (Chapter 5) recalls Jean-Paul Sartre's essential observations (made in 1944) about *prelogical archaisms* as the origin of hatred towards the Other, and shows how two French productions of *The Merchant of Venice* (2001 and 2017) staged the post-modern resurgence of such *archaic* motivations, it may come as no surprise that, tracing back the linear perspective of the composite mental landscape in this collection, one finds the vanishing point in that amazing storehouse of archaic knowledge, both prelogical and logical, the Bible. The analyses of all productions presented here fall into a pattern around a latent centre: the biblical archetype of the perennial Other and the devastating collateral damage of hostile othering. This can serve as a *tertium comparationis* to highlight the most relevant features of the two plays at a critical moment of European history.

The Other, when desperately needed in a crisis

When director Plamen Markov (Chapter 13) reveals that the germinal idea for his 2020 Varna production of *Othello* was that 'the Moor Othello is made Commander-in-Chief at a critical moment for Venice, a recognition that the city lacks able leaders for its maritime wars', he adds that it is the Turkish danger that compels the Duke and the Senate to 'legalize Desdemona's abduction by Othello in order to use his exceptional military abilities to save their skins', and that 'these are acts of sheer expediency, overriding racial, class, or moral considerations'. Markov is talking about this play only, but the gist of his interpretation could apply to *The Merchant of Venice* as well. After all, it is a similar crisis, not military but financial, that makes another alien, Shylock, desperately needed. Without the crisis the alien would be openly despised and alienated, but now, for a delicate moment, the despisers have to negotiate the discrepancy between their own hostile feelings and the veneer of civility that their sheer self-interest dictates.

It is at this point that tracing the common biblical archetype can reveal the plays' insidious ways of alienating the Other. The text is from the story of Jephthah in Judges 11–12, arguably one of the most Shakespearean books of the Bible in its theme and concerns, which (11.30–40) is famously echoed in *Hamlet* (2.2.339–58) and *Henry VI Part 3* (5.1.90–2). Its major episodes and its entire dramatic structure can illuminate the question of why European directors focus on problems of otherness in the Venice plays.

Recasting a biblical ancestor of Othello and Shylock: Enter Jephthah

In the Geneva Bible, which inspired Shakespeare by its main text and marginal glosses (Mowat 2012), the very first verse of Judges 11 says that 'Iphtáh the Gileadite was a valiant man, but the sonne of an harlot'.[1] Here 'valiant', explained in the margin as 'a man of mightie force', reminds us of the epithet usually applied to Othello. As it is counterpointed by 'harlot', implying Jephthah's vulnerable social status due to his illegitimate birth, the dramaturgy of this biblical narrative foreshadows a clash of interests with dark consequences, not unlike the Shakespearean conflict between a talented bastard and the rightful yet unfitting heir. The expulsion of Jephthah comes in due course: Gilead's wife bore sons and when they 'were come to age, they thrust out Iphtáh, and said vnto him, Thou shalt not inherit in our fathers house: for thou art the sonne of a strange woman' (Judg. 11.2).

Calling her a 'strange' woman (i.e. a Stranger) may be less rude than the biblical narrator's 'harlot', but it is enough to deprive her son of his rights in the family and make him an outcast. This alienating linguistic device is even more discreetly efficient in the original Hebrew text where the adjective is *aheret*, that is, 'another' woman or 'the other' woman. As *aheret* literally means 'one coming behind' or 'one further away', few epithets could be as apt for indexing the process of *othering* as 'the son of *another* woman'. The label constructs an easy target when self-interest wishes to find reasons for treating a close relative as the Other who should be kept apart, at a safe distance, well behind the 'real' members of the family.

Alienated, Jephthah fled to the land of Tob, gathered some dubious followers there, made forays with them and soon got the reputation of a formidable warrior. When the Ammonites attacked Israel, the Gileadites needed him more than ever. They approached him, and the ensuing bargain sounds like some crucial scenes in Shakespeare's Venetian plays.

Bargains with the alienated: Jephthah, Shakespeare's Strangers and recent European politics

The elders of Gilead said: 'Come and be our captaine, that we may fight with the children of Ammón', but Jephthah's evasive counter-question reminded them of the uncomfortable past: 'Did not ye hate me, and expel me out of my fathers house? how then come you vnto me now in time of your tribulation?' This indignant yet calculating response (implying the elders' share of responsibility in his expulsion) sufficed to make them upgrade their offer from captain to 'head ouer all the inhabitants of Gileád', and when Jephthah made them confirm the terms of their pact, he was appointed both captain and head (Judg. 11.6–11).

The expediencies of the impending war with a frightening enemy make this negotiation similar to the Duke's straightforward offer to Othello: 'Valiant Othello, we must straight employ you / Against the general enemy Ottoman' (*Oth* 1.3.49–50). This, too, is followed by a more urgent plea when news about the approaching enemy reaches Venice, and this time the Duke acknowledges Othello's irreplaceable merits: 'The Turk with a most mighty preparation makes for Cyprus. Othello, the fortitude of the place is best known to you, and though we have there a substitute of most allowed sufficiency, yet opinion . . . throws a more safer voice on you' (1.3.222–6). The Moor's promotion must have also produced resentment, fear and disdain; Brabantio's fury when hearing about Othello abducting and marrying Desdemona represents not only the father's worry: 'For if such actions may have passage free / Bond-slaves and pagans shall our statesmen be' (1.2.98–9). In spite of such lurking sentiments Othello, the alien needed in crisis, is offered his high military rank.

The rhetoric and psychology of Jephthah's reluctant first reply is even nearer to Shylock's answer to Antonio's request, similarly pointing out the self-contradiction in his opponent's behaviour: 'Well, then, it now appears you need my help. / Go to, then, you come to me, and you say, / "Shylock, we would have moneys." You say so. / You, that did void your rheum upon my beard / And foot me as you spurn a stranger cur / Over your threshold' (1.3.110–15). Exposed, Antonio cynically answers that he would spit again on Shylock, who should therefore lend him the money as to an enemy and hope for the opportunity to retaliate.

In the background of all three dialogues there is the same desire to use the Stranger for gaining power and to preserve his negative stereotype for the same purpose, thus exploiting the Other ruthlessly both as an aid and as a scapegoat. The sad political relevance of all this is not difficult to find in Europe today. When Natália Pikli (Chapter 7) remarks that 'George Soros, a Hungarian-born Jewish-American businessman, became the [Hungarian] government's favourite scapegoat, for, as they were still claiming at the time of writing, financing the refugees' migration to Hungary', the unsurpassable irony was that in recent decades he has been utilized both as a friend in times of need and as an enemy responsible for all evils, sometimes both simultaneously. Many are eager to forget that in 1989 the Soros Foundation generously financed Western scholarships for Hungarian intellectuals, including the future prime minister Viktor Orbán and several members of his staff. Moreover, in October 2010, when an industrial disaster spilled toxic sludge over entire settlements in West Hungary, Soros, as chair of his Open Society Foundation, quickly responded to prime minister Orbán's appeal for help and donated one million US dollars, uneradicable photos showing them laughing together in the Hungarian Parliament. At the onset of the Covid-19 pandemic, in March 2020, amidst a campaign of hostile propaganda painting Soros as one of Hungary's arch-enemies, with large posters all over the country urging that 'we should not let Soros have the last laugh', he still donated one million euros to his birthplace, Budapest, for medical aid, a sum promptly labelled in the government media as shamelessly mean almsgiving. The senators in *Othello*, Antonio in *Merchant* and even the elders of Gilead could not have played more adeptly the dubious game of alienating *and* instrumentalizing the Other.

Othered by language: From the 'Shibboleth' test to modern dialects on the stage

The rationalization of hostile othering required no less ingenuity in the war between Jephthah's Gileadites and their various enemies than in the productions of the two plays. Recent performances tend to replace differences of race and religion with much less visible cultural markers of the peoples living in modern Europe. Othello is played as white (or everybody as black), the visible signs of Shylock's Jewishness are downplayed, costumes are radically modernized and otherness is often signalled only by the subtler acoustic differences between regional languages or dialects.

Different accents have always been exploited for delimiting communal identity, but when Jephthah's triumphant Gileadites wanted to prevent the defeated Ephraimites from escaping unrecognized at the passages of the Jordan, their cultural similarity was so great that they had to devise a cunning test to identify them. They asked each of them, 'Say now Shibboleth', but each said 'Sibboleth' ('for he colde not so pronounce') and all were killed, 42,000 men altogether (Judg. 12.6).

This story attracted highly imaginative literary allusions, including those by Paul Celan (Redfield 2020: 50–85), but recent stagings of Shakespeare's aliens expose a further connection. The merciless use of the Shibboleth test is typical of the violence unleashed by what is perceived as an alarming threat posed by the almost-identical, an anxiety that hinders social integration and assimilation. The psychological message here is close to Sigmund Freud's formula of 'the narcissism of minor differences' in 'The Taboo of Virginity' (1918), inspired by Ernest Crawley, suggesting that 'it is precisely the minor differences in people who are otherwise alike that form the basis of feelings of strangeness and hostility between them' (Freud 1955: vol. 11, 199). Recent productions of Shakespeare's two plays tend to affirm this thesis. Writing about a 2004 Belgrade performance of *The Merchant of Venice*, Zorica Bećanović Nikolić (Chapter 4) cites Freud's phrase to pinpoint an 'intra-European disdain for otherness' when the 'Italian' Portia ridicules Monsieur Le Bon and Baron Falconbridge in a performance that is based on the post-humanist tenet that there is no such thing as a universal human nature since, owing to our unique situations, we are all Others. While making effective use of dialects on the stage, productions today cannot help recasting the biblical arch-story and its message of just how small a difference can suffice to be turned into a lethal weapon.

The sacrifice of Jephthah's daughter, femicides and alienated women in twenty-first-century productions

Jephthah, zealous to win the decisive battle and become the ruler of those who had expelled him, made a vow to God that if He delivered the Ammonites into his hands he would sacrifice the first living being he met on his return – thus he had to sacrifice his own daughter (11.30–40). Deplored by commentators over the centuries as the 'rash' vow (Thompson 2001: 100–78), it is Jephthah's fatal act that Hamlet was hinting at when he quoted a ballad adaptation, thereby warning Polonius not to expose Ophelia to the dangers of the court. This is all the more disturbing when we remember that Jephthah's vow promised not just any sacrifice but a burnt offering, and the minute biblical description of that process (Lev. 1.3–17) talks about killing, flaying and cutting to pieces before burning, not to speak of the later accreted meanings of his vow in the Vulgate translation of Judg. 11.31, 'eum holocaustum offeram' (Dávidházi 2015). Modern feminist and post-colonial readings (Exum 2007; Kim 2007) radically revaluate this story, refuse most of its traditional moral implications and resent the message of its pious ending (11.40) that wanted to commemorate the obedient daughter without a name of her own.

This critical turn is very similar to some recent interpretations of *Othello* which see it as an enactment of domestic violence ending in femicide, a play in which every woman is labelled a whore by her man. As Sara Barros Leitão, the assistant director of a Portuguese staging puts it (Chapter 9), the protagonist is the unforgivable murderer of a woman: the play is not about jealousy but about women's liberation. Considering the damage, it is difficult to find consolation in the biblical idea, spelled out also in Judges 9.57 and figuring as a phrase both in *Othello* (1.3.192) and *Merchant* (4.1.206), that finally it is the wickedness of men that God visits upon them. Several contributions in this volume make the point that two wives are killed by their husbands in *Othello* and, although nobody dies in *Merchant*, once meant to be a comedy after all, the alienated Shylock in pursuit of revenge loses his daughter and his faith; Antonio's life is broken; and no marriage remains unharmed. In the end the alienated Other is left on the stage, dead or alive, surrounded by devastation.

Looking for orientation in crisis: From 'the Other-within' to 'strangers and sojourners'

From theatres we cannot expect solutions for the enormous problem of how to save civilized life on the planet, yet their overall warning sounds right: we cannot afford to alienate the Other much longer. Boika Sokolova and Kirilka Stavreva

(Chapter 2) justly praise two Bulgarian adaptations of *Othello* because 'their aesthetic forges powerful affective connections with the Other-within' and 'their spectators are given a space to take the civilizing step of recognizing the humanity of the Other'. In France, director Arnaud Churin (Chapter 12), refusing all 'authoritarian, divisive responses to the question of the Other', convincingly argues that 'our planet is not well: given the number of us living on this planet, we are going to have to allow the Other into our lives'. This insight is not far from Chancellor Angela Merkel's ideal of a *Willkommenskultur*, which is deeply rooted in the Bible, even if its practical difficulties (as we learn from Bettina Boecker in Chapter 10) have become painfully obvious.

Probably there is not much time left to guard our lives and lands from the 'Other' at all costs (even for those who would advocate such policies). It is vital to rethink the meaning of both 'ours' and the Stranger's. When Jephthah and the King of Ammon debated over the ownership of the territory east of Jordan, which they both called 'my land', Jephthah referred to the divine help received in a former battle as legitimating its possession (Judg. 11.12–23). Yet, in his argument, we may detect an unintended further implication, less helpful for his purposes but more relevant to our global queries today. Even if it was the Lord who helped an army occupy a land, it is still *His* land, so the winners have no right to expel its inhabitants as forever dispossessed strangers, especially because ultimately that is what we all are. This sublime thesis is laid down in the same biblical book, Leviticus, which also contains the rules of the burnt offering Jephthah so fatally vowed to God. In Shakespeare's closely read Geneva Bible, the Lord explains (Lev. 25.23) why the land cannot be sold forever: 'the land is mine, *and* ye be but strangers and sojourners with me'.

Note

1 I am quoting from a facsimile of the 1560 edition (Berry 2007).

References

Austin, J. L. (1979), *Philosophical Papers*, ed. J. O. Urmson and G. J. Warnock, Oxford: Oxford University Press.

Berry, L. E. (introd.) (2007), *The Geneva Bible: A Facsimile of the 1560 Edition*, Peabody: Hendrickson.

Dávidházi, P. (2015), '"O Jephthah, judge of Israel": From Original to Accreted Meanings in Hamlet's Allusion', *Shakespeare Survey*, 68: 48–61.

Exum, J. C. (2007), 'Whose Interests Are Being Served?', in G. A. Yee (ed.), *Judges & Method: New Approaches in Biblical Studies*, 65–89, Minneapolis: Fortress Press.

Freud, S. (1955), *The Standard Edition of the Complete Psychological Works of Sigmund Freud*, gen. ed. transl. J. Strachey, with A. Freud, A. Strachey and A. Tyson, 24 vols, London: The Hogarth Press and the Institute of Psycho-Analysis.

Kim, U. Y. (2007), 'Who Is the Other in the Book of Judges?', in G. A. Yee (ed.), *Judges & Method: New Approaches in Biblical Studies*, 161–82, Minneapolis: Fortress Press.

Mowat, B. A. (2012), 'Shakespeare Reads the Geneva Bible', in T. DeCook and A. Galey (eds), *Shakespeare, the Bible, and the Form of the Book: Contested Scriptures*, 25–39, New York: Routledge.

Redfield, M. (2020), *Shibboleth: Judges, Derrida, Celan*, New York: Fordham University Press.

Shakespeare, W. ([2010] 2014), *The Merchant of Venice*, ed. J. Drakakis, The Arden Shakespeare, third series, London: Bloomsbury.

Shakespeare, W. (2016), *Othello*, ed. E. A. J. Honigmann, rev. ed., intr. A. Thompson, The Arden Shakespeare, third series, London: Bloomsbury.

Thompson, J. L. (2001), *Writing the Wrongs: Women of the Old Testament among Biblical Commentators from Philo through the Reformation*, Oxford: Oxford University Press.

INDEX

Abadjiev, Vassil 53
Abadjieva, Liliya 15, 16, 50, 52, 53–9, 66 nn.1, 4
Ackermann, Zeno 3–5, 132
adaptation 16, 24, 25, 70–2, 81, 174, 233, 253, 259, 276, *see also The Merchant of Venice*; *Othello*
Adriaanse, Aram 12, 13, 17, 174, 179–85
Africa 2, 4, 8, 13, 128, 200, 260
  West 262–4 (*see also* Mauritania)
African(s) 99, 102, 103, 248, 255
  North- 181, 247, 255
Agamben, Giorgio 7
age 1, 12, 25, 71, 74, 161, 166, *see also* Desdemona; Portia
Alföldi, Róbert 154–6
Al-Qaeda 108
Amisi, Serge 250, 257 n.4
anti-feminism 137, *see also* femicide; violence
anti-Semitism 2–4, 12, 14, 109–11, 114, 118–19, 121, 122, 128–9, 134, 137, 140–2, 146–7, 153–6, 161, 166–7, 172, 173, 181–5, 230, 236

Antonio (*MV*) 16, 75, 90, 96–8, 115–20, 123, 135–8, 143, 157–60, 162–3, 166, 180, 185, 218, 237, 241–3, 274, 275, 277
  anti-Semitism 74, 97, 113, 116
  homosexuality 15, 74, 75, 96, 98, 136
  similarity with Shylock 112, 117
Aragon, Louis 116
archaism(s) 111, 114, 270
Arendt, Hannah 8–10
Ariosto, Ludovico 35
Armenia 1
Armstrong, Gareth 138–45, 147
Aron, Raymond 119
Arragon (*MV*) 15–16, 91–2, 110, 115–16, 119–20, 137, 162, 182
Aschenbach, Gustav von 103
As You Like It 259
audience(s) 2–4, 11–12, 16, 17, 26–7, 32–4, 37, 39, 49–52, 54, 56–9, 65–6, 69–70, 79–82, 99–100, 103, 110–17, 120–1, 136, 138, 141, 143–6, 154, 157–9, 161–4, 167–8, 177,

179, 183–5, 193, 201,
203–4, 214–18, 231,
234–9, 241–3, 250–6,
259, 262–3, 266–7,
see also reception
  Anglo-American 12, 15,
   108, 182
  French 12, 113, 122–3,
   256
  German 216, 218
  Hungarian 156, 164–5
  international 26, 139
  Polish 26, 80
  Portuguese 195, 197–8
  Romanian 80, 133, 139
  Serbian 91, 95–6
  sympathy 57, 97, 159,
   162, 191, 192, 195
Austin, A. J. 269

Bagó, Bertalan 154–5,
   164–7
Bancou, Marielle 111, 122,
   124 n.1
Bassanio (*MV*) 74–7, 91, 96,
   114–15, 117–20, 136,
   144, 158–60, 162,
   181, 241, 244
Bassi, Shaul 5–6, 14, 44,
   45 n.4, 100
Bauman, Zygmunt 25, 73,
   83 n.8, 84 n.19
Bayser, Clotilde de 113
Bečanović Nikolić, Zorica 10,
   26, 89, 94, 276
Beckett, Samuel 59, 244
Bianca (*Oth*) 100, 178, 201,
   231, 253, 265, 266
Bible 200–1, 270, 271, 278
  Geneva 11, 272, 278

blackface 12, 13, 50, 51,
   70, 77–9, 176, 179,
   215–16, 224–5 n.5,
   249, 264
Blackmore, Josiah 200,
   206 n.7
blackness 6, 25, 29, 34,
   37, 40, 42, 94,
   102, 106 n.2, 200,
   206 nn.7, 8
  -within 14, 44
Blanc, Christian 113
Blixen, Karen 181
Bocsárdi, Laszlo 16, 132,
   135–8, 145, 146
Boecker, Bettina 10, 130,
   186 n.2, 209, 278
Boissery, Jean 256 n.2
Bolsonaro, Jair 191, 199, 205
Bondy, Luc 249
Bonell, Andrew 5
Branco, Dinarte 193, 199
Braudel, Fernand 37
Brexit 205
Brinkema, Eugenie 59
Brugnera, Andrea 243
Busi, Anna 5

Callaghan, Dympna 102, 103
Calvino, Italo 40
Camilleri, Andrea 39
Capelo Cardoso, Paulo 194
Caravaggio 102
Cardoso, João 198, 207 n.11
Cardoso, Nuno M. 193–8,
   205 n.1
Carinhas, Nuno 15, 193,
   198–204, 207 n.11
Cassio (*Oth*) 33, 46 n.15, 61,
   63–4, 100, 101, 178,

197, 249, 253, 254, 260, 263
critical conscience 35
Stranger 36, 55
Castorf, Frank 211
Catholic(s) 3, 77, 85 n.26, 86 nn.30–1, 92, 121
Celan, Paul 275
Cetera, Anna 5
Ćetković, Vojin 99
Ceylan, Nuri Bilge 29, 30
Charlie Hebdo 109
Cheek by Jowl 193
Chekhov, Anton 259, 266
Christian(s) 3, 74, 75, 77, 90, 92, 94, 95, 101, 114, 118, 129, 137, 140, 143–5, 147, 155, 162, 182, 204, 240
Churin, Arnaud 11, 230–1, 245–6, 256 n.3, 257 nn.4, 6, 270, 278
Cimitile, Anna Maria 10, 25, 29
Cinpoeş, Nicoleta 10, 128, 130, 131, 134, 135, 140–5, 148 n.11
Cioran, E. M. 38
Cloarec, Christian 116
Coetzee, J. M. 82
Cohen, Stephen 2
colonial/ism/ization 1, 4, 6, 12, 16, 45, 46 n.16, 49, 84 n.19, 106 n.2, 186, 195, 199, 200, 212, 264
Coluche (Colucci, Michel) 246
Comaroff, J. and J. L. 45

Comédie-Française, Paris 108, 109, 110, 113, 116, 124 nn.1, 7
Comedy Theatre, Bucharest
commedia dell'arte 15, 110, 141, 142, 213, 236
communism/t 6, 8, 13, 49–52, 128–9, 134, 138, 153, 155, 211, *see also* post-communism
Compagnia de' Colombari 233
Coonrod, Karin 11, 14, 46 n.5, 230, 233–4
coronavirus, *see* Covid-19 pandemic
Coryat, Thomas 37
Covid-19 pandemic 18 n.4, 122, 124 n.1, 125 n.14, 191–2, 234, 245, 255, 268, 269, 274
Craiova International Shakespeare Festival 1, 80, 138, 139
Crawley, Ernest 276
crisis 10, 171, 191–2, 211
archetypal 11, 269–78
migrant/refugee 9, 17, 80, 130, 154, 164, 209–27
and the Other 271–2, 274
Cyprus 16, 45 n.4, 51, 100–1, 103, 196, 203, 212, 213, 231, 265, 273
Czechoslovakia 8

Daisme, Johan 113
daughter(s) 63, 74, 77, 93, 112, 116, 120, 137,

144, 161–2, 236, 255,
260, 267, 276–7,
see also Desdemona;
Jessica
Dávidházi, Péter 11, 269, 277
De Filippo, Eduardo 39
Delabastita, Dirk 4
Déprats, Jean-Michel 124
nn.3, 10, 246
Derrida, Jacques 38
Desdemona (*Oth*) 13, 32–4,
51, 55, 57–9, 61–2,
75, 78–9, 90–1, 95,
99–100, 102–3,
105, 176, 178, 205,
213–16, 249, 251,
254–5, 260, 273–4
age difference with
Othello 1, 231, 266
disgrace 79
mirror image of
Othello 203–4
nun 81, 202
responsible for her own
death 203
sense of guilt 263–4
Stranger 14, 35–6, 44
victim of domestic
violence 15, 33, 59,
196–8, 201–2, 253
Devos, Raymond 246
Diagne, Souleymane
Bachir 255
dialect(s) 14, 25, 30–1, 36–46,
216, 230, 275–6
difference 1, 6–7, 9, 13,
31, 37, 39, 91, 92,
95, 96, 99, 137–8,
195–6, 199, 266,
275–6

cultural 40, 42, 187 n.3,
196
ethnic 12–13, 44, 175,
275
gender/sexual 26–7, 205,
207 n.11
religious 92, 99, 175, 275
disability 25, 71
displacement 4, 13, 30, 38,
44, 54, *see also* exile;
migration
D'Jazzy 115
Dobson, Michael 133, 146
Doesburg, Johan 12, 174–9
Doireau, Pierre-François 121
Donkov, Deyan 54
Donnellan, Declan 193
Draganov, Ivo 60–1
Drakakis, John 18 n.5, 84
n.12, 124 nn.4, 9,
132, 147, 148 n.12
Dreyfus, Alfred (affair) 110,
111, 119
Dubus, Théophile 118

Eagleton, Terry 92, 94
Eisenberg, Ned 243, 244
Ejdus, Predrag 96
Elaui-Stoicheva, Regina 264
El Hamus, Sabri Saad 180,
182, 184
Emilia (*Oth*) 35, 36, 57–8, 67
n.6, 100, 101, 178,
198, 201, 216, 231,
260
death 103, 253
helplessness 179
empathy 93, 190–3, 215,
220–4, *see also*
audience sympathy

between characters 16, 93, 129
  with Desdemona 263
  with Iago 2, 197
  lack of 113, 197
  with Othello 196, 204
  radical 129–30, 190–208
  with Shylock 159, 161
  and sympathy 191, 195
Entzinger, Han 173
ethnicity 6, 7, 13–14, 25, 34, 44, 70, 71, 73, 78, 84 n.18, 85 n.22, 101, 128
Europe 1–17, 24, 29, 37–8, 50, 80, 82, 85 n.22, 86 n.30, 91–4, 128, 134, 146, 191–3, 198, 199, 210, 233, 265, 273–5
  Balkan(s) 98, 99
  borders 6, 7, 92, 93, 134, 193, 222
  Eastern 4, 5, 8, 106 n.1, 129, 133
  Iberian 8, 200
  North/South divide(s) 6, 8, 44
  regions 2, 5–7, 14, 25, 30, 31, 38–44, 98, 216
  West(ern) 4, 6, 8, 30, 44, 147 n.2, 211, 274
European Union 4, 86 n.31, 129, 135
exclusion 8, 25, 53, 60, 73, 80, 85 n.22, 103, 128, 146, 167

Fassbinder, Rainer Werner 12, 181

Felder, Franz Xaver 133, 147 n.1
femicide 36, 254, 276–7
feminism/t (anti-) 54, 81, 137, 201, 255, 277
Ferency, Andrzej 73–4, 78
First World War 7
Fischer, Laurence 254
Fischer, Susan L. 5, 109, 113, 121, 123
Fisk, Robert 183
Fo, Dario 40
Folias d'Arte 193
Fortuyn, Pim 172–4
Foucault, Michel 100
Freud, Sigmund 91, 254, 257 n.6, 276
Funès, Louis de 18 n.4, 113

Gadamer, Hans-Georg 26, 89, 91
Gadda, Carlo Emilio 40
Gáspár, Sándor 165
gay(s), *see* homosexual(s)
gender 4, 8, 12, 15, 25–7, 66, 85 n.22, 90, 96, 98, 129, 178, 193, 196, 203, 206 n.4, 270, *see also* difference
  MV 76, 78, 146, 240–2
  Oth 2, 24–5, 53–9, 66 n.3, 193, 198, 200–1, 203–5, 207 n.12, 253–5
Genet, Mathieu 254
Geyer-Ryan, Helga 93–4, 98, 104
Ghetto Sheriff 153
Gibbons, Brian 39
Gibińska, Marta 10
Gilead 272–3, 275

Glass, Philip 58
global/ization 3, 29, 45,
    46 n.12, 73, 84 n.19,
    100–1, 114, 191, 278
Gobetti, Piero 40
God 77, 92, 160, 177, 276–8
Goethe, Johann Wolfgang
    von 37–8
Gogh, Theo van 129, 172–5,
    179–80, 186
Gogh, Vincent van 173
Gonzalez Thomas 118
Görög, László 156
Gospodinov, Penko 262
*The Government
    Inspector* 267
Gramsci, Antonio 25, 31,
    40–1, 44–6 n.15, 156
Gratiano
    MV 96, 118, 121, 158,
        159, 162
    Oth 253, 263
Greenblatt, Stephen 93, 95,
    101, 103, 106 n.2,
    129, 190–1, 205
Gregor, Keith 2
Grois, Lyuben 13, 50–2, 65,
    66 n.1
Gross, John 186 n.3
Guidi, Michele 244
Guntner, Lawrence 11, 24,
    128, 230

Hamlet/Hamlet 34, 72,
    83 n.2, 130, 138,
    147 n.1, 148 n.8, 155,
    223 n.2, 271, 276
hate/hatred 77, 145, 147, 192,
    240, 273
    hate speech 9, 155–8

Héga, Julie 254
Heidegger, Martin 38, 89
Heijden, Hein van der 172,
    173, 180
Heijes, Coen 10, 15, 129, 173,
    175
Henry VI Part 3 271
Hermanis, Alvis 210
hermeneutics 91, 94
Hevér, Gábor 158
Hillje, Jens 212
Hirsi Ali, Ayaan 173
Holbus, Jasmina 99
Holocaust 70, 80, 85 n.24,
    129, 153, 173, 277,
    see also Jews; post-
    Holocaust; Roma
homosexual(s/-ity) 15, 26, 71,
    72, 74–5, 83 n.6, 96,
    98, 136
Hove, Ivo van 179
Hungarian National Theatre,
    Budapest 133

Iago 13, 31, 32–3, 34, 35, 42,
    46 nn.6, 15, 56, 61,
    64–5, 75, 85 n.23,
    90–5, 100–4, 129,
    176–9, 190, 199, 201,
    213, 215, 225 n.5,
    231, 247, 253, 261–3,
    266, 267
    (aggressive)
        masculinity 55, 57–8
    cold rationality 195
    empathy with 2, 190–1,
        205
    infantilized 57
    as Moor 13, 260, 265
    as Neapolitan 36

and the Other 249, 252
patriarchal 255
populist
   attractiveness 191, 197
racist 193, 195, 200, 248
sexist 193
identification 2–3, 7, 9, 11, 14, 42, 49, 57, 105, 193, 213–14, 223–4
identity/ies 1, 2, 14, 25, 31, 40, 66, 70, 82, 99, 117, 136, 144, 174, 212
   artistic 137
   blended 71, 73
   collective 9, 27, 146, 275
   deconstruction 95, 104
   feigned 119
   fluid 78, 220
   hybrid 13, 93, 101
   layered 6–7, 31
   national 4, 7, 134
   politics 71
immigrants 2, 3, 14, 184, 191, 199, 262, 264
immigration 8, 172, 173, 179, 191, 199, 209, *see also* immigrants; migration; refugees
Imre, Zoltán 153, 156, 168 n.2
Ingarden, Roman 71
intermediality 36, 70, 73
Irving, Henry 155
Iser, Wolfgang 89

Jamois, Marguerite 110
jealousy 2, 34, 36, 37, 44, 91, 101–3, 176–9, 186, 194, 195, 201, 266, 277

Jeanne, Anthony 118
Jelesijević, Marija 99
Jelinek, Elfriede 218
Jephthah 271–8
Jessica 74, 75, 96, 112, 113, 115, 116, 118, 120, 123, 143–4, 157, 161–4, 185, 236–40
   adolescent 120, 236, 241
   American tourist 114
   conversion 75, 98, 114
   otherer 115
   silence of 241, 243
Jewishness 94, 97, 98, 108, 119, 140, 142, 154, 161, 164, 165, 167, 171, 172, 275
Jew(s) 4, 5, 7, 13, 14, 17, 26, 72–7, 83 n.6, 90, 92, 94, 96–8, 109, 111, 113, 117–19, 121, 122, 129, 132, 133, 135, 140, 144, 146, 148 n.5, 152–3, 155, 158–64, 166, 173, 180–4, 186, 218, 230, 234, 239–42, *see also* Holocaust
   assimilation/pressure to assimilate 8–9, 159, 276
   extermination 8, 80, 153
   figure of 3, 153
   stereotypes 12, 136, 143, 157
João Pinho, Maria 201, 207 n.11
Jonas, Daniel 199, 201, 202
jouissance 104
Joyce, James 42

Julius Caesar 259

Karamazov, Vladimir 54
Kern, András 164
Khamphommala,
 Vanasay 121, 123,
 125 n.12
King Lear 25, 69, 74, 79,
 147 n.1, 238
Klajn, Hugo 96
Koblišková, Zuzana 5
Konstantinov, Aleko 265,
 268 n.1
Kovács, Márton 157, 167
Ksander, Peter 237
Kujawińska, Krystina
 Courtney 5

Lacan, Jacques 83 n.4, 104
Lancelet/ot 16, 96, 114, 115,
 121, 123, 125 n.11,
 143, 158
Lancillotto, *see* Lancelet/ot
Lange, Bob de 171
Langhoff, Shermin 212
language(s) 1, 4, 7, 10, 13,
 16, 32, 34, 38, 58, 70,
 132, 168 n.4, 197,
 231, 235–6, 244 n.1,
 246, 248, 263–4,
 see also dialect(s);
 Shibboleth
 barrier 11, 42, 92, 128,
  262, 275
 body language 14, 25, 76
 comic 253
 of hatred 152, 163
 historically conditioned 91
 multiple 14, 111, 230,
  234, 236, 265

regional 14, 24, 39, 41,
 46 n.15
László, Zsolt 166, 167
Lea-Jones, Jenni 241
Lear 12, 25, 26, 35, 69, 73–4,
 79, 147 n.1, 238
Lemoine Jean-René 117
Le Poulain, Jean 110
Lessing, Gotthold
 Ephraim 221
Levinas, Emmanuel 7, 9, 10,
 16, 105, 115
LGBTQI 191
Lilienthal, Matthias 217–18,
 221–3
Limon, Jerzy 73
locality 29, 30, 37, 44
Lo Cascio, Luigi 14, 16, 31–7,
 41, 42, 46 n.6
Lolić, Miloš 13, 90, 99, 102,
 104
London, Frank 236
Lormeau, Nicolas 114
Lorry-Dupuy, Mathieu 117
Loureiro, Rita 196
Love's Labour's Lost 259
Lyutakov, Simeon 262

Macbeth 259
McConachie, Bruce 203
Macron, Emmanuel 109
Madel Nelson-Rafaell 253
Maffesoli, Michel 26, 54, 60,
 109, 111, 118
Mălăele, Bogdan 143
Mălăele, Horațiu 11, 132,
 139, 144, 147
Malaparte, Curzio 37, 38
marginalization 7, 9, 26, 71,
 219

marionettes 262, 263, 266
Markov, Plamen 11, 13, 15, 230, 251, 258, 271
masculinity 15, 52, 53, 55, 57, 58, 66
Mauritanian(s) 263–5
Mediterranean 2, 7, 175
Meneghello, Luigi 40, 41, 44
Mensur, Irfan 96–7
The Merchant in Venice 233–4
The Merchant of Venice, *see also* gender; names of characters
   adaptations of 12, 60–5, 108, 129, 133–5, 139–40, 147, 174, 179–84, 233–44
   in prison 234, 243–4
mercy 120, 133, 134, 145, 147 n.2, 185, 230, 235, 242, 243
Merkel, Angela 209, 278
Merleau-Ponty, Maurice 250, 257 n.5
Mesu, Costiaan 177, 178
métissage 123
#MeToo 252, 253
Meyer-Plantureux, Chantal 5, 12
Mićanović, Dragan 96
A Midsummer Night's Dream 231, 246, 259
migrant(s)/migration 8, 13, 116, 127, 175, 212, 216, 231, 258
   migrant crisis 17, 80, 128, 129, 209
   migrant-led initiatives 220

   migrant *Oth* 258
Milutinović, Dobrica 96
minority 4, 6, 7, 98, 250, 255, 262
   cultural 39, 40, 46 n.14
   ethnic 11, 254, 256
Mira, Virginie 251
Mladenov, Ivan 50, 52, 53, 60, 62, 66
Mohácsi, András (designer) 156
Mohácsi, István (dramaturge) 156
Mohácsi, János (director) 153, 156, 157, 160
Mohácsi brothers 12, 154, 155, 158–60
Molière (Jean-Baptiste Poquelin) 113, 122
Montale, Eugenio 40
Moor 1, 2, 30, 38, 39, 42–4, 50, 93, 94, 104, 171, 190, 195, 200, 206 n.7, 213–15, 219, 225 n.5, 231, 252, 259, 260, 271, 273, *see also* Muslim(s); Ottoman Empire
   Moorish community 13
Morelli, Domenico 100
Morin, Edgar 255, 256
Morocco (char. *MV*) 15, 16, 91, 92, 97, 98, 110, 115, 116, 119, 137, 158, 163, 167, 175, 182
mother 63, 162, 230, 238, 240–1
Mouawad, Wajdi 76, 77
Mozas, Océane 119

multiculturalism 4, 9, 172, 173, 180, 185, 186
music 25, 32, 36, 54, 55, 58, 111, 118, 157, 165, 166, 196, 233, 236–7, 239, 240, 243, 246, 264
Muslim(s) 4, 14, 93, 95, 103, 118, 122, 172, 173, 175, 183–6, 191, 219, 265

Nádasdy, Ádám 152, 164, 165, 168 n.1
Naples 37, 38, 43
 Teatro Bellini 36
nationalism(s) 2, 4, 7, 8, 53, 80, 127, 128, 146, 193
National Theatre, Miskolc 156
National Theatre 'Ivan Vazov', Sofia 53, 267
Nazi/sm 5, 75, 80, 85 n.25, 110, 116, 119, 124 n.6, 148 n.6, 217, 256
Nedkova, Paulina 263
Nekrošius, Eimuntas 193
Nicolao, Stefano 239
Nietzsche, Friedrich 223
9/11 108, 129, 130, 172, 173, 182
Novy, Marianne 139, 195, 196, 201

Oel, Justus van 180–4, 186
Okereke, Bistra 264, 265
Orban, Victor 274
Ostermeier, Thomas 224–5 n.5

Othello, *see also* blackface; Other-within
 Catholic nuptials 78
 Christian 93, 103, 106 n.2, 248
 hybrid identity 13, 93, 101
 imaginary ethnicity 14, 44
 jealousy 2, 34, 36, 37, 44, 91, 101–3, 176, 177, 179, 186, 194, 195, 201, 266, 267
 mercenary 129
 pirate 260, 261, 263
 (West) African 260
 white actors 12, 36, 77, 216, 252, 264
Othello, *see also* gender; names of characters
 adaptations 3, 15, 130, 212–17, 253, 278
 all-male performance 53–9
 chorus 16, 32, 34, 76, 212–15, 219
 Clown in 13, 123, 231, 253, 262–6
 communication 194
 difference within 42
 exclusion 25, 60
 handkerchief 32–4, 36, 57, 59, 201, 251, 266
 jealousy 2, 177
 love 177
 in prison 11, 25, 50, 53, 60–3, 67 nn.7–8
 recognition 2
 Soldier (char.) 16, 32, 34, 35, 46 n.7

Other-within, the 23, 24, 49, 51, 52, 66, 277, 278
Ottoman Empire/Ottomans 2, 6, 49, 128, 134, 216, 273
Oury, Gérard 12, 113

Pacino, Al 243
Parker, Patricia 95
Pasolini, Pier Paolo 35, 39, 40, 43, 44
Pasternak, Boris 1
patriarchy 12, 81, 102, 231, 248
Pegida 14, 210, 216
Perczel, Enikő 156, 159–63
Pesti Színház (theatre), Budapest 164
Petkov, Nikola 51
Pfeifer, Anniek 176
phenomenology 71, 72
Pikli, Natalia 10, 129, 152, 274
Pinter, Harold 263
pity 62, 203, 207, 214, 233
   terror and 16, 105
Pollock, Jackson 101
Pontecorvo, Gillo 256 n.3
Portia 3, 16, 74–81, 90, 91, 96–8, 113–22, 133, 136, 137, 145, 159, 161–6, 182, 185, 218, 241–4
   ageing 76
   Catholic vow 77
   drag queen 96
post-colonial/ism 3, 17, 71, 83 n.9, 195, 212, 255, 277

post-communist 8, 9, 13, 25, 51–66
post-dramatic 24, 70, 72, 83 n.3, 104, 217–23
post-Holocaust 70, 85 n.24, 110, 122, 129
post-modern 16, 54, 83 n.4, 95, 97, 111, 122, 270
post-totalitarian 2, 3, 15, 17
Pouly, Jérôme 113
Powell, Linda 244
prejudice 25, 91, 119, 146, 147, 152, 219, see also racism; stereotypes
   against dialects 14
   anti-African 16, 119, 214, 215
   intra-European 91
presentism 4, 27, 100–5, 132, 136, 142, 147, 164, 198
prison, see *The Merchant of Venice*; *Othello*

Rabkin, Norman 94
race, performance of 1, 2, 4, 5, 6, 12, 13, 15, 24, 25, 37, 51, 52, 59, 65, 70, 71, 78, 81, 84 n.18, 85 n.22, 90, 92, 171, 175, 200, 204, 206 n.8, 212, 213, 215, 216, 231, 266, 270, 275, see also blackface
Rachkov, Dimitar 55
racism 2–4, 8, 15, 44, 71, 80, 110, 128, 129, 145, 153, 155, 156, 158–60, 163, 164,

167, 172, 179, 184,
    186, 213–14, 216,
    224, 231, 247–50, 266
Radev, Stoyan   263
Radnay, Csilla   165
Rayner, Francesca   10, 66 n.3,
    129, 270
reception   14, 30, 69, 79, 140,
    156, 172, 173, 177,
    179, 184, 186, 256,
    see also audience(s)
refugees   4, 8, 9, 128–30, 154,
    191, 198–9, 210–11,
    220–1, 274, *see also*
    migration
religion   7, 37, 85 n.26, 90–2,
    98, 144, 235, 255,
    270, 275
Rétoré, Guy   110
Richard III   100, 177, 259,
    267
right-wing   14, 80, 84–6 n.30,
    118, 129, 154, 216,
    219, 222
Rivette, Jacques   248, 256–7
    n.3
Roderigo   14, 35, 55, 57, 62,
    103, 178, 197, 216,
    253, 261
Rodin, Auguste   240
Roma/ni   7, 14, 99
Römer, Thijs   174–6, 178
Ronconi, Luca   110
Rota, Nino   237
Ruzante   40, 237, 244 n.1

Sakowska, Aleksandra   10, 25,
    69, 72, 73, 148 n.9
Sambo, Raymi   181
Samie, Céline   114

Sartre, Jean-Paul   26, 110,
    111, 119, 123–5 n.15,
    270
Savin, Egon   90, 96, 98,
    106 n.1
Schenk, Tom   178
Schiller, Friedrich   221
Schmitt, Dominique   111
Schülting, Sabine   3–6
Second World War   7, 8, 49,
    63, 75, 80, 110, 122,
    148 n.6, 155, 170,
    184, 217
Seneca   246
Şerban, Andrei   11, 14, 16,
    108, 109, 110, 111,
    113, 115, 117, 122,
    123, 124 nn.1, 10
Serôdio, Maria Helena   204
Seweryn, Andrzej   112, 113
Shakespeare, William, *see also*
    names of individual
    works
    global   17, 31, 44–5
Shakespeare in Love   259, 267
Shibboleth   11, 275
Shylock   5, 6, 11, 26, 69–70, 76,
    78, 90, 92–4, 97, 98,
    108–9, 111, 115, 119,
    120, 123, 130, 139–41,
    147, 152, 165–6, 167,
    168 n.5, 169 n.10, 185,
    218, 242–4, 275
    assimilated/secular
        Jew   14, 117–18,
        122, 172
    collective character   238–41
    conversion to
        Christianity   91, 98,
        162, 167, 241

loss of Jessica 144, 161–2, 236, 238–9, 277
as mother 230, 238, 240–1
as Muslim 4, 13, 219
necessary Other and scapegoat 174, 271
old 137, 142, 160
patriarch 74
post-historical 70, 80
post-humanist 96
racist 15, 163
religious Jew 237
revenge 182
Romanian 128
shared fates with Antonio 158, 162
stereotypical Jew 12, 81, 113, 135, 143
victim 3, 73, 133, 145, 181
  of anti-Semitism 75, 110, 112–14, 116, 121–2, 156, 159, 180, 183–4, 234
Shylock or the Blood Bond 133
Sicily 16, 35, 37, 38
Sluysmans, Michel 177, 178
Smith, Emma 3
Smith, Ian 251
Sofrenović, Ana 96
Sokolova, Boika 5, 8, 10, 12, 25, 49–51, 66 n.2, 80, 124, 133, 146, 153, 277
Soros, George 154, 174, 274, 275
Sousa, Geraldo de 97
Sousa, Sonia de 251

Spezzano, Gianni 31, 42
Spiegelman, Art 75
Spivak, Gayatri 212
Spriet, Pierre 110
State Jewish Theatre, Bucharest 134, 148 n.6
Stavreva, Kirilka 8, 10, 25, 66 nn.2–3, 67 nn.7–8, 277
Steenbergen, Paul 172
Stein, Peter 211
Stelling, Lieke 9
Stemann, Nicolas 14, 211, 217–19
stereotypes 11, 12, 25, 37, 41, 70–3, 75, 78, 79, 81, 83 n.8, 91, 110, 113, 119, 142, 143, 166, 180, 191, 193, 196, 204, 215, 216, 224 n.5, 254, 274
  Jewish (*see* Shylock)
Swados, Elisabeth 111, 124 n.1

Tamási Áron Hungarian Theatre, Sfântu Gheorghe 132, 136, 148 n.7
The Tempest 39, 235
texts&beheadings/ Elizabeth R 238
Thalheimer, Michael 222, 223, 225 n.6
Three Jews 132
Todorov, Tzvetan 6, 7, 9, 10, 25, 60, 65, 68
Toich, Francesca Sarah 242, 243

Torre, Roberta 39, 195
Torres, Ângelo 195
Torreton, Philippe 249
translation 1, 5, 24, 25, 55, 56, 70, 105, 122, 124 nn.5, 10, 133–5, 138, 154, 164, 165, 194, 205 n.3, 212, 219, 230, 246, 252, 265, 277
   cultural translation 37, 43
   into dialects 39, 40
tribalism 15, 118, 123
   masculine/military 54, 56, 66
   neo-tribalism 26, 53, 111
tribe(s) 15, 120, 121, 213, 239, 267
   linguistic 14, 43, 264
   neo-tribes 51, 54, 60, 109, 118, 122
Trump, Donald J. 191, 205
Tubal 75, 113, 119, 140–5, 147

Uncle Vanya 267
UNITER 138
universalism 250, 255, 256, 257 n.5

Valló, Péter 14, 164, 167
Valls-Russell, Janice 1, 10, 26, 245, 256, 270
Varna Dramatic Theatre 'Stoyan Bachvarov' 258, 259, 263, 267, 271
Varna prison 60, 67 nn.7–8
Venetian Ghetto 11, 14, 30, 142, 143, 230, 236–43

Venetians, *see under The Merchant of Venice; Othello*
Verdi, Giuseppe 100
Vergov, Yulian 57
Vienne-Guerrin, Nathalie 169 n.9
Vigny, Alfred de 108, 124 n.2
Vincey, Jacques 16, 109, 110, 117–23
violence 9, 54, 64, 75, 109, 132, 143, 196, 254–6, 275
   domestic 15, 52–3, 58, 66, 86 n.31, 130, 200–1, 203, 205 n.9, 269, 277
Violinov, Vladisla 55
Voima, Soeren 212–15
Vörösmarty Theatre, Székesfehérvár 154

Waller, Gary 94
Warlikowski, Krzysztof 12, 15, 25, 69, 70–80, 82 n.1, 84 nn.14, 17, 18, 85 nn.22, 24, 139, 148 n.9
Weise, Christian 14–17, 211, 216, 219
Werktreue 217
whiteness 6, 14, 101, 199–200, 206 nn.7–8
Willkommenskultur 23, 209, 278
women 14, 15, 25, 36, 51, 53–8, 66, 71, 72, 75, 82, 86 nn.30–1, 103, 136, 158, 162, 173, 191, 198–202, 205,

240–54, 264–6, 276, 277, *see also* femicide; gender
xenophobia 4, 8, 80, 113, 115, 128, 136, 156, 181, 185, 186

Yacine, Kateb 247
Yugoslav Drama Theatre 90, 106 n.1
Yugoslavia 8, 98, 106 n.1
Young, Lisa 200
Young, Sandra 2, 31, 44, 45, 46 nn.12, 13, 16

Zadek, Peter 3, 211, 224–5 n.5
Závada, Pál 153
Zhechev, Toncho 265

www.ingramcontent.com/pod-product-compliance
Lightning Source LLC
Chambersburg PA
CBHW052151300426
44115CB00011B/1624